The
Pink and Blue
Toddler and
Preschooler
Pages

Practical Tips and Advice for Parents

Laurie Waldstein ❤ **Leslie Zinberg**

CONTEMPORARY BOOKS

Library of Congress Cataloging-in-Publication Data

Waldstein, Laurie.
    The pink and blue toddler and preschooler pages : practical tips
and advice for parents / by Laurie Waldstein and Leslie Zinberg.
        p.   cm.
    Includes index.
    ISBN 0-8092-2790-8
    1. Infants.   2. Infants—Care.   3. Toddlers—Care.   4. Child
rearing.   5. Parent and child.   I. Zinberg, Leslie.   II. Title.
    HQ774.W3515   1999
    649'.122—dc21
                                                            99-29188
                                                            CIP

Pronouns alternate gender from chapter to chapter in the interest of balance.

Notice: The information contained in this book is true and complete to the best of our knowledge. All recommendations are made without any guarantees on the part of the author or of NTC/Contemporary Publishing Group, Inc. The authors and publisher disclaim all liability in connection with the use of this information.

Cover design by Todd Petersen
Interior production by Susan H. Hartman
Cover and interior illustrations by Steve Gillig
Authors photograph by Charles William Bush

Published by Contemporary Books
A division of NTC/Contemporary Publishing Group, Inc.
4255 West Touhy Avenue, Lincolnwood (Chicago), Illinois 60712-1975 U.S.A.
Printed in the United States of America
International Standard Book Number: 0-8092-2790-8

99 00 01 02 03 04 CU 18 17 16 15 14 13 12 11 10 9 8 7 6 5 4 3 2 1

To our parents, who showered us with love and devotion and encouraged us to fulfill our lifelong dreams . . .

In loving memory of Muriel D. Slavin and Rabbi Floyd S. Fierman

and

In honor of Edythe B. Fierman and Warren J. Slavin

Contents

Foreword

Since the release of their first book, *The Pink and Blue Baby Pages*, my wife, Laurie, and her coauthor, Leslie, have received enthusiastic responses from new parents all over the country. Their fresh and simple approach to answering the innumerable questions every pediatrician gets daily from inexperienced parents proved to be a success. In keeping with that tradition, they have collaborated again and written *The Pink and Blue Toddler and Preschooler Pages*. This invaluable book guides the parent through the many challenging stages of a toddler and preschooler's life.

Unfortunately, pediatricians no longer have the luxury of spending quality time answering everyday questions most parents of toddlers and preschoolers have. As a result, parents must look to other sources besides the doctor for more in-depth information. As mothers who have raised children of their own, Laurie and Leslie are sensitive to the issues parents are confronted with daily, such as toilet training and discipline.

No one has prepared us to become mothers and fathers; parenting is an experience learned through on-the-job training. In *The Pink and Blue Toddler and Preschooler Pages*, Laurie and Leslie have compiled a concise, pleasurable, well-referenced book that all parents will find enormously useful.

Peter S. Waldstein, M.D., F.A.A.P.
Clinical Assistant Professor of Pediatrics, UCLA
Attending Physician, Cedars-Sinai Medical Center
Los Angeles, California

Acknowledgments

Writing this book has been a huge undertaking, and our families have been very patient along the way. Thank you to our husbands, Michael and Peter, who continue to encourage all our endeavors. And an extra thank-you to our medical consultant, Peter S. Waldstein, M.D., F.A.A.P. (Laurie's husband), who took the time out of his busy pediatric practice not only to advise us, but also to answer our myriad of questions.

This book required the assistance and expertise of many professionals, who reviewed specific chapters and offered valuable suggestions. We could not have written this book without their help and their support. Our heartfelt thanks go to the specialists in the field of child and family psychology: Don Fleming, Ph.D.; Barbara W. Guggenheim, Ph.D., licensed clinical psychologist; and Sat Kaur Khalsa, Ed.D.,

M.F.C.C. We are also grateful to Mary Donkersloot, R.D., author and nutrition therapist; Soram Singh Khalsa, M.D., medical director of the East/West Medical Research Institute; Mark H. Goldenberg, D.D.S., M.S., pediatric dentist; and Donna DeGaetani, M.S. in early-childhood education, M.A. in human development, M.F.C.C.

We thank Kara Leverte, our editor, for her time and input. A special thank-you to our agent and resident "mom," Jillian Manus, for all her support and encouragement. And an additional thanks to her efficient team.

Introduction

Just when things are starting to feel comfortable in your parenting role, something happens to your angelic baby: he becomes a toddler. After changing thousands of diapers and coping with countless hours of lost sleep, you thought parenting would become easier. In fact, the daily challenges increase, and the issues become more complex as your toddler begins to assert his autonomy, struggling between independence and dependence. On one hand he wants to put his shoes on all by himself, and on the other he still needs your help because he doesn't know which foot fits into which shoe. And if you think life is getting a bit more complicated with a toddler or preschooler, wait until you've lived through one of his many mood swings. In a split second a relatively sweet, well-behaved, and rational child can transform into a Gila monster!

Active toddlers and preschoolers keep their busy parents on their toes, leaving them little free time to peruse lengthy books searching for assistance and information on how to raise their child. In our first book, *The Pink and Blue Baby Pages*, we recognized the need to provide direct, practical, and simple tips to parents of infants from birth to twenty-four months. The positive response we received from our readers proved to us that parents want to be informed but not intimidated. In *The Pink and Blue Toddler and Preschooler Pages*, we continue the Pink and Blue tradition by offering guidance with concise answers to and options for everyday dilemmas.

We have grouped together the toddler and preschooler ages in this book because so many issues begin to develop around two years old and overlap into the preschool years. For example, some toddlers are ready to begin toilet training as early as two years old, while some preschoolers are not ready until they are three years old.

Is it the "terrible twos, threes, and fours" or the "terrific twos, threes, and fours"? It all depends on how you approach these years. Every child is different, even in the same family. What works best for one child may not work for another. There's no cut-and-dried formula or one right way for raising a child because parenting is not an exact science.

As mothers who have been there and experienced the daily goings-on of raising our own children, we understand the trials and tribulations parents encounter. We want you to feel empowered when using our child-rearing tools and organizational skills. And, since children don't come with a set of instructions, we provide plenty of practical information, enabling you to feel more comfortable and confident in your parenting role. Whether you have a problem or just a simple question, having this book is like being able to call your mother, sister, or best friend.

As always, use it in the best of health and happiness.

⊚ 1 ⊚

The Caregivers

More and more working parents today are confronted with the agonizing dilemma concerning child care. Whether you need full-time or part-time help, the decision to let someone else care for your child is never easy. How do you choose such a person, and how will you know if you can trust him or her? Do you need day care, or would you prefer to have a daily baby-sitter? Do you have the space for a live-in house-keeper or nanny? It takes time, patience, and careful scrutiny to decide which avenue to take.

Regardless of your decision, it's important your child be in a fun, stimulating, nonsmoking, and safe environment that encourages her physical, mental, and social develop-ment. A toddler's day must include gross motor movement, such as climbing, running, and jumping; intellectual stimula-tion, including exposure to books, music, and creative play;

PINK AND BLUE HINT

 Speak to a Certified Public Accountant regarding child care deductions for tax purposes. Save all your receipts.

I

PINK AND BLUE HINT

 Leave a notarized authorization slip giving the caretaker permission to authorize emergency medical treatment if you can't be reached.

and social interaction with other young children, as well as adults.

As a parent, you are responsible for shaping your child's development. A good caregiver will share this desire, welcome your input, and help you achieve this goal. After all, if your child is happy and secure in the environment you have carefully arranged, what else could you ask for? When considering a day care center, family day care, a baby-sitter in your home, or a grandparent or other relative, the following guidelines will help you to make this extremely important selection.

Day Care Centers

When researching day care centers for your family, visit and compare at least two facilities. Be sure to do your homework well because this is your child's home away from home. And as emotional as it is, keep in mind that child care is a business arrangement. If possible, give yourself at least six months' lead time to research the programs available in your community, especially if there's a shortage of centers.

Here's a list of questions to consider when visiting a potential day care center:

❀ Is the day care center state-licensed and accredited?

❀ What are the credentials of the caregivers? Are they specially trained in early-childhood development?

❀ Does the day care center require all children to be immunized, and does it keep records on each child?

❀ Is the caregiver warm and responsive to the children's needs? Does she seem genuinely interested in the children? Does she talk to them at eye level?

❁ What is the rate of employee turnover? Children need consistency.

❁ What is the toddler-to-caregiver ratio? The National Association for the Education of Young Children (NAEYC) recommends two adults for every twelve children two years and older.

❁ How long has the center been in existence?

❁ How many children are enrolled, and is it mixed-age?

❁ Are caregivers certified in cardiopulmonary resuscitation (CPR) and first aid? Is a well-stocked first-aid kit available?

❁ If your child has an accident, will the center contact you first? Is an emergency facility nearby?

❁ In cases of emergency, such as a natural disaster (hurricane, tornado, or earthquake), what are the evacuation procedures?

❁ Does the center practice fire drills? Is it equipped with smoke detectors and fire extinguishers?

❁ Is it childproofed? For example, are the electrical outlets covered, and are toxic substances such as cleaning products kept locked in a cabinet out of children's reach?

❁ Is the location convenient for you (close to home or office)?

❁ What are the operating hours? Are early and late hours available? Is the schedule flexible? Is the center open on holidays?

❁ Is the facility clean, cheerful, inviting, and stimulating?

PINK AND BLUE ALERT

Considering the occasional news stories about abuse by child care providers, you may want to run a police check to determine whether a caregiver has a criminal record. To do so, call your local police department and ask for assistance.

❧ Are there separate areas for diapering, sleeping, eating, and different activities? Do children have their own bedding?

❧ Is there a fully equipped kitchen? Does the center provide meals and snacks? If so, does it offer choices, and are they nutritious?

❧ What is the policy regarding sick children? Will the staff administer medication when necessary?

❧ Is there a good selection of toys, books, music, and outdoor equipment? Are they in good condition?

❧ Is the outdoor play space large enough for the number of children attending the program? Is the play equipment (i.e., jungle gym, slide, and swings) resting on a soft protective surface, such as mulch or wood chips?

❧ What kind of daily activities are provided?

❧ How does the center handle separation anxiety between parent and child? Are caregivers patient and helpful in this transitional period?

❧ Will the staff assist your child in toilet training?

❧ How do staff members discipline the children? What is the policy on biting?

❧ What is the cost? Are there payment options—monthly or weekly?

❧ Are parents welcome to visit anytime? Will the center accept phone calls during the day?

It's a good idea to contact other parents whose children attend the same day care center to confirm your findings and ask any other questions you may have.

Time-Tested Advice

❤ Talk to your child care provider about any changes in your child's life.

❤ Be sure to stay in communication about the daily routines and any other concerns you may have.

❤ Never sneak out without saying good-bye to your child. If you make a surreptitious exit, your child may angrily resist future separations. Always tell her you'll be back later to pick her up.

❤ If your child has a problem with biting or is being bitten often, speak with the day care supervisor. If the problem isn't rectified in a timely fashion, consider changing your child to a smaller day care facility.

❤ Remember to supply all the items your child will need throughout each day, and be sure to include a change of clothing.

❤ Always label or put an identifying mark on items taken to the center. This will eliminate any confusion about which possessions belong to your child.

❤ Make sure the center has a record of emergency and medical information pertaining to your child. Be sure the staff always has a phone number or pager number where you or your spouse can be reached.

❤ Be on time when picking up your child. If you're running late, call ahead so the caregiver can prepare your child.

PINK AND BLUE HINT

 If your child takes a lunch box, put a small photograph of her on the box for easy recognition.

PINK AND BLUE HINT

To help your child become more comfortable with her new friends, arrange a one- to two-hour play date with another child from the day care program.

❤ Spouses should share responsibility for dropping off and picking up. This makes everyone familiar with the day care staff and program.

❤ On sunny days apply sunscreen to your child's skin before leaving the house, since child care workers may not always remember.

❤ Read your child a book about day care and working parents. Be sure the book is age appropriate. A few suggestions are *Carl Goes to Daycare* by Alexandra Day, *Busy at Day Care Head to Toe* by Patricia Brennan Demuth, *Who's Going to Take Care of Me?* by Michelle Magorian, *Day Care ABC* by Tamara Phillips, and *Jessie's Day Care* by Amy Valens. Consult your local librarian, bookstore, or day care provider for more recommendations.

On-Site Day Care

There's a growing trend in American businesses toward on-site day care centers. Companies that have implemented this kind of program for their employees have seen an increase in job performance and a decrease in stress and fatigue. If your employer does not have a center and enough coworkers are interested, approach your boss about instituting such a program. For more information on how to start an on-site facility, call the Association of Work/Life Professionals at (800) 874-9383.

Family Day Care

Family day care, which offers care for the young child in a person's home, is an option parents find appealing. Many parents prefer family day care to a day care center because the environment is cozier, the fees are generally lower, the number of children attending is smaller (so the atmosphere is less chaotic), and there's greater flexibility within the program. Every state has different regulations for in-home care. Therefore, check with your local department of social or human services, which can identify the agency responsible for regulating family day care in your state.

To find an at-home provider, check with local preschools, churches, synagogues, senior-citizen centers, your pediatrician's and obstetrician's offices, and community centers. Talk to everyone you know. Also try calling the National Association for Family Child Care at (800) 359-3817 and ask if the family in-home child care facility you're interested in is accredited by it.

In addition to the questions listed under Day Care Centers, here are some other factors to consider when researching family day care:

※ Is the home safe, clean, and childproofed?

※ What are the arrangements for backup care in case of an emergency with one of the children?

※ Does the caregiver have home and car insurance?

※ What happens when the caregiver is sick? Is there a reliable substitute?

※ Has the provider passed a TB screening test?

※ Do the other children at the home have up-to-date immunizations?

※ How many children are being cared for in the home? The National Association for the Education of Young Children recommends a ratio of six children per caregiver.

❈ Does the provider know CPR and first-aid techniques?

❈ How does the caregiver structure a typical day? Are there planned activities to stimulate the young child's mental, physical, and emotional growth?

❈ Is there a variety of age-appropriate toys and books? Are they in good condition? What kind of outdoor equipment is available? Is it in safe, working order?

❈ Who watches the children while the provider goes to the bathroom?

❈ Does the provider have young children of her own? If so, what happens when her children are sick?

❈ Is a potty available for the child who is toilet training? Are sinks reachable for the children to wash their hands? If not, are step stools available, and will someone assist the children?

❈ Does anyone smoke in the house? You do not want your child exposed to secondhand smoke.

❈ Are the caregiver's child care philosophy and style compatible with yours?

❈ How would the provider handle two or more children crying at the same time? Or accidents occurring at the same moment?

❈ Has the provider had any early-childhood education and special training?

❈ Is the caregiver flexible with your schedule?

❈ If the provider has to transport a child in the car, is a car seat available?

❈ Is television used to entertain the children?

When selecting this type of care, you must do your homework thoroughly. Get references from at least three other parents who have used this provider's services. In addition to checking Time-Tested Advice in the section on Day Care Centers, consider the following information.

Time-Tested Advice

* When first visiting the day care home, spend several hours observing the caregiver with the children. She should be warm, friendly, and responsive to their needs.

* Make sure the home is child-proofed with smoke detectors, fire extinguishers, covered outlets, gated stairs, locked cabinets, secured windows with no long cords, and enclosed porches and balconies. (For more information, see Chapter 8, "Safety.")

* The home should not have any medicines, paint cans, insecticides, or other poisonous materials within the child's reach. A telephone number for the local poison control center should be posted by the telephone.

* Ask about emergency plans in case of fire, hurricanes, tornadoes, earthquakes, or any other unpredictable circumstances.

* Provide the caregiver with your child's current schedules and routines, including eating, sleeping, self-dressing, and toilet training. Insist that your toddler's individual needs be met to maintain consistency in her life.

❦ Solicit your caretaker's help and advice when introducing new skills or reinforcing old ones.

❦ To avoid boredom and encourage stimulation, the caregiver should rotate toys periodically.

❦ While television viewing should not be a part of the daily program, an occasional age-appropriate show or video is OK.

In-Home Care

Many parents prefer to keep their toddler at home in a one-on-one situation. The comfort of being in familiar surroundings, without having to drop off and pick up, makes life less complicated. And if your child gets sick, you won't have to take time off work. You may be fortunate enough to keep it all in the family with a grandparent or relative helping out. Or perhaps a baby-sitter who comes and goes will fit your bill. If you have the space available at home, you may want a live-in person, such as a housekeeper or nanny. In any case, whomever you hire, be sure to create a detailed job description and be very clear about what your expectations and objectives are.

To find a person to care for your child at home, contact employment or baby-sitting/nanny agencies; your local newspaper (place an ad); college bulletin boards; schools, churches, and synagogues; friends and coworkers. Before you interview anyone, make a list of your requirements, such as experience with young children, job references, age, English fluency, salary, driving availability, scheduling flexibility, cooking, personal appearance, and demeanor. Based on your requirements, ask interview questions such as the following:

❀ Why did the caregiver leave her last job? How long was she there?

❀ What were the ages and genders of the children she took care of?

❀ Does she have children of her own? How old are they? Who takes care of them when she's not home?

❀ Are her hours flexible?

❀ Will she do household chores? Can she cook?

❀ Does she smoke?

❀ Are there any health problems you need to be aware of?

❀ Does she know what to do in case of an emergency? (Teach her what to do in case of an accident involving your child, a fire, or a natural disaster.)

Always get at least two to three referrals and check them thoroughly, even if you're using an agency. When speaking to past employers, listen to the tone of their voice and determine whether the responses are enthusiastic or hesitant. Ask questions that require in-depth responses, not one-word replies. If a caregiver's referral doesn't return your call or is unreachable, think twice.

If the caregiver will drive your child anywhere, check the person's driving record. To do so, contact your insurance company or your state's department of motor vehicles.

PINK AND BLUE HINT

When using an employment agency, confirm its fee and carefully read its contract. Make certain the agency is state licensed. Interview as many individuals as you like, and don't be persuaded to select one of the first few candidates. Don't be intimidated by the agency, and demand to check more than one reference. Should the person you hire not work out or meet your needs, what is the agency's guarantee policy?

Time-Tested Advice for a Baby-Sitter, Housekeeper, or Nanny

❀ Whether you're out during the day or the evening, always leave a phone number or pager number where you can be reached.

PINK AND BLUE HINT

Post all emergency information in a visually accessible place. Include parents' work numbers, pediatrician's phone number, poison control number, closest emergency room, neighbor's and relative's phone numbers, age and weight of child, home address and phone number, and closest cross streets.

❀ Before leaving your child alone with the sitter, arrange for child, parent, and sitter to spend time together. Then allow yourself some time around the house in a noninterfering way.

❀ Start separating gradually by leaving your child with the sitter for short intervals of time.

❀ Detail the rules and routines to be followed. Post a chart so the sitter knows what you and your child expect. Carefully review sleeping and eating schedules.

❀ Have the sitter keep a log of daily activities.

❀ If household chores are part of the sitter's responsibility, set up a schedule of how and when you want them completed.

❀ Teach her how to cook your family's favorite recipes.

❀ Discuss the way you want your child to be disciplined.

❀ Insist television viewing be limited. Decide which age-appropriate shows your child may watch.

❀ Make sure your sitter follows the same procedures you implement when your child is learning new skills, such as toilet training and dressing herself.

❀ Keep the relationship professional, and don't get involved in her life.

❀ Set up performance reviews on a monthly basis.

❀ Let your child help compile a list of important things she wants the sitter to know.

* If the sitter is a relatively new driver, it's not advisable to let her practice with your child. Driving with young children is an added challenge and requires experience. Reassure the sitter you have confidence in her, but driving is a matter of safety.

* Pay for a CPR and first-aid class.

* Set some time aside each week to discuss any problems or observations you or the sitter may have. Communication is the key to a successful relationship.

* Listen to suggestions from your sitter, and consider her point of view.

* Make a surprise visit every once in a while.

* Leave a notarized authorization slip giving your sitter permission to get emergency medical assistance for your child if you cannot be reached. Also, leave the same authorization slip with your pediatrician.

If you hire a person who does not speak English fluently, there will be some other things to consider carefully, besides whether the person is child focused, attentive, and friendly. Ask these questions:

* Can this person communicate with your child?

* Can she handle an emergency and effectively call for assistance?

* Will you be able to communicate with each other regarding household duties and your child's routines (such as eating and napping)?

PINK AND BLUE HINT

Role-play possible emergencies with your sitter, and have her pretend to call 911 or your local fire and police departments.

※ Can she answer the telephone and take messages?

※ Can she read any English (such as cleaning and medicine labels, directions for cooking)?

Daily exposure to a foreign language at the toddler stage is a wonderful bonus to your child's intellectual development. Therefore, if your gut reaction to this person is positive, invest some time in developing her skills:

※ Point out potential hazards throughout the house.

※ Remind her to keep all cleaning products out of the child's reach.

※ Discuss daily routines, and practice emergency procedures.

※ Buy English instruction cassettes for the baby-sitter or housekeeper, or send her to adult evening school.

Changing Caregivers

Changes in child care are inevitable. If a caregiver leaves the job (either at home or at the day care center), a child may feel sad and anxious. Therefore, the more accepting you are of the departure, the more quickly your child will adjust. After all, you are the constant in her life.

If a parent or child is not satisfied or connected with a caregiver, make a change. Use simple language to explain what's happening, and follow the time-tested advice to make a smooth transition.

PINK AND BLUE ALERT

Your child needs to understand that caregivers sometimes leave their job, but parents, the most important people in her life, will always be there for her.

Time-Tested Advice

❀ Rather than dwell on the baby-sitter's departure, focus on the new person and explain that she will do everything the old baby-sitter did and more.

❀ Introduce the new baby-sitter gradually. Have her spend time with your child before her first day of work.

❀ Let your child participate in the transition. Have her help you list important things she wants the caregiver to know (for example, favorite food or toy).

❀ If your caregiver is leaving on a positive note, give her a small send-off and keep the relationship open between everyone.

Cooperative Baby-Sitting

Not all families need a full-time baby-sitter. However, everyone needs a break. If you want an occasional night or day free, consider forming a baby-sitting co-op. This may involve just two families taking turns caring for one another's children, or a few families may exchange sitting services. Cooperative baby-sitting can be both financially and socially rewarding. For you and your child, this is an opportunity to develop long-lasting friendships.

The easiest way to start a group is with friends you trust. If you cannot find other interested families, check with your pediatrician's office, neighbors, local PTA, church or synagogue, bulletin boards at the local market or community center, YMCA, preschools, health clubs, or businesses that cater to young children.

PINK AND BLUE HINT

Make an index card on each child. Include home address and phone number, emergency telephone number, birth date, weight, any medical problems (such as allergies), pediatrician's telephone number, and food likes and dislikes.

PINK AND BLUE HINT

Families can chip in and buy pagers for the group. The parents going out can carry one of the pagers, while their child is being cared for at the co-op home.

Time-Tested Advice

❧ Spend some time with potential members, and make sure you're comfortable with them and their philosophies on raising children.

❧ Check the other homes for proper childproofing. Speak up if you are concerned about any safety issues.

❧ It's advisable for all parents to be trained in CPR and simple first-aid techniques.

❧ A complete first-aid kit should be available at all homes.

Separation Anxiety

Regardless of who is caring for your child, at some point she may experience separation anxiety when you leave. This is a perfectly normal phase young children go through, although it can be taxing on the parents' nerves. Always reassure your child that every time you leave, you will come back. The following advice should help soothe the separation transition.

Time-Tested Advice

❧ Never sneak out without saying good-bye. You don't want your child to develop a sense of mistrust.

❧ Plan on spending time with your child while making the transition. For example, visit the day care center together and allow your child to get comfortable in the new surroundings while you're still there. Even if the transition is at home, parent and baby-sitter should spend some time together with the child.

- ❈ The first time you leave your child, make it for a short period. Then gradually work up to longer periods. Work with the caregiver on this transition.

- ❈ Talk to your child about the new arrangements so there are no surprises.

- ❈ Allow yourself and your child plenty of time in the morning. A rushed situation is not a good way to start the day and may not promote a smooth separation.

- ❈ If you find a routine that eases your departure, use it each day. Children feel confident with familiar routines.

- ❈ Prepare as much as possible the night before by laying out clothes and making lunches.

- ❈ When you first see your child after the separation, make it a big deal. Give her extra time and attention, discuss what her day was like, and tell her about yours.

- ❈ Act confident when leaving your toddler, because she will sense any guilt or apprehension you may be feeling.

- ❈ Once your child has adapted to her new situation, give her a kiss and a short good-bye in a positive, upbeat manner.

When you return from a day away from your child, it is not unusual for her to misbehave and whine when she sees you. When the caretaker tells you, "She's been so good all day long," don't be surprised. It's the end of the day, and your child is overtired, hungry, and wound up. She has controlled herself for a very long time and cannot hold herself together any longer, anticipating your arrival. Children are most secure with their parents and typically "unravel at the seams" because they intuitively know your bonds are made of unconditional love.

ꙮ 2 ꙮ

Toilet Training

You're sound asleep, and once again that recurring nightmare awakens you. It's your son's first day of high school, and as he leaves the house, car keys in hand, the picture's just not right. He's all decked out in the newest outfit, but wait a minute, he's still wearing *diapers*!

Don't fret. While toilet training is a big transition, you can be reassured your child won't go off to high school wearing diapers. In fact, most children are open to toilet training between the ages of two and three. However, let their behavior, not the calendar, be the guide. Most girls learn the art of toilet training a little bit faster than most boys, but boys have an "equipment" advantage and can easily find a convenient location when the need to go strikes.

The toilet training experience can go smoothly or can become your worst nightmare, depending on how you

PINK AND BLUE ALERT

It's probably better not to introduce toilet training if there's a major transition taking place in your family (for example, last trimester of pregnancy, new sibling, house move, new caregiver, parents separating or divorcing). Wait so that the child can be in a more relaxed frame of mind.

approach it. Just because you want to say good-bye to changing diapers doesn't necessarily mean your child feels the same way. Remember two things: your *child* (not you) must be ready, and *you* have to relax.

Readiness

Starting the toilet training process on a positive note is essential to your child's success. Let him be the guide. If you start your child when he's not interested, you will set yourself up for an unhappy, unsuccessful, lengthy experience. Some children show signs of interest as early as two to two and a half years, while others are just not ready until three or older. Sometimes delaying toilet training can make the process quicker and easier.

So, how will you know when he's ready? These are the signs:

- Your child is able to stay dry for a couple of hours and may even wake up from a nap dry.

- He recognizes the elimination process. He may tell you with either words or bodily gestures. It's not unusual for a child to squat, grunt, hold his genitals, or pause from play.

- Your child has regular bowel movements about the same time every day.

- He understands and follows simple directions.

- Your child understands the concept of wet and dry, and finds the dirty diaper unpleasant and uncomfortable. He may even refuse to wear the diaper altogether.

- ❧ He has a strong interest in cleanliness and orderliness. To instill and encourage his choice to be clean, change his diapers frequently.

- ❧ Your child imitates adult and older-sibling behavior.

- ❧ He verbally expresses the desire to wear underwear.

- ❧ He has a general curiosity about bathroom habits. He can walk to and from the potty and sit on it without help.

Toilet Terminology

As you toilet train your child, be sure your family members and caregivers consistently use the same toilet terminology, such as "wee-wee," "pee-pee," or "tinkle" for urinating, and "poop," "BM," "doo-doo," "poo-poo," or "doody" for bowel movements.

Teach the correct anatomical terms for body parts to encourage a child's healthy body image. It's confusing for your child if you make up names that only your family understands and recognizes. The bottom line is a penis should be called a penis, and a vagina should be called a vagina.

PINK AND BLUE HINT

If your child is in preschool or attends a day care center, consider using its toilet terminology for consistency.

Equipment

Once your toddler shows signs of readiness, you'll need to make some purchases. Being prepared in advance will help your efforts. Here are the items you'll need:

- ❧ A child's potty chair with a sturdy base

- ❧ An attachment seat adaptable to your toilet

- ❧ A sturdy, evenly balanced step stool

PINK AND BLUE HINT

Take your child to the store and let him pick out his new underwear.

※ Training pants (cloth and/or disposable)

※ Six pairs of underwear

※ Clothing that is easy for the child to take off and put on (clothing with elastic waistbands rather than overalls or clothing with buttons, snaps, or zippers)

※ A doll that wets (not a necessity, but helpful for some children)

※ A child's book and/or video about toilet training

※ Cloth diapers (optional as a way to help the child recognize the sensation of wet and dirty much faster than wearing a disposable)

Potty Chair Versus Toilet

While many experts advocate the child-sized potty chair, others support using a regular toilet right from the beginning. The choice is ultimately what's comfortable for your child. There are three basic seat styles: the one-piece potty, the convertible potty with a removable bowl and removable adaptable seat, and the adaptable seat ring, which fits directly onto the toilet. If you begin by using the potty chair, then once your child has mastered it, have him practice on the toilet so he can eventually make the transition. Just keep in mind that the ultimate goal is the standard-sized toilet.

Advantages of the Potty Chair

※ A potty chair is portable and convenient.

※ The child's feet can touch the ground.

❈ Many children feel safer with equipment that's scaled to their size.

❈ A child can use the potty unassisted.

❈ A child likes the idea of having his own personal potty.

❈ You can take a potty chair in the car.

❈ A child using a potty chair has no fear of falling in or falling off, as may be the case with the big toilet.

Disadvantages of the Potty Chair

❈ If you start with a potty chair, you will have to retrain your child on the big toilet.

❈ A child who is used to a potty chair may not want to use a regular toilet when he's away from home.

❈ The potty chair not only requires extra cleanup but also has to be disinfected after each use.

❈ The one-piece potty chair tends to be lightweight and slides too easily.

❈ If you have limited floor space in the bathroom, the potty may take up too much room.

Advantages of the Toilet

❈ If you start with the toilet, all you need is an adaptable seat ring and a well-balanced step stool.

❈ If you buy the flat folding adaptable seat, you can take it with you anywhere.

❈ The child feels very grown-up when he can use the toilet as the rest of the family does.

PINK AND BLUE HINT

A squishy, soft toilet seat is more comfortable for the toddler's bare bottom than a hard seat. The softness may encourage sitting on the toilet.

❀ It eliminates an extra teaching step from potty chair to toilet.

❀ There's no extra cleanup (unless the male toddler or preschooler has trouble aiming).

❀ It makes the transition to toilet use easier when he's away from home.

Disadvantages of the Toilet

❀ Climbing on and off a toilet is difficult and usually requires adult assistance.

❀ You have to remove the adaptable seat for others to use the toilet.

❀ A child may fear falling in or falling off.

Getting Ready for the Next Step

Certain explanations and simple suggestions can help you introduce the concept of toilet training.

Time-Tested Advice

❤ Create a relaxed, positive, fun environment where the child doesn't feel any pressure or anxiety.

❤ Pay attention to your toddler's urination and bowel movement patterns. You may even want to keep a log to determine his clock.

❤ *Every* time you or anyone else goes to the bathroom, take the child with you so he can watch what you're doing. Young children enjoy imitating role models.

- Your child may get motivated to toilet train by watching his peers who are already trained.

- Have the child assist you by lifting the toilet seat (for dad, grandpa, or older brother), pulling and tearing the toilet paper, and flushing. Including him in these activities makes him more aware of what's going on in the bathroom.

- Place the potty chair in the bathroom so it becomes a familiar object; do this at least one month in advance. Make it clear that this is his special chair.

- Let your child sit on the potty or the adaptable toilet ring with his clothes on and praise him.

- Once your child feels comfortable sitting on the potty, let him sit on it bare-bottomed.

- Change your toddler's diapers as soon as they're wet or soiled so he learns to know the difference and enjoys being clean and dry.

- While you're changing the diaper, explain to your child what you're doing, using the family's toilet terminology. Remind him how good it feels to be dry and clean.

- Start changing diapers in the bathroom so your child understands the association between elimination and the bathroom. When he has a bowel movement, have him watch you empty the contents into the toilet.

- Don't make negative comments about the contents or odor of his diapers. The last thing you want is for him to feel embarrassed or ashamed.

- Dress your child in clothing that is easy for him to pull up and down when he goes to the bathroom.

- Purchase a doll that wets so you and your child can practice potty training with the doll. Have your child mimic your words and actions with the doll.

- Make sure your child understands simple instructions, such as "Please bring me your doll" or "Please put your shoes in your bedroom." In this way you know your child is able and willing to follow directions as you begin the road to toilet training.

- Books are a nice way to introduce potty training without pressure. Suggested books are *The Toddler's Potty Book* by Alida Allison, *Dry Days, Wet Nights* by Maribeth Boelts, *No More Diapers* by Joae Graham Brooks, M.D., *Potty Time* by Anne Civardi, *Sam's Potty* by Barbro Lindgren, and *My Potty Chair* by Ruth Young. Visit your local library or bookstore for other recommendations.

On Your Mark, Get Set, Go

Now that you know your child is ready and you have established his toilet timetable, proceed slowly. Your goal is to help him get familiar with the potty chair and/or toilet, whichever equipment you have decided on. If you're using the potty chair, keep it in the bathroom so your child will associate elimination with the proper room. For two-story homes with bathrooms on both floors, invest in an extra potty.

As you go through the toilet training process, be consistent, patient, and positive. Don't be discouraged by false starts and regressions. Set aside as much uninterrupted time as possible to work consistently with your child on this new milestone. This should be a serious commitment on your part.

Diapers, Training Pants, and Underwear

Decisions, decisions, decisions . . . whoever thought there would be so much to take into consideration? Should you continue to use diapers on occasion or go cold turkey? What about disposable versus cloth training pants? Do you go straight to underwear and forget about the other items? While everyone has opinions, keep in mind that each child is an individual, and what works for one may not work for another.

Begin by having your child spend his waking hours at home without diapers. This will facilitate his understanding and awareness of his bodily functions. In warm weather, romping around with nothing on in the house or in the backyard makes getting to the potty easier. If accidents occur outside, it's not such a big deal.

When you are dressing your child, introduce the training pants instead of the diapers. You may want to use the disposable type to cut down on your laundering; however, the disposable is so absorbent the child doesn't feel the wetness as quickly as in the cloth training pants. Once he stays dry for longer periods of time, graduate to the cotton training pants. When accidents happen, the child will feel cold and uncomfortable and will probably dislike this feeling. Your hope is that this will motivate him to use the potty or toilet. Let him step in and out of these pants unassisted so that he can develop self-confidence and a greater sense of independence. He'll master a new skill and feel very grown-up.

Many parents choose to pass on the training pants because the pants feel too much like diapers. Others prefer using underpants immediately to speed up the toilet training process. A good incentive for wearing underpants is to take

PINK AND BLUE HINT

Buy training pants at least one size larger than your child's other clothes, because the child can pull them on and off more easily. It also allows for shrinkage, since you'll be washing them often.

the child shopping and let him select his favorite "big boy" underwear. Since accidents invariably occur, there's more cleanup involved with underpants because everything gets wet and dirty. However, graduating from training pants to underwear can make the training process smoother. In the end, the choice is yours.

Basic Training

There are different approaches to training, and no one way is the right way. It's whatever works for your child. One method is to pay close attention to your child's elimination schedule, body language, and facial expressions. Learn to read his signals. When you see him holding his crotch, grunting, pacing, squirming, or squatting in a corner, you'll know what is happening. Say, "Bobby has to go pee-pee or poo-poo," and take him to the bathroom. By gently encouraging him at the right moment, you can instill success on his part.

Another technique, similar to the first, is for the parent to initiate the visits to the bathroom many times a day for the first couple of weeks, timing it around when you think he needs to go (after meals, before and after a nap). Have him sit on the potty and/or toilet for a few minutes. If he wants to get off without "going," let him. Don't be confrontational; the last thing you want to do is wage war over something you don't ultimately control. Always take a positive approach!

Time-Tested Advice

❧ Continue to have your child go to the bathroom with you or other members of the family whenever you need to go. Mimicking this behavior is an effective method of toilet training.

❦ Do practice runs to the potty whenever your child gives a signal (body language) that he needs to "go."

❦ Remind your child to tell you when he needs to go to the potty so you can assist him.

❦ Have your child practice pulling his training pants and clothing up and down by himself.

❦ Approximately twenty to forty minutes after your child drinks fluids, take him to the bathroom. Let him sit for as long or as short a period of time as he wants. Praise him whether he "goes" or not.

❦ While your child is sitting on the potty, try running water in the bathroom faucet for a few minutes. It may stimulate the urge to urinate.

❦ Sometimes a child will leave the potty too soon and then have an accident. Don't fret—with plenty of practice, he'll get his timing down.

❦ It's not unusual for your child to tell you he needs to go to the bathroom after he has already wet or soiled himself. It takes a while for the young child to distinguish between the urge and actually "going."

❦ Usually children can control bowel movements more easily than urination because there are more physical signals.

PINK AND BLUE ALERT

 Never force or physically restrain your child to sit on the potty or toilet.

PINK AND BLUE HINT

Keep a box of new picture books and toys in the bathroom so your child will be encouraged to sit as long as necessary when he has a bowel movement. These special items are *only* to be used in the bathroom! Every few weeks, bring in a few new selections to keep him interested.

❧ If your child has difficulty passing bowel movements and his stool is hard, consult your pediatrician regarding changes in the child's diet.

❧ To help your child relax when sitting on the potty and/or toilet, read him a book.

❧ Regardless of whether your child uses the potty or the toilet, it's a good idea in the beginning to keep a potty seat in the car for emergencies. Once you are confident your child has acquired the skills to control himself and he's comfortable using the toilet, there will be no need to carry the potty. Another tip for outside the home is to carry an adaptable toilet seat that can easily fit onto any public rest room toilet.

❧ To prevent power struggles, avoid asking whether he needs to go to the bathroom. Instead, just say, "It's time to go to the bathroom."

❧ If your child becomes resistant to the toilet training, stop all your efforts for a week or two. Some children become resistant to the process because they are reminded or lectured too much. In addition, when a child sees he has control over you, he can learn to be manipulative.

❧ Using rewards can be a great incentive to motivate your child to master this new skill. Make a chart or calendar showing your child's progress. Let him fill it in with his favorite stickers or brightly colored stars immediately after his success. Once he achieves a goal of five stickers or stars, give him a small toy for his proud accomplishments. Another idea is to take an empty coffee can or an undecorated piggy bank and let the toddler decorate it. Then each time he's successful, reward him with a penny that he can deposit in his bank.

* Good bathroom hygiene is important, and children need to learn to wash their hands each time they go to the bathroom.

* Some children display a fear of toilet training because the flushing sound scares them. If that's the case, flush the toilet after your child leaves the bathroom.

* Some children are afraid of eliminating bowel movements on the toilet because they don't like losing a part of themselves. Be patient if your child experiences such a fear. Let him go to the bathroom with you so he can see and understand that everyone eliminates into a toilet.

For Girls

* Teach your daughter to wipe from the front to the back to prevent urinary infections.

* Make sure she wipes gently and doesn't irritate herself.

* Explain that girls, unlike boys, sit on the potty for all elimination.

For Boys

* Start a boy by sitting on the potty. Not only will it minimize sprays and drips on the floor and walls, it also will keep him from getting easily distracted and leaving too soon. In addition, this gets him

PINK AND BLUE HINT

Buy pump soap instead of bars of soap. It's easier, neater, and more fun to use.

PINK AND BLUE HINT

Boys need to practice aiming, so help them learn this skill by putting a target into the toilet bowl. Take a brightly colored lipstick and draw an X, a happy face, a heart, or a kiss at the point in the toilet where the water levels. Reapply as needed.

accustomed to sitting on the potty for a bowel movement.

❤ Teach your son to point his penis down when he's seated on the potty and/or toilet.

❤ Since young children enjoy imitating behavior, have your son go to the bathroom with dad. When he shows signs of wanting to stand (just like dad), let him try the toilet. It's much easier to aim into a toilet bowl, because it's larger than the potty and requires no cleanup.

❤ Be sure to have a sturdy-based step stool available for your son to stand on.

❤ A mother can teach her son how to stand at the toilet by straddling over the bowl, facing the lid.

Staying Dry Through the Night

Once your child is toilet trained during the day and wakes up dry from his naps, you can begin to think about overnight training. Continue with the overnight diaper or training pants, because if accidents occur in the middle of the night, it's easier to change a diaper than to change all the linens and the child's pajamas. Don't rush into this next stage since it can take six months or longer (after giving up diapers) for the child to stay dry all night long. To expect a young child to go ten to twelve hours when he's in a deep sleep is a big stretch.

Time-Tested Advice

❦ Stop all drinks at least two hours before bedtime.

❦ Make it a routine to visit the bathroom before going to bed. This is an important rule.

❦ Put a rubber pad or sheet over the mattress pad to protect the mattress. Buy extra pads for those middle-of-the-night accidents.

❦ As an incentive, let your child select sheets with his favorite characters.

❦ Have your child wear pajamas that are easy to remove.

❦ Keep a night-light in your child's room and in the bathroom he'll be using.

❦ Practice dry runs to the bathroom with your child. Pretend it's the middle of the night, and have him demonstrate getting up, walking to the bathroom, using the toilet, and climbing back into bed.

Bed-Wetting

Bed-wetting is a normal problem many children, especially boys, experience after they have mastered toilet training. Medical studies indicate there are a few contributing factors to this problem. One theory suggests family history, usually on the father's side, while other evidence points to a young child's bladder that's not yet fully developed. Some children may wet their beds because they are in such a deep sleep they haven't learned to wake up from the feelings of a full bladder.

If your child has been staying dry regularly and then all of a sudden starts wetting, speak to your pediatrician and have him rule out any possible medical problems, such as a urinary tract infection or constipation. Sometimes wetting occurs when there's a major change in your home, such as birth of a sibling, a move to a new home, parents separating, a new preschool, or a new caregiver. And as frustrating as it can be, a parent must never punish, criticize, or allow any teasing. It's best just to change his pajamas and sheets and not make a big deal about it. The key for the parent is to be patient and tolerant, reassuring the child that he will overcome this obstacle.

In addition to the Time-Tested Advice in the section Staying Dry Through the Night, use the following suggestions.

Time-Tested Advice

* Don't allow any fluid intake at least two hours before bedtime, and avoid carbonated drinks, citric juices, and drinks with caffeine.

* Make a chart and let the child put a star or sticker for each night he stays dry. After three or four consecutive nights, reward him with a small toy. Keep a bag of small toys for the child to select from.

* Take him to the bathroom before *you* go to sleep.

* If your child resists the overnight diaper, try using extra-absorbent training pants.

* Praise the child with words of encouragement.

* Ask your pediatrician about the bed-wetting alarm (only for the preschooler).

Accidents Happen

Nobody is perfect, especially a child who's learning to control his bodily functions. Accidents are inevitable. Regression is typical behavior for a young child, who can display inconsistency, taking two steps forward and one step back. Even when a child has been trained for a long time, it's not unusual for him to have an occasional mishap. He could be overly tired or excited, thoroughly engrossed in an activity, experiencing separation anxiety, or dealing with new and stressful events in his life (new sibling, move, new preschool, new baby-sitter, separation or divorce). When accidents occur, have your child help clean up the mess, and don't be judgmental.

❧ 3 ❧

Your Child's Health

The Pediatrician

At this time in your child's life, you have been visiting
the pediatrician regularly for routine checkups and the
inevitable sick visits. As a toddler's memory becomes more
acute, it is not unusual for her to develop a fear of the
doctor because she associates "shots" and general prodding
and poking with that particular person. This is normal
toddler/preschooler behavior that she will eventually
outgrow. In fact, many children begin to understand that
the doctor is their friend and wants to make them feel
better when they're feeling sick.

The rapport you and your child have established with
your pediatrician should continue to solidify through the
years. When your child can communicate well enough, let

her tell the pediatrician how she feels, and let her respond to the doctor's questions. Of course, the parent should always elaborate when necessary.

Unfortunately, health care in America has changed dramatically in the past five years, often with insurance companies dictating what the doctor can and cannot do. If your doctor is affiliated with a group practice, you might not get to see the same physician each time. Therefore, be sure to schedule visits with as many of the doctors as possible so that you and your child will be more comfortable, and the doctors will get to know your family.

In many offices, nurse practitioners handle the majority of the calls and visits. While they are either registered nurses with additional accreditations in child development or nurses with master's degrees, you have to decide whether you're comfortable dealing with them instead of the pediatrician. Regardless of who cares for your child, it's important you continue to share similar philosophies on raising your child and not be intimidated by the doctor's approach. Be honest at all times with the doctor; the more information you can provide, the better. If at any time you find yourself reevaluating the medical care or attitudes of the doctor's office, perhaps this is the time to make a change.

Scheduled Checkups with the Pediatrician

At this point in your child's life, well checkups to the pediatrician are less frequent. It is not unusual for toddlers and preschoolers to be afraid of these visits to the pediatrician. To help alleviate the child's fear, read her books such as *The Berenstain Bears Go to the Doctor* by Jan and Stan Berenstain,

Corduroy Goes to the Doctor by Don Freeman, *Bungle Jungle Doctor* by Robert Kraus, and *My Friend the Doctor* by Jane Werner Watson, Robert E. Switzer, and J. Cotter Hirschberg.

At each checkup, your doctor will keep your child's immunizations up-to-date and review whether your child is reaching major developmental milestones typical for that age. Remember, every child develops differently.

Two Years

❧ General checkup including TB Tine test

Two and a Half Years

❧ General checkup (If your child is behind on any immunizations, this is a good time to get caught up.)

Three Years

❧ General checkup, including:

- TB Tine test
- Urinalysis

Four Years

❧ General checkup, including:

- Urinalysis
- Blood stick test (checks blood count and cholesterol)
- DT (diphtheria/tetanus) booster
- OPV (oral polio vaccine)
- Mantoux/PPD test (TB test)
- Eye examination

⊚ Hearing test (especially if child has had chronic ear infections)

The Home Medicine Cabinet

Even with checkups, immunizations, and careful supervision, accidents and illnesses will occur. Being prepared for the unexpected is always the best bet. Keep the following items on hand and remember to restock when necessary. Always purchase products that are specifically for children.

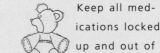

PINK AND BLUE ALERT
Keep all medications locked up and out of children's reach.

※ Vitamins (your pediatrician will recommend what kind your child should take daily)

※ Acetaminophen (such as Children's Tylenol or Children's Panadol)

※ Ibuprofen (such as Children's Motrin or Children's Advil)

※ Antibiotic ointment, cream, or spray

※ Hydrocortisone cream

※ Hydrogen peroxide

※ Rubbing alcohol

※ Electrolyte solution (available in liquid form and frozen ice sticks)

※ Suppositories for vomiting or high fever (require a doctor's prescription)

※ Thermometer (see the section on thermometers later in this chapter)

※ Petroleum jelly

※ Antibacterial soap

PINK AND BLUE ALERT

When administering prescription and nonprescription medicine, always read the instructions carefully, using a proper measuring spoon for the exact dosage specified. Never give medicine to your child at night in the dark; turn the light on to see properly.

- Antihistamine (check with your pediatrician for preference)
- Cough medicine (check with your pediatrician for preference)
- Calamine lotion
- Bicarbonate of soda
- Insect repellent
- Assorted sizes of bandages
- Sterile gauze pads
- Hypoallergenic adhesive tape
- Cool-mist humidifier
- Cotton balls or pads
- Ginger ale, decaffeinated cola drinks, or cola syrup
- Syrup of ipecac
- Measuring syringe or spoon
- Tweezers
- Scissors
- Ice packs in the freezer (the best are the reusable cold packs)

Time-Tested Advice for Using Nonprescription Medicines

- Consult your pediatrician before administering any medication. Ask the doctor whether there are any specific side effects to watch for.

- Tell the doctor which dosage form your child prefers (liquid or chewable).

- Be sure to tell your doctor if your child is taking any other medication.

- Always read the labels carefully.

- Follow dosage directions, and do not exceed the recommended dose of any over-the-counter medicine.

- Always administer the proper medicine for your child's age and weight.

- Never use adult medicines to treat a child.

- Purchase products with tamper-resistant packaging, and always make sure they are intact.

- For most products, store in a cool, dry place.

- Check the expiration date on all medications. Out-of-date items can lose their effectiveness.

- Never discard expired medications in an accessible trash can; it's best to flush them down the toilet.

- Your local pharmacist is also an excellent resource who'll be happy to answer any questions you may have.

The Alternative Medicine Home Kit

Alternative medicine has become more acceptable and popular in the last few years. Homeopathic pharmacies and health food stores are opening in cities throughout the country. Even drugstores and supermarkets are stocking their shelves with vitamins and homeopathic remedies. Many doctors are recommending homeopathy not only as a preventive measure for their young patients, but also as a supplement to traditional medical therapies. Consult your doctor before purchasing the following items:

Homeopathic Remedies

- ☿ Chamomilla 6x or 30x (can be very useful in children's earaches)

- ☿ Hepar sulfuris (can be useful in certain types of coughs)

- ☿ Arnica montana pellets 6x or 30x and cream (for healing of cuts, scrapes, bruises, and fractures)

- ☿ Belladonna 6x or 30x (for fever with cold and flu)

- ☿ Aconite 30x (for onset of cold and flu)

- ☿ Nux vomica 6x or 30x (for stomach problems)

- ☿ Apis mell pellets 6x (for mosquito bites)

Other Remedies

- ☿ Echinacea junior (especially during flu season)

- ☿ Chewable vitamin C

- ☿ Chamomile tea (to alleviate stomach spasms; also good for cold or flu)

- ☿ Acidophilus (to be taken in conjunction with antibiotics)

Some stores sell a general homeopathic home kit, containing the most common remedies. Remember to administer child-sized dosages. Speak to the homeopathic pharmacist or doctor for other recommendations.

Childhood Illnesses

Now that your child is more social and spends time with other children, don't be surprised if she gets sick frequently. This is especially true of children attending day care or any toddler or preschool program. The most common illnesses are upper respiratory infections (colds and bronchitis), ear infections, viral syndromes, and viral gastroenteritis. You should call the doctor when your child has any of the following symptoms:

❧ Fever

❧ Diarrhea or constipation

❧ Yellowish green mucus discharging from the nose

❧ Coughing or wheezing

❧ Tugging on the ear or complaining of earache

❧ Complaining of sore throat

❧ Redness or discharge in eyes

❧ Rapid, labored breathing

❧ Stomach pains or distended, gassy stomach

❧ Vomiting

❧ Loss of appetite and listlessness

❧ Symptoms of dehydration (lack of urination, dry eyes, dry mouth)

❧ Skin rash

❧ Inconsolable crying and overall change in temperament

❧ Unusual bleeding (in urine or stools, excessive nosebleeds)

Call the doctor at the onset of any of the above symptoms. Don't procrastinate, because symptoms usually worsen as the day progresses, and fever always escalates at night. Save yourself and your pediatrician a sleepless night by calling first thing in the morning so that your child can be seen as quickly as possible. Be considerate and call during regular office hours; no doctor wants to receive phone calls after office hours that should have been handled during the day.

When you call, be prepared with the following information:

- Child's age and weight

- Temperature

- Symptoms

- Changes in child's behavior or routines (e.g., appetite, sleep patterns, disposition)

- Allergies

- Any significant family history

- Past reactions to medication or injections

- Pharmacy telephone number

Fever

Many parents worry when their child has a fever. In actuality, a fever is a good sign because it's the body's natural response to infection, which may be viral or bacterial. Normal temperature is 98.6 degrees Fahrenheit. If your child has a fever under 102 degrees, dress her in lightweight clothing and push lots of fluids, such as water, juice, or flat lemon-lime soda or cola. To make the child more comfort-

PINK AND BLUE HINT

If your pediatrician prescribes medication and your child is well enough to return to day care or preschool, ask the pharmacist to put the medicine into two bottles. Leave one at home and take the other to the caregiver, with explicit directions (for example, that the medication needs to be refrigerated).

able, lower her temperature by administering acetaminophen. Follow the directions on the package, or call your pediatrician to determine the dosage.

If the child is spiking a temperature of over 102.5 degrees, switch to ibuprofen and call your doctor. Alert her to any symptoms accompanying the fever, such as dehydration (dry mouth and lips, little urination, and lethargy), irritable behavior, vomiting or diarrhea, difficulty breathing, rash, or pain in the stomach, throat, or ears. Besides giving her the medicine, try putting the child in a tepid bath. Dip a washcloth in the bathwater, wipe it over her body and forehead, and then let the water evaporate. After the bath, towel-dry the child. The temperature should come down within twenty minutes. Repeat the bath as often as necessary. Continue to push fluids in order to prevent dehydration.

Parents tend to overreact to a high temperature; however, brain injury and other harmful effects from high fevers are extremely rare. Fevers produce febrile convulsions in some children. Doctors don't know why, but they believe family history plays a role. A febrile seizure is a rapid rise in temperature, often accompanied by uncontrollable shaking, leaving the body limp and listless. Other characteristics are pale, clammy skin and eyes rolling back or fluttering. These seizures are not generally dangerous, but you must call the doctor immediately. Don't leave the child alone, even to make the call; take her with you. Lay the child flat, remove any heavy clothing (especially shirts with drawstring collars), turn her head to one side, and make sure there's nothing in her mouth to obstruct breathing. If a convulsion lasts longer than three to five minutes, or if the child cannot breathe properly after the seizure and continues to display irrational behavior, call 911 immediately.

PINK AND BLUE ALERT

Before taking the child's temperature, always shake a mercury thermometer so that the mercury falls below 97 degrees. Disinfect rectal and oral thermometers with alcohol after each usage; then rinse off with tepid water.

PINK AND BLUE ALERT

Never use rubbing alcohol to lower the child's temperature. The skin can absorb the alcohol, and inhaling the fumes is dangerous.

PINK AND BLUE ALERT

Aspirin should not be used for treating pain or fever in young children, specifically when chicken pox or viral illnesses occur. It can cause dangerous side effects, such as Reye's syndrome, a potentially fatal disease.

Time-Tested Advice

❤ If your child is running a fever, do not send her to day care or school because she infects everyone else around her, which ultimately perpetuates the problem.

❤ A child should be fever-free for twenty-four hours before returning to her regular activities.

❤ If you need to cool down your child's body temperature and she resists getting into the bathtub, entertain her with a few favorite bath toys to keep her content and distracted.

❤ If your child resists drinking fluids, try giving her a frozen electrolyte ice stick or a Popsicle. They're available in popular fruit flavors at most pharmacies and supermarkets.

Diarrhea

When diarrhea strikes, check for frequency and consistency of stool so when you call your doctor you have all the specifics. The biggest concern is dehydration, and the signs are diminished urine flow, dry mouth, no tears when crying, and lack of skin elasticity (pinch a small area of skin and see if it bounces back). If any of these conditions are present, consult your pediatrician immediately.

PINK AND BLUE HINT

When your child has mild diarrhea, remember the BRAT diet: bananas, rice, apples, toast. All these foods are binding, but a word of caution—don't overdo it. Let the child's tummy rest.

If there's no dehydration and a general diarrhea condition exists, treat your child with plenty of liquids, including electrolyte solution (either the liquid form or the frozen ones like Popsicles). Avoid all dairy products, especially milk. Consult your physician if the condition persists for more than twenty-four hours. Don't administer any antidiarrhea medication without your doctor's consent.

Vomiting

You never know when the "upchucks" are going to hit or how long they may last. Don't be surprised if your child acts upset and cries. This is a natural response to quite an ordeal. While you really can't be prepared for the first accident, you can take precautions for future vomiting bouts.

Time-Tested Advice

- ❧ Ice chips help your child stay hydrated and will also help remove the bad taste in her mouth.

- ❧ An excellent alternative to ice chips is frozen electrolyte solution on a stick. Just be sure she doesn't eat it too fast.

- ❧ Give her very tiny sips of water so she can hold down the liquids.

- ❧ If you're lucky enough to get your child to the toilet, stand and support her by gently holding her forehead while she vomits.

- ❧ Keep a plastic trash can by the bed, and demonstrate to your child what to do when she feels like vomiting.

- ❧ Place a few large towels over her pillow and blanket to keep cleanups down to a minimum.

Constipation

When constipation occurs, change your child's diet. Encourage lots of fluids, high-fiber foods (bran cereal or muffins, multigrain bread), roughage (salads, legumes, fresh

PINK AND BLUE ALERT

 For severe diarrhea, give your child only liquids, then gradually move to the BRAT diet. Once her body tolerates this diet, continue with bland, easily digestible foods such as plain pasta, plain baked potato, gelatin, or poached chicken.

PINK AND BLUE ALERT

 Your child will probably regain her appetite and want to eat too soon after vomiting. A word of caution: Don't let her whining and nagging persuade you to feed her. Stick to a bland diet till her tummy is rested and she is retaining all foods. The diet should consist of clear broth, toast, and gelatin. Avoid all dairy products.

fruits, and vegetables), and dried fruit free of preservatives. Serve food in bite-sized pieces to the toddler.

Also make sure your child is getting plenty of exercise, which is an excellent stimulant for regularity. Apply some petroleum jelly to her rectum to ease bowel movement passage. Consult your pediatrician if the constipation lasts more than two days, or if the child is experiencing any pain or discomfort. The doctor may prescribe a stool softener if constipation persists.

Colds, Flu, and Upper Respiratory Infections

When the weather changes and winter months approach, young children are a breeding ground for colds, flu, coughs, sore throats, bronchitis, and croup. It is virtually impossible to prevent these germs from attacking. Usually, colds, flu, and other viral infections are contagious just before the symptoms appear. This is why day care and nursery schools can be a hotbed for infection.

It takes a while for the child's body to build up immunities against these airborne viruses. Always call the pediatrician and be prepared with all the information she needs in order to evaluate your child's condition. For more information, consult the section on fever, earlier in this chapter.

PINK AND BLUE ALERT

If your child continues to have labored breathing after steaming or going outside, call your doctor immediately. If you cannot reach the doctor, go to the nearest emergency room.

Time-Tested Advice

❀ To protect you and your family from infection, everyone should wash hands often with soap and warm water, especially after going to the bathroom or changing diapers, before and after handling food, and before eating.

❀ Don't allow family members to share utensils, cups, or food.

❧ Change bedding and towels daily.

❧ Wipe clean and disinfect all toys and objects that your child has sneezed, coughed, or drooled on. This will inhibit the germs from spreading.

❧ Teach your child to cover her mouth when she coughs or sneezes.

❧ It's healthier to use disposable tissues as opposed to handkerchiefs.

❧ Even though it's hard, avoid kissing your child, especially on the mouth.

❧ Do not allow anyone to smoke around your child, especially if she has any kind of respiratory problem. Secondhand smoke is dangerous under healthy, normal circumstances, let alone when a child is having difficulty breathing.

❧ Some children's medications don't taste very good. If a medicine is in liquid form, try mixing it with her favorite juice. If the medicine is in tablet form, crush it and mix it with applesauce, mashed banana, or fruit yogurt.

❧ If your child resists taking medication, state in a matter-of-fact way, "It's medicine time." Do not ask for permission or plead for her cooperation. Instead, offer a favorite treat when she is cooperative.

❧ At bedtime, run a cool-mist humidifier in your child's bedroom to help open up the airway passages.

❧ For bronchitis or croup, run hot water in the shower and sit with your child in the bathroom, letting the steam ease her labored breathing.

PINK AND BLUE ALERT

 Always complete the prescribed antibiotic, even if your child is feeling better after two or three days. If you stop the medication before the full course is finished, the harmful bacteria may not be completely eliminated.

* If the night air is cool and misty, an alternative remedy for croup is to take your well-bundled child outside for a few minutes to ease her breathing.

* To ease breathing with colds or coughs, try elevating the head of the mattress with either some books or folded towels or blankets.

* To thin mucus, make a home remedy of warm water mixed with lemon juice and a little honey. (Honey should only be given to children over one year old.)

* To prevent sore nostrils, dab some petroleum jelly on a tissue or soft handkerchief before wiping your child's nose.

* Push a lot of fluids so the toxins in the body will be flushed out.

* Once your child is feeling a little better and is not running a temperature, it's OK to let her go outdoors to get some fresh air. Don't allow her to run around and get overheated. Keep the activity low-key.

PINK AND BLUE HINT

A good home remedy for an ear infection is garlic oil or olive oil. Warm the oil and place it in a dropper. Be sure to test the temperature of the oil before administering. Put a few drops in the infected ear.

PINK AND BLUE HINT

After swimming in the pool or ocean, try dipping a cotton swab in rubbing alcohol and then gently insert it into the child's ear. This will make the water in the ear evaporate and help prevent an outer ear infection (swimmer's ear).

Ear Infections

Otitis media (ear infection) is one of the most common illnesses young children develop. It can affect one or both ears and is usually a buildup of fluid within the middle ear. An ear infection is not directly contagious and often follows a cold, flu, or eye infection, which are all contagious. If your child complains and/or tugs on her ear, has a restless night, and acts irritable, call the pediatrician immediately.

When infection is evident, antibiotics are usually the course of action. Avoid dairy products to reduce the mucus.

In addition, if your child is put on antibiotics, acidophilus is recommended for her diet in order to protect the lining of her stomach and ward off yeast infections. If your child is in extreme discomfort, the doctor may also prescribe ear drops.

Injuries and Insects

Besides the occasional illness, your child will surely experience the ouches and itches that result from accidents and from encounters with insects. You'll have to be ready to treat bee stings, bumps, bruises, and, yes, even lice. While these occurrences may be traumatic for both of you, staying calm and collected is the best advice. When your child is hurt and you have any concerns, call your pediatrician.

Head Injuries

It is not unusual for young children to bump their heads. However, if your child falls or receives a severe blow to her head, take these precautions. First, determine whether she has lost consciousness. If not, check to see if she's alert and easily aroused. If she's unconscious and/or bleeding, vomiting, or disoriented, complains of a headache, cries uncontrollably for more than ten minutes, has slurred speech, or displays unusual behavior, call 911 and your pediatrician right away.

To control the swelling, apply an ice pack to the injured area. Your child will probably not like the feeling of the ice, but it is very important to contain the inflammation immediately. Do not allow your child to go to sleep immediately after the fall, and continue to observe her behavior. It's not advisable to administer acetaminophen or any pain reliever because the symptoms could be masked. When in doubt, call your doctor.

PINK AND BLUE ALERT

Never swing, drag, or pull a young child by the arm because you can easily pull her arm out of joint and cause "nursemaid's elbow." If this accidentally occurs, call your pediatrician immediately and go to the office or the closest emergency room.

PINK AND BLUE ALERT

Never leave your child unattended with a severe head injury. If someone else is at home with you, have her make the call. If the pediatrician advises you to go to the nearest emergency room, try not to go alone, so you can attend to your child on the way to the hospital.

PINK AND BLUE ALERT

Always wrap an ice pack with a towel or washcloth to avoid ice burns.

PINK AND BLUE HINT

A bag of frozen vegetables is a good substitute for an ice pack because it easily molds to the child's injury.

PINK AND BLUE ALERT

Never apply butter, vegetable shortening, petroleum jelly, or powder to a burn because that can lead to infection. In addition, do not pop blisters, because bacterial infection can develop.

Bruises

There's no escaping the inevitable bruise, cut, or scrape all children experience in their daily lives. Generally speaking, bruises can usually be treated with ice, antibacterial and antiseptic lotion, a bandage, and some tender loving care. Mishaps are to be expected, and you need to be prepared. (Please see the Home Medicine Cabinet checklist earlier in this chapter.)

Usually a bruise is not a big deal. It may hurt, turn black and blue, swell a little, and heal within a week. However, some bruises can indicate a more serious problem, such as sprained or fractured bones. If your child is favoring a limb or has limited mobility, or if extreme swelling appears, consult your physician at once.

Burns

Burns are divided into three categories, depending on the severity. The least damaging is the first-degree burn, where the skin is mildly red, has slight swelling, and can be very painful for a short period of time. Second-degree burns are bright red, blister, and swell instantly. The most serious burns are third-degree and are characterized by white or charred skin. In all cases, contact the doctor.

Time-Tested Advice

❤ When a child suffers a burn, immediately immerse the area in cool water for a minimum of ten minutes. Never use ice.

❤ If something hot is spilled on your child, run cool water on her—and the clothing because any skin that might be sticking to a garment can be damaged even more.

- If the injured area is small and not oozing, apply aloe or prescription Silvadene cream and a sterile nonadhesive dressing.

- If the child is in pain, administer acetaminophen or ibuprofen, and call your doctor.

- If the burn is serious and requires immediate medical attention, call 911 or take her to the nearest emergency room.

PINK AND BLUE ALERT

 Don't leave your child unattended. If you're alone, take the child with you when you make the emergency call.

Scrapes

A scrape usually covers a larger area than a cut. Scrapes tend to be more painful because more nerve endings are exposed. The most common areas that young children scrape are their knees, shins, and elbows.

Time-Tested Advice

- Clean the scraped area carefully with water and antibacterial soap, and gently remove the dirt and any debris.

- If any foreign matter is deeply embedded in the skin, leave it alone, and call the doctor at once.

- Apply antiseptic spray, antibiotic ointment, or healing ointment (such as Aquaphor) to the wound, then loosely cover with a sterile bandage or gauze pad.

- If bleeding occurs, apply pressure to the wound. If there's no bleeding, leave the scraped area open to air.

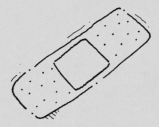

PINK AND BLUE HINT

Buy decorative bandages with your child's favorite characters. When she gets a cut and becomes upset, distract her by asking her to pick out the bandage. She won't be so resistant to covering the cut and will be proud to display her new boo-boo.

PINK AND BLUE HINT

When removing a bandage from a young child's tender skin, try rubbing the outside of the adhesive strip with petroleum jelly or lotion. This helps soften the glue's grip, allowing you to pull off the bandage with less stinging, pain, and hysterical fanfare from your child.

* Clean the wound daily until it has scabbed.

* While the scraped area is healing, keep your child out of dirt and sandboxes.

* Encourage your child not to pick at her scab, because it can cause infection.

Cuts

In a young child's active life, it is not unusual for her to fall and cut herself. She may become somewhat hysterical at the sight of her own blood, so it's very important you stay calm and collected while helping her stop the bleeding. As always, lots of TLC can help soothe the discomfort, too!

Time-Tested Advice

* Apply pressure directly on the wound with a sterile gauze pad or clean washcloth for at least five minutes. If a cut appears deep and doesn't stop bleeding after ten to fifteen minutes, call your doctor immediately.

* If your child is spurting blood or appears to be going into shock, call 911 at once. While waiting for the emergency assistance, continue to apply pressure over the wound.

* For simple cuts, once the bleeding has stopped, clean the wound with soap and water or hydrogen peroxide. Dab dry with a sterile gauze pad, apply antibiotic cream or ointment, and then place a bandage over the cut.

❤ Change the bandage and reapply the topical ointment at least once a day.

❤ If the bandage gets dirty or extremely wet, change the dressing on the cut.

❤ Keep the cut covered with a bandage for at least two days. Then when it's starting to heal, remove the bandage, allowing air to get to it.

❤ If signs of infection such as oozing, redness, swelling, or increased pain occur, call your doctor.

❤ Whenever scarring or infection poses a risk, seek medical attention immediately.

❤ If a child or animal bites your child and the skin is broken, wash the wound with antibacterial soap and water, and call your pediatrician immediately.

❤ If a deep laceration to the face occurs, your child might need sutures (stitches). A plastic surgeon is the best choice because she is specially trained and will help minimize scarring; call your pediatrician for a referral.

❤ If a wound is deep and jagged, call your pediatrician or go to the nearest emergency room.

❤ If a cut is deep, be sure your child is up-to-date with her tetanus booster shot.

Insect Bites

Along with the pleasures of playing outdoors come natural risks. Insect bites can be a nuisance at best and dangerous at worst.

PINK AND BLUE HINT

When changing a bandage daily, remember to change its position—vertically one time, horizontally the next time. There's less chance the gluey material will irritate the child's sensitive skin.

PINK AND BLUE ALERT

If your child picks at her scabs, she could develop impetigo, a contagious bacterial skin infection caused by staphylococci or streptococci. If a cut starts to look honey-colored and crusty, and little lesions begin to spread on your child's skin, call your doctor at once.

Bees

At the top of the list is the unpredictable bee sting. Unfortunately, there is no way of knowing whether your child is allergic to bee stings, regardless of whether you or your spouse is allergic. If the child has difficulty breathing after being stung, call 911 for immediate help.

Usually, most children will have a local reaction that should be treated immediately. Remove the stinger by either gently scraping it off with a flat-edged object such as a credit card or knife. The area will become red, swollen, and painful to the touch. Wash it with soap and water, then apply ice to control the swelling and ease the discomfort. In addition, to relieve itching, dab calamine lotion onto the sting, or make a paste of either bicarbonate of soda or meat tenderizer and water.

If your child breaks out in hives or begins to vomit, call your doctor at once. If the redness or swelling persists more than twenty-four hours or you notice red streaking lines near the area, call your doctor immediately.

Spiders

Spider bites can be equally uncomfortable and dangerous if left untreated. Should you notice unusual redness or streaking lines around the bitten area, call your doctor immediately.

Mosquitoes

Protect your child against mosquito and other common insect bites by applying insect repellent to clothing, shoes, and exposed skin areas before your child plays outdoors. Since mosquitoes are attracted to water, don't let your child play in standing pools of dirty water. Be particularly aware of these annoying insects during the summer season, both day and night.

Mosquito bites can be treated by dabbing calamine lotion on them. You can also try using Apis mell 6x pellets, which can be found at your local homeopathic pharmacy.

Fleas

If you have a dog or cat, beware of fleas because they can easily infest your home and leave multiple bites on the skin. At least one month before the flea season (usually around June), it's a good idea to preventively treat your house against the flea invasion. Vacuum your home daily to catch any fleas living in the carpet, and discard the bag when you are done (or else you'll release the fleas back into the carpet the next time you vacuum). If anyone in your home has bites from fleas, try calamine lotion or oatmeal baths for relief.

Ticks

Within the last decade there has been an outbreak of Lyme disease. This is caused by a bacterium called a spirochete, which is transmitted by tiny deer ticks that are very difficult to see. If you're planning on hiking, picnicking, or taking your child to a woody or tall-grassy area where deer are prevalent, be sure everyone is covered well with insect repellent containing deet (carefully follow package instructions) to avoid tick bites. Wear long pants and either tuck them into your socks or pull the socks over the pants tightly to eliminate the possibility of bugs crawling inside your pant leg; also, wear a long-sleeved shirt with a tight-fitting neckline. While you hike or picnic, periodically have tick checks. When you return home, make sure everyone takes a shower, using very warm water, soap, and shampoo to remove the

PINK AND BLUE ALERT

Deet must be used with caution on young children. It's best to apply it to clothing and shoes, always avoiding the mouth and eyes. In addition, since young children tend to put their fingers and hands in their mouths, do not put the repellent containing deet on the hands. An adult should apply this particular repellent to the child, and in small quantities. Avoid areas with sunburns and rashes.

deet and any ticks that may be hiding in the scalp, neck, armpit, and general torso area.

If you see a tick on your child's skin, try not to kill it. Just gently remove it with tweezers as close to the skin as possible, without squeezing or crushing it. After removing the tick, put it in a well-sealed plastic bag or container to take to the doctor for medical analysis.

Common symptoms of Lyme disease are a raised red, bull's-eye rash (at the site of the bite), fever, flulike symptoms, headaches, sore throat, fatigue, joint swelling and aches (as in arthritis), facial tics or numbness, stiff neck, and sometimes heart arrhythmia. If your child experiences any of these symptoms after a deer tick bite, consult your pediatrician immediately. A Lyme disease vaccination has been approved by the FDA and will be available to the public in the very near future.

Human Bites

Bites by other children are usually not serious, but they are frightening to the child and parent. Immediately comfort the child who has been bitten. Then clean the bite with soap and water, followed by hydrogen peroxide. If the skin has been broken, apply an ice pack and then an antibiotic ointment. Call your pediatrician if swelling and redness occur.

Nosebleeds

Although nosebleeds are a common childhood occurrence, they are definitely frightening to the young child. Here are a few simple procedures to follow; they will usually stop the bleeding.

Time-Tested Advice

- Have your child sit with her head tilted forward. (Tilting the head backward causes the blood to run down the throat.)

- Gently pinch the nostrils together and hold for approximately ten minutes. Make sure your child breathes through her mouth! Check to see if the bleeding has stopped, and if it hasn't, continue squeezing for another ten minutes.

- Carefully put a cold, wet cotton ball in the bloody nostril. Don't pack it in the nose too tightly or too far into the nostril.

- If bleeding hasn't stopped or slowed noticeably after twenty minutes, call your doctor.

- To prevent nosebleeds during dry or cold weather, swab the inside of the nose with petroleum jelly. Placing a cool-mist humidifier in the child's room at night also can help alleviate dryness.

Head Lice

Even the cleanest family with good hygiene can fall prey to lice. It is not uncommon for your child to pick them up at day care, school, or the park, especially around the sandbox. Head lice are extremely contagious and must be treated immediately. Lice can be spread rapidly by wearing someone's infected hat, by using another person's comb or brush, or even leaning the head against a headrest in a car or airplane. Signs of head lice are head scratching, scalp rash, and actually seeing the nits (white eggs).

Follow these steps to remove this uncomfortable, highly contagious problem.

PINK AND BLUE HINT

Set a kitchen timer, and shampoo the hair and scalp thoroughly for exactly ten minutes.

PINK AND BLUE HINT

Tea tree oil shampoo is an excellent deterrent for head lice because it contains natural antibacterial and antiseptic properties. After your child has had lice, use this shampoo frequently.

Time-Tested Advice

❤ Inspect the scalp for lice, which are small, gray bugs, and the hair follicles for the nits, which are hard, white eggs, under a bright light.

❤ If you find either bugs or nits, call your pediatrician. She'll either prescribe a medicated shampoo or tell you to use an over-the-counter shampoo designed to destroy the lice. Some shampoo packages include a fine-toothed comb and a spray disinfectant, although antilice sprays are not necessary. Carefully follow the directions on the package, and don't overuse the product.

❤ After towel-drying the hair, back comb with a fine-toothed comb to remove the nits and lice. It's best to work in small sections at a time. Be patient when removing lice and nits, because it's an arduous process, especially if the hair is long. Don't forget to rinse the comb in hot water each time you pass the comb through the hair.

❤ Brushes and combs can be sprayed first with the disinfectant (again not mandatory), and then must soak for one hour in a solution of the medicated shampoo and hot water. To be on the safe side, do the same thing with everyone else's combs and brushes in your home.

❤ Wash your child's towels, sheets, pillowcases, blankets, bedspreads, clothing, and cloth-covered toys (and those of anyone else in the home infected with lice) in hot water to kill any remaining lice. Next, vacuum carpets, pillows, upholstered items, and mattresses, and throw away the vacuum cleaner bag upon completion.

❧ Hats and clothing that can't be laundered need to be put in tightly sealed plastic bags and set aside for three weeks (that's the longest time nits can survive). At the end of this period, you can safely send those items to the dry cleaner.

❧ If nits appear on eyelashes, lightly apply petroleum jelly on lashes twice a day for one week.

❧ Repeat all head treatments one week to ten days later to eliminate lice that may hatch in the interim.

❧ Check the scalp of all family members and anyone else living in your home daily for the next two to three weeks.

❧ Notify day care, school, or anyone who has been in close contact with your child.

❧ If rash doesn't clear after treatment or it clears and then returns and new eggs appear in the hair, consult your doctor.

❧ If you prefer to try the homeopathic method, visit your local homeopathic pharmacy and ask for recommendations.

PINK AND BLUE ALERT

Do not use products containing the compound lindane. It is not as effective in eliminating head lice as the other recommended products.

PINK AND BLUE HINT

If nits are particularly difficult to remove from hair after shampooing, use an even mixture of vinegar and rubbing alcohol to loosen the eggs.

PINK AND BLUE HINT

In extreme cases of lice, try smothering the nits and eggs by applying mayonnaise to the scalp and hair follicles.

Nourishing the Sick Child

When a child is not feeling well, it is common for her appetite to decrease. Although it may pose a challenge, keeping the child well hydrated is very important. Many parents obsess about their child not eating solid food, but fluid intake is far more vital for keeping the body's organs functioning properly. If the child is not drinking enough fluid, watch for signs of dehydration. They can include diminished urine flow, crying without tears, lethargy, dry mouth, and lack of skin elasticity. If your child displays any of these symptoms, call your doctor at once.

Feeding your sick child depends upon what ails her. In some children, dairy products can be hard on the stomach and create more mucus. The following list includes the most common ailments that affect a child's appetite.

Vomiting and Diarrhea

PINK AND BLUE HINT

To remove the carbonation from soda, either quickly stir the soda in a cup with a spoon, or pour the liquid from one cup to another.

A child's small body can dehydrate quickly. Encourage frequent sips of water, diluted juice, sports drinks, or flat cola or ginger ale. Once your child tolerates the clear liquids, slowly start a bland diet. Begin with small portions of the BRAT diet: bananas, rice, applesauce, and toast. In addition, while gelatin has little nutritional value, it is filling and gentle on a queasy stomach. Let the belly rest for a few days before returning to a normal diet.

Upper Respiratory Illnesses

Colds, coughs, and sore throats can diminish a child's appetite. Push plenty of fluids and encourage her to eat. In addition to clear liquids, serve warm chicken soup or weak tea. Soft, cool foods, such as applesauce, fruit smoothies, frozen ices, and gelatin are soothing for a sore throat. Avoid dairy products.

Fever

When your child is running a fever with no other symptoms, push lots of liquids. If the child resists drinking, try ice chips or frozen ices. It's perfectly fine for her to eat solid foods and maintain a normal diet as long as her stomach is not upset.

Activities for the Sick Toddler or Preschooler

When your youngster is sick at home, you will need plenty of activities and tricks up your sleeve to keep her entertained. It is not unusual for a child to be clingy when she's not feeling well, so it's important to give her extra hugs and kisses as you reassure her she is going to get better. If you act anxious or worry excessively when your child becomes sick, you risk creating that same fearfulness in the child. Be optimistic, stay calm and lift the sick child's spirits by providing fun, interesting activities that entertain her, distracting her so she doesn't think too much about her current condition.

If she is particularly uncomfortable, she will probably want to stay in bed, so let her rest quietly and watch a video or read her a favorite book. As she starts to feel better, she will need activities to stimulate her mind and hold her interest. Instead of parking your child in front of the television all day, do some of the following activities together. Most of these activities can be done while she's recuperating in bed; however, if the child is up to it, let her do them in your designated arts and crafts workplace.

❀ Make necklaces with different materials:

   ◎ Thin licorice strands and O-shaped cereal

PINK AND BLUE ALERT
Make sure art supplies are nontoxic and age appropriate for toddlers and preschoolers. Use paintbrushes with rounded handles.

- String and different-shaped pastas (for three- and four-year olds)

- Yarn and large, colorful beads (for three- and four-year olds)

❀ Make puppets:

- Use paper lunch bags, old gloves, Popsicle sticks, or tongue depressors.

- Decorate with crayons, colored markers, or washable paint.

- Glue on yarn, doilies, ribbon, fabric, buttons, etc.

❀ Make face masks with paper plates:

- Cut out holes for the eyes, nose, and mouth. (An adult should do this.)

- Decorate facial features with crayons, colored markers, or washable paint.

- Punch a hole on both sides of the plate, and tie string or yarn in each of the holes. Tie the string in a a bow or loose knot behind the child's head so she can wear the mask.

❀ Make a collage or picture on a paper plate, construction paper, or poster board:

- Decorate with thick crayons, colored markers, washable paint.

- Cut out pictures from old magazines and glue them on.

- Glue on different shapes of pasta. (When the glue is dry, paint the pasta.)

๑ Glue on odds and ends from around the house, such as buttons, beads, and assorted cereals.

❀ Either make your own play dough (a recipe is in Chapter 11, "Home Sweet Home") or buy ready-made Play-Doh. Use it with cookie cutters, bottle tops, garlic press, blunt scissors, plastic spoon or dull-edged knife, potato ricer, and rolling pin, or purchase Play-Doh accessories.

❀ Paint an old white T-shirt with washable paints.

❀ Make your own Mr. Potato Head from a raw potato and decorate, or buy the Mr. Potato Head toy.

❀ Create pictures with rubber stamps or cut-up sponges and nontoxic ink pads.

❀ If your child is not required to stay in bed, let your preschooler construct her own little hideaway using chairs, stools, end of a sofa, or a card table along with blankets, sheets, and pillows. Let her imagination run wild as she creates a special space that belongs only to her.

๑ 4 ๑

Personal Hygiene

PINK AND BLUE HINT

To teach your child the difference between left and right, have him hold up his left hand so that his left thumb and index finger form an L. (Show him what an L looks like by drawing the letter on a piece of paper.)

Instilling good hygiene habits at an early age sets an important precedent for your child. Naturally, it's the parents' responsibility to teach the young child how to care for himself.

Bath Time

At the end of a child's busy day, one thing is certain: the grime's got to go. Some children take baths willingly and even look forward to them, while others find baths sheer torture and terrifying. The key for the parent is to make bath time as much fun as possible. Being prepared eliminates the hassles and makes bath time a pleasurable experience.

In today's child-oriented market, manufacturers have developed an array of bath gear and accessories to delight the little consumer. Here are some basic items you'll need to have on hand:

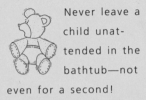

❧ *Nontoxic soap*—It can be purchased in bar form, animal or character shapes, or special scents. Also, many manufacturers make a liquid body wash.

❧ *Shampoo*—Some manufacturers make a shampoo and conditioner all in one. Be sure to purchase products that are specifically for children and nonirritating to the eyes.

❧ *Washcloths*—It's handy to have one for the body and another one to protect the eyes when shampooing. Puppet or decorative washcloths add extra fun to bath time.

❧ *Towel*—The regular kind is fine, but there are also terry cloth poncho towels that cover the child from head to toe.

❧ *Bath toys* and plastic books

❧ *Nonskid bath mat or decals*—a *must* for safety's sake

❧ *Handheld sprayer attachment* for rinsing off (optional)

Time-Tested Advice

❧ Make sure the bathroom is warm enough so your child won't catch a chill when stepping out of the tub.

❧ Have everything you need for bath time in the bathroom and readily accessible at your fingertips.

PINK AND BLUE HINT
Store bath toys in a mesh laundry bag and hang it from either the faucet or shower head. Every so often, clean the toys, since soap scum accumulates.

PINK AND BLUE HINT
A bath bonnet (shampoo hat) is an excellent way to keep shampoo and water out of the child's eyes.

❦ Run the bathwater and test the temperature before allowing your child to get into the tub. Make sure the bathwater is not higher than the child's waist.

❦ Keep child-resistant safety knobs on the hot and cold valves so your child can't play with them.

❦ Since a child can easily bump his head on the bathtub spout, place a safety cover over it.

❦ Always help the child step in and out of the tub carefully. Unless your child is getting out of the tub, there should be no standing allowed in it.

❦ Buy bath toys and books specifically designed for the bath.

❦ Rotate the toys, and every once in a while bring in kitchen items, such as plastic measuring cups, containers, and funnels, so he can practice measuring and pouring without making a mess.

❦ Since some children are either resistant to or fearful of shampooing, it's a good idea to let them play first and then wash their hair and body last.

❦ A handheld sprayer attachment is handy because it makes rinsing out shampoo easier and faster, and provides clean water.

❦ If you don't want to use a spray attachment, try using a small, lightweight watering can to rinse hair.

❦ Another technique for removing shampoo is to lean the child back and cradle his head and neck in the crease of your arm and carefully rinse. To protect his eyes, let him hold a washcloth over his face or eyes.

Fear of Bathing

It is not uncommon for a young child to be fearful of the bathtub and water. However, just because he acts out and refuses doesn't mean you let him get his way. Instead, you'll need some resourceful tactics for helping him clean up his act.

PINK AND BLUE HINT

For the child who is fearful of shampooing his hair and getting soap in his eyes, try having him wear swimming goggles.

Time-Tested Advice

- If your child is afraid of the bath, try taking one with him (wear a bathing suit if you feel uncomfortable being naked), or have a sibling or friend join him.

- Talk to your child about his fears, and see if you can determine how and where the fear began. Be understanding and don't be critical of his feelings.

- When you fill the bathtub, start with only a few inches of water. As your child becomes more comfortable, slowly increase the amount of water.

- Take your child to the store and let him select a few new bath toys.

- Go to your local library or bookstore and pick out a few books on bath time. Some suggested books are *Bernard's Bath* by Joan Elizabeth Goodman, *I Hate to Take a Bath* by Judi Barrett, and *Sam's Bath* by Barbro Lindgren.

- Purchase soap crayons, and let him draw pictures in the bathtub.

- Sing songs or play a musical tape to calm his nerves. (Use a battery-operated recorder.)

♥ Puppet washcloths or terry cloth hand mitts help the parent and child role-play and talk about the child's fears through the words of the puppet.

♥ If your child displays a fear that he may go down the drain with the water, then let the water out after he leaves the tub.

♥ If he is completely hysterical and resistant to the bath, start off with sponge baths and gradually move into the tub.

♥ Try taking your child into the shower with you, keeping the water pressure as low as possible.

♥ Have the child bathe a waterproof doll in the kitchen or bathroom sink. Then, when he takes a bath, let him bring the doll into the tub so they can bathe together.

Good Grooming

Encouraging good grooming habits and initiating high standards of hygiene at an early age are important because they teach the child to take responsibility for his personal appearance and general well-being. The parent has to be patient, persistent, and consistent in promoting these efforts. It will pay off.

Hair Care

Whether your child's hair is short or long, it still requires attention. An active child needs a shampoo at least every other day to wash away the food and dirt he has accumulated in his lovely locks. Use a good mild shampoo that does not dry the scalp. (See Bath Time for shampooing tips.)

As the hair grows, you'll be introducing haircuts, either at home or at a professional salon. The following information should help alleviate any hair struggles.

Time-Tested Advice

- ❤ Be sure to have a good brush and wide-toothed comb (no sharp, pointy teeth or bristles) for daily brushings. Don't share these items with anyone else; each family member should have his or her own grooming set.

- ❤ Don't brush hair when it's wet; use a wide-toothed comb.

- ❤ To detangle long, wet hair, start at the bottom and comb one section at a time, slowly working your way up to the top of the head.

- ❤ For hair that easily tangles or knots, try using conditioner after washing, or use a detangling spray.

- ❤ Let your child practice combing and brushing a doll's hair. Or if you're brave enough, let him practice on you.

- ❤ Most little girls love colorful barrettes, bows, and fancy ponytail holders. When removing these items, be careful to avoid pulling and breaking the hair. To prevent breakage, use only coated rubber bands specifically made for hair. Don't pull the hair too tightly, because this can cause headaches.

- ❤ If you choose to cut your child's hair yourself, invest in a good pair of haircutting scissors. Keep these sharp scissors out of your child's reach!

PINK AND BLUE HINT

 If gum mysteriously gets stuck in your child's hair, use peanut butter or cold cream lotion to remove it. Comb it through the gummy section, then wash the hair thoroughly.

When cutting your child's hair, have him sit in his high chair in front of a mirror. Wrap a towel gently around his shoulders, and put newspaper on the floor for easy cleanup. Play music to distract and relax him. To avoid big mistakes, cut a little at a time. Don't expect your child to sit perfectly still and be completely cooperative—you are dealing with a toddler.

Take your child to a local barbershop or salon that specializes in cutting children's hair. These shops cater to the young child, offering simple treats and rewards, and understand that time is of the essence when it comes to cutting a child's hair.

For the first few visits, let the child sit on your lap if he resists sitting by himself.

Don't make an appointment around mealtime or naptime, when your child may be hungry or cranky.

PINK AND BLUE HINT

To introduce your child to the hair salon or barber, visit the shop with your child before the first appointment. You can get a haircut to familiarize him with the process.

Hand and Nail Care

Maintaining clean hands and nails is essential. Have you ever watched where a young child puts his hands? Everywhere! Since dirty hands and nails carry germs, which lead to infection, teach and encourage your child to wash his hands regularly.

Time-Tested Advice

Insist that your child wash his hands after using the toilet, before and after meals, and after playtime. Make sure an adult accompanies him to the bathroom for safety's sake.

- Keep a sturdy stool by the sink, along with antibacterial liquid pump soap and a fresh hand towel.

- If you use bar soap, be sure to rinse off the dirty bar after each use to eliminate the germs left on the soap.

- Teach your preschooler how to adjust the water temperature, turning the cold water on first and then slowly adding a small amount of hot water. Also, show him how much water pressure to use.

- Once your child is capable of washing his hands without your assistance, let him do it himself. As he becomes more independent, there will be fewer power struggles in completing this task. Do a spot check to make sure the grime has been removed.

- Be sure to praise the child for his efforts, even if he makes a big mess.

- If your child balks at washing his hands, give him something fun to wash, like a toy or a doll or plastic dishes. Or, fill the sink with dishwashing liquid or shampoo, and lure him with the bubbles.

- Keep your child's nails shortly trimmed to avoid dirt accumulating underneath the nails and to prevent him from scratching himself and others.

- To keep nails clean, use a nailbrush daily at bath time. For lodged-in dirt, cover a rounded wooden toothpick with a tissue and gently remove the particles.

- The easiest time to cut nails is immediately after a bath, when the nails are pliable. Use round-headed scissors or a soft nail file.

PINK AND BLUE HINT

Place a plastic hook at your child's eye level so he can easily reach the hand towel.

PINK AND BLUE HINT

When you're away from home, carry disposable wipes or a small bottle of instant hand sanitizer gel in your bag for quick cleanups.

PINK AND BLUE HINT

If bath time is not a convenient time to cut nails, and your young child is fidgety, complete the task while he's sleeping or distract him with a video or television.

Dental Care

The official position of the American Academy of Pediatric Dentistry is that a child's first visit to the dentist should be at the age of one. It is a get-acquainted visit and introduction to early child dental care. By the age of three, your child will have twenty teeth, which make up the full set of primary teeth. And that, of course, will eventually mean twenty visits from the tooth fairy!

Ideally, you have been diligent about cleaning your child's teeth ever since that first tooth emerged. By now your child should be brushing his teeth every day with your assistance. When teeth are not brushed and flossed regularly, plaque builds up, forming harmful bacteria, even at this early age. Taking care of baby teeth is important, because decay can affect the adult teeth forming beneath the gums. Good dental hygiene keeps your child's little teeth pearly white.

Time-Tested Advice

- Be a role model and have your child watch you brush your teeth, then do it together.

- Select pleasant-tasting toothpaste that your child will like. Try the new flavors especially created for children.

- To encourage your child to brush his teeth, buy one of the soft-bristled child toothbrushes that come in a variety of designs, such as a favorite character, a unique shape, or a design that glows in the dark.

- A parent needs to help the toddler brush his teeth, because at this stage his manual dexterity is not fully developed, and his cleaning is not effective enough.

- Encourage brushing teeth after every meal and before bedtime.

- Teach your child to brush in a circular motion on the front and back of each tooth. He should also brush his tongue to remove bacteria that causes bad breath.

- A child should stand on his bathroom step stool in order to see himself in the mirror as he brushes.

- When baby teeth touch each other, it's time to floss to prevent cavities from forming between the teeth. The parent needs to do the flossing because a young child does not have the dexterity to perform this skill and could easily hurt his gums.

- Don't give your child too many foods and drinks with high sugar content such as presweetened drinks, juices, sodas, candy, cookies, cake, dried fruits, and chips (in other words, junk food). They can cause cavities.

- When it's logistically impossible to get your child to brush his teeth, give him water to drink. It will rinse the food and bacteria off his teeth.

- Ask your pediatrician or dentist whether your child needs fluoride supplements, such as a prescription multivitamin with fluoride. Taking fluoride helps to protect your child's teeth from unwanted cavities. If you have any questions about the fluoride content in your water, call your local water agency.

- ❀ Many dentists recommend fluoride toothpaste for their young patients. A young child should use only small amounts of fluoridated toothpaste, because if he swallows too much fluoride, it can lead to mottling (discoloration and speckling) on his permanent adult teeth.

- ❀ If you notice your child grinding his teeth, consult the dentist.

- ❀ If your child breaks a baby tooth, see the dentist to make sure a portion of the tooth and/or root is not remaining in the gums. (Baby teeth do not need to be reattached.)

- ❀ Should your child express fear about visiting the dentist, get a few books or videos on the subject.

- ❀ Ask your pediatrician whether he can recommend a pediatric dentist who is specially trained to work with young children.

Clothing

Toddlers and preschoolers have very definite opinions, especially when it comes to clothing they want—or don't want—to wear. Typically, at the age of three, children begin to develop a sense of independence and self-expression, and they exhibit it through their choice of clothing.

Purchase clothing that is practical, comfortable, durable, and easy for a young child to put on and take off. In general, buy clothes that are one size larger than necessary, because your child is still growing and many fabrics tend to shrink with frequent washings.

Time-Tested Advice

- Choose clothing that is appropriate to the occasion and place. Fancy clothing doesn't belong at school or the park, and pajamas should be worn only at home. Your child will begin to learn what clothing is suitable for school versus a party.

- Teach your child to dress suitably for the weather outside—for example, shorts for warm weather, a jacket for cold weather.

- Buy clothing that is easy to dress your youngster in and simple enough for him to dress himself. Buttons are hard for little fingers to manipulate, so purchase clothing with elastic waistbands and Velcro closings.

- To avoid catching your child's skin on a zipper, pull the garment away from his body.

- Don't bother with shirts that need to be tucked in. They never stay in.

- Tight-fitting necklines are difficult for the parent to put on the child and uncomfortable to slip over the child's head.

- Remove neck/hood drawstrings and toggles from T-shirts, sweatshirts, and jackets because they can get caught and easily choke the child. If necessary, replace the drawstrings with a Velcro closure or a snap.

- Shorten waist drawstrings to avoid catching on doors, handrails, playground equipment, or hardware.

PINK AND BLUE HINT
Run a bar of dry soap over a sticky zipper.

PINK AND BLUE HINT
If your child attends day care or preschool, label all clothing with either name tags or indelible ink.

- ❤ Avoid fabrics that are scratchy and itchy to the touch.

- ❤ Remove labels that rub against the child's skin.

- ❤ When the knees wear out on a pair of pants, purchase iron-on knee patches.

- ❤ If there's a hole in clothing, buy an appliqué and sew it on.

- ❤ When pant legs get too short, lengthen them by sewing on decorative trim. Or cut the legs and turn the pants into summer shorts.

Pajamas

Pajamas should be flame-retardant. If your child has a favorite pair of pajamas, purchase a few of the same ones to avoid nighttime battles. It's a good idea to purchase two-piece pajamas for the child who is toilet training or is already diaper-free.

Outerwear

When the seasons change and cold or rainy weather hits, dressing your youngster can be a challenge. Covering his body from head to toe won't be at the top of his list; however, he needs to be protected from the elements. By the time he's dressed in a sweater, jacket, hat, mittens, and boots, you'll be sorry you ever wanted to leave the house.

PINK AND BLUE HINT

To save some money, in warm weather let your child sleep in an old T-shirt and underpants.

Time-Tested Advice

- ❤ In rainy weather, dress your child in a waterproof raincoat or jacket or a slicker with a hood and water-resistant shoes or galoshes. Do not give a young child an umbrella, as he can hurt himself or someone else with its pointy tip.

❧ In cold weather, dress your child in layers. If the temperature is extreme, consider layering your child in long underwear, turtleneck, sweater, and a jacket. If he gets too hot, he can always peel off a layer.

❧ If anyone offers you hand-me-downs, accept. Kids grow out of clothing quickly, and cold-weather apparel is expensive.

❧ When purchasing a winter jacket, make sure there's enough room for the under layers. There are new lightweight, insulating materials that retain body heat and aren't too bulky or uncomfortable for the child.

❧ Buy at least two pairs of mittens or gloves, because one is bound to be missing or lost. To help alleviate this problem, use mitten/glove clips attached to the sleeves of the jacket.

❧ Make sure the hat or knit cap covers the ears and is comfortable for the child.

Shoes and Socks

While clothing can be a little oversized, shoes must fit right. Visit a child's shoe store where the salespeople are knowledgeable about proper sizing (and patient with the fidgety toddler and preschooler). Look for nonslip, well-grooved, flexible shoes for daily wearing.

Buy comfortable socks that allow the feet to breathe. Try a few different styles and textures of socks to see what your child prefers. Different thickness in socks can alter the fit of a shoe.

PINK AND BLUE ALERT

 Don't allow your child to run around the house in socks. He can slip and easily hurt himself. To avoid accidents, buy nonslip socks for home use.

Time-Tested Advice

❤ When you go to the shoe store, make sure your child is wearing the correct socks for the shoes you're purchasing—athletic socks for tennis shoes and winter boots, dress socks for dress shoes.

❤ Make sure the salesperson who assists you has your child stand up when he measures your child's feet.

❤ When your child is trying on a new pair of shoes, both you and the salesperson should check the fit. Push down on the front of the shoe with your thumb, and make sure there is a space about the size of your thumb between his big toe or second toe (whichever is longer) and the front of the shoe.

❤ After your child has tried on a pair of shoes, remove the socks and check for any red or indentation marks. You want your child to be comfortable in his brand-new shoes!

❤ Don't accept hand-me-down shoes because they are already shaped to another child's foot.

❤ Velcro fasteners are much easier for the toddler and parent to put on and take off. When the child starts dressing (and undressing) himself, he'll need little assistance with Velcro.

❤ Dress shoes usually have smoother soles, so rub the bottom of the shoes either with a piece of sandpaper or on a cement surface to improve their traction, or put a piece of masking tape on the soles to prevent slipping.

- The active toddler or preschooler's feet often perspire. Buy at least two pairs of shoes to allow one pair to air out between wearing. In addition, if the shoes are dirty, it will give you an opportunity to clean and dry them.

- Avoid pointy-toed shoes or boots because they force the toes into an unnatural position.

- Once you've decided which shoes you're buying, have your child wear them in the store to make sure the shoes fit properly and are comfortable.

- Have plenty of extra shoelaces on hand.

- To help a child recognize the left shoe from the right shoe, mark L in bright red indelible ink on the inside of the left shoe. Teach him which foot is left, and practice putting that shoe on first.

- If you're teaching the preschooler how to tie his shoelaces, make sure laces are even and not too long. Spend time practicing this challenging task with the shoes off your child's feet. Be patient.

- You can usually tell your child has outgrown his shoes because he refuses to wear them, tells you the shoes hurt, or walks with a limp.

PINK AND BLUE HINT

Show your child that shoes are on the correct feet when both shoes touch at the toe and heel and form a little gap in the center.

Clothing Struggles

Some kids may want to wear the same outfit every single day, while others may prefer to wear no clothing at all. To minimize the clothing conflicts, set limits that everyone can live with.

PINK AND BLUE HINT

If your child is stuck on a particular clothing item, try enticing him with a new piece of clothing decorated with one of his favorite characters.

Time-Tested Advice

❧ Let your child select what he wants to wear, but give him direction by offering him three choices that are acceptable to you. This helps in his decision-making process and builds his self-esteem.

❧ Some children are so attached to a particular clothing item that they want to wear it every day because it gives them a sense of security. This item becomes a transitional object, just like a blanket or stuffed animal. If it poses no problems, keep it clean and allow the child to work through this phase, or buy duplicates.

❧ If your child resists dressing, try these distractions:

   ❧ Playing musical tapes

   ❧ Singing songs together

   ❧ Making up a story

   ❧ Playing peekaboo when putting hands through sleeves, pulling shirts over his head, and putting legs through pants

❧ To motivate your child to dress without a struggle, make a chart and let him put a star or sticker on the chart each time he cooperates. When he receives five consecutive stars, tell him he has earned an extra day at the park, a trip to the zoo, or something special he really enjoys.

❧ Praise your child when he's cooperative getting dressed.

Learning How to Get Dressed

Just when you thought you had total control, your child decides he wants to dress himself. Encourage the process, be patient, and know you won't love every outfit he coordinates. Allow plenty of time; rushing won't make him dress any faster. Learning the art of buttoning and zipping, determining the front from the back, and putting the left foot in the left shoe require lots of practice. Praise him for his efforts, even if he needs your assistance.

Time-Tested Advice

❧ Buy pants and skirts with elasticized waistbands to make dressing and undressing easier for the toddler or preschooler.

❧ Teach your child that labels help determine the front and back of clothing. If there's no label in the garment, or if labels bother the child's skin, put an X or your child's initials on the back of the neckline for easy recognition.

❧ Show your youngster how to zip and unzip an item by pulling it away from his body to avoid catching his skin.

❧ Practice buttoning and snapping from the bottom up so both sides match evenly.

❧ Over-the-head shirts should have loose-fitting or flexible necklines for comfort and ease.

❧ Children love to get dressed up in costumes. Let him practice dressing and undressing with his favorite costume.

PINK AND BLUE HINT

 To help your child easily find his clothing in the dresser, tape (use masking tape) a picture to the outside of each drawer, identifying what type of clothing is stored in that particular space. For instance, cut out a picture of underwear and socks, and affix it to the underwear and sock drawer. Label each picture with the clothing word so he begins to recognize and learn the word as well.

- Don't hover over the child when he's getting dressed; it may make him nervous and be frustrating for you. Be available in case he asks for your help.

- Tube socks are easier to put on because they don't have heels.

- Let your child practice dressing and undressing his favorite doll. Just be sure the doll and its clothing aren't too tiny for him to work with to eliminate frustration.

- Buy an interactive book that teaches the child how to button, snap, zip, and tie.

- Praise your child once he's dressed, even if you dislike the combination!

- If you're concerned about color and style, temporarily fill your child's wardrobe with solid colors.

೦ 5 ೦

Food, Nutrition, and Exercise

Getting a young child to eat can be an exasperating experience for a parent. When it comes to food and mealtime, don't be surprised if your youngster acts indifferent, uninterested, and downright resistant to the thought of stopping what she's doing just to eat! Toddlers and preschoolers want to be in control, so battles between child and parent do flare up. Young children exhibit their independence and assertiveness by making food an issue.

Things can backfire if the parent wrongly attempts to force-feed the child, loses patience with the slow or finicky eater, or uses food as a threat. However, it is the parents' responsibility to provide their child with healthful, nutritious foods, which are essential for the child's well-being. It is also equally important for her to like food, enjoy sitting at the table, recognize when she is hungry, and stop when she is

85

full. The types of food presented to children represent culture, family preference, and individual likes and dislikes. If you help establish healthful eating and exercise patterns in the early childhood years, they will last your child a lifetime.

Even if your child is a picky eater, it's not likely she'll be undernourished. A toddler doesn't need to eat as much as an infant because she does not grow as fast. It is actually quite common for a toddler's appetite to decrease, fluctuating not only from meal to meal but also from one year to the next. Remember, this is a phase your child will outgrow if you just remain patient. She surely will not starve herself. As she enters the preschool age, she will come to understand that eating well gives her more energy to play and learn. Keeping a relaxed attitude may make all the difference in how your child approaches healthful eating habits.

Well-Balanced Eating

Just like an automobile, our bodies need fuel to function. Food supplies the body with important nutrients, such as vitamins, minerals, and fiber, which enable the body to thrive. Proper nourishment stimulates the immune system and helps fight off infection. Right from the beginning, every young child's normal, healthy growth and development depend upon good nutritional habits. According to the U.S. Department of Agriculture and the U.S. Department of Health and Human Services, a child's daily diet should include grains, vegetables, fruits, dairy products, and proteins, along with small amounts of fats, oils, and sugars. To meet this goal, a young child must eat three well-rounded meals a day, with healthful snacks interspersed throughout the day. Thus, a well-balanced diet comprises a variety of foods, moderately low in fat, and moderate in sugars and salt.

To educate consumers and encourage healthful eating through variety, balance, and moderation, the U.S. Department of Agriculture has developed the Food Guide Pyramid. For an overall healthful diet, a child should eat from each of the food groups in the pyramid daily. The pyramid is a recommended guideline. Be flexible and do not worry if your child misses one of the suggested food groups on occasion. Remember, the "independent" toddler and preschooler's mood and appetite fluctuate.

Bread, Cereal, Rice, and Pasta Group

At the base of the Food Guide Pyramid is the bread, cereal, rice, and pasta group, which should compose most of the diet. These grains provide complex carbohydrates, minerals, vitamins, and fiber. They are a good energy source.

Vegetable Group

Vegetables are a good source of vitamins, minerals, protein, carbohydrates, and fiber. In addition, they are free of cholesterol and fat, and may even protect against some forms of cancer.

Fruit Group

Fruits are excellent sources of vitamins A and C, potassium, folic acid, and fiber. While many toddlers and preschoolers enjoy drinking fruit juice, they also need to eat whole fruit to get an adequate amount of fiber in the daily diet. Fruits and vegetables are equally important in nutritional value, and one shouldn't be substituted for the other.

Milk, Yogurt, and Cheese Group

The foods in the milk, yogurt, and cheese group are good sources of calcium, riboflavin, protein, and other essential vitamins and minerals. At the age of two, the toddler should begin to consume low-fat and nonfat products to reduce the fat intake. A two-year-old needs sixteen ounces of low-fat milk per day, a three-year-old needs approximately eight to

PINK AND BLUE HINT

 If a child doesn't drink enough milk or consume enough dairy products, supplement her diet with liquid or powdered calcium (available over the counter at pharmacies). Consult your pediatrician for her recommendations.

PINK AND BLUE ALERT

If your child has an allergic reaction after consuming a dairy product (rash, hives, diarrhea, vomiting), call your pediatrician immediately.

ten ounces of low fat milk per day, and a four-year-old needs eight ounces of low-fat milk per day.

For children who are lactose-intolerant, allergic to dairy, or vegetarian, substitute a lactose-free beverage such as Rice Dream or soy milk. Some allergic children tolerate goat's milk well. Talk to your pediatrician for more information.

Meat, Poultry, Fish, Legumes, Eggs, and Nuts Group

The foods in the meat, poultry, fish, legumes, eggs, and nuts group are good sources of protein, iron, zinc, and B vitamins. Prepare lean meat and skinless poultry to cut down on the fat. Although nuts fall into this group, they are not safe for a young child to eat because nuts can cause choking, unless they are prepared as a nut spread. In addition, many children are allergic to nuts.

Fats, Oils, and Sugars

At the top of the Food Guide Pyramid are fats, oils, and sugars. This category is not actually one of the basic food groups; however, foods are often prepared with these items. They contain calories but few, if any, nutrients. Fats, oils, and sugars consumed in excess can contribute to obesity in a child. In addition, too many sweets and starches can cause dental cavities at a young age. Therefore, use fats, oils, and sugars sparingly.

With all of this in mind, however, it is not realistic, healthy, or necessary to keep your child totally away from sugars and fats. Depriving a child of sweets only makes her want them more. Instead, a parent needs to set limits. Offering your child a treat a few times a week is not going to ruin her eating habits, as long as it does not displace needed nutrients or lead to excess calories. Some foods classified in this group are candy, cookies, ice cream, chips, doughnuts, jelly, jam, gelatin desserts, cream cheese, oils, butter, margarine, gravy, and sodas.

Food Strategy for Toddlers and Preschoolers

Variety is the spice of life. Even a young child who thinks she only likes one food may change her mind when presented with good healthful options. A child may not eat a variety of foods at one particular meal, but it is important for her to eat a variety of foods throughout the day. Encourage the food each day, but don't make it a big deal if your child doesn't want to eat a particular item.

Since a child works best with a routine, set up a consistent schedule for meals and snacks, allowing for flexibility when necessary. It's not unusual for the toddler or preschooler to be cranky at the end of the day. While you may want your child to eat with the rest of the family, she may not be able to wait until dinnertime. Either feed her earlier or offer her one of the courses to be served at the meal before the family's dinnertime. In this way you can satisfy her hunger and appease her mood.

The parents' role is to determine the environment and what food is served. The child's role is to determine what and how much she will eat. A parent should not overload a child's plate nor demand she eat everything on her plate. If she wants more, she can always ask. A child has a smaller stomach than an adult and, therefore, a smaller appetite. Offering limited nutritious choices encourages the child to take responsibility for eating, promotes decision making, and helps avoid food battles.

PINK AND BLUE ALERT
Never serve hot food to a young child.

Help your child become a content and cooperative eater by following these tips.

PINK AND BLUE HINT

Food heated in a microwave oven should be mixed thoroughly before serving. Often the temperature of the food is uneven, hot on top and cool on the bottom.

Time-Tested Advice

❤ Create a relaxed, stress-free atmosphere during mealtime.

❤ Serve small portions on small plates at room temperature.

❤ Teach your child to take small bites and chew the food well before swallowing. Don't let her stuff too much food into her mouth at once. Teach her not to talk with a mouthful of food.

❤ Keep distractions to a minimum. Turn the answering machine on, and give your family your undivided attention during mealtime.

❤ Never serve your child a meal in front of the television.

❤ Always feed your child when she's hungry. A child who waits too long to eat may lose her appetite and become cranky.

❤ Try introducing a new food with a favorite food when the child is hungry.

❤ Praise the child when she tries new food.

❤ While it is not unusual for the toddler to refuse new foods, do not give up introducing them. Sometimes it takes numerous tries before a child accepts the taste of something new. Often a child will suddenly like something she detested if she sees a friend or family member enjoying that food. Remember, we all eat what we are familiar with.

❧ Be creative when introducing a new food. If you cook it a variety of ways, your child is bound to find one recipe she likes.

❧ Set rules and limits for acceptable table behavior— for example, never allow your child to stand and eat. Praise her for good behavior.

❧ A parent should set a good example by exhibiting healthy eating habits. Let your child observe you enjoying your meal. This is also a good time to reinforce proper table manners.

❧ To encourage sitting at the table, make sure your child has a comfortable, safe seat to sit on. If she cannot reach the table sitting in a regular chair, purchase a booster seat.

❧ Many toddlers are slow eaters when they are first feeding themselves. Allow them enough time to eat, but once they start playing with their food, end mealtime.

❧ When the toddler is more proficient at feeding herself and is eating with the family, don't expect her to sit at the table the same length of time as the adults and older siblings. Excuse her from the table when she is finished, and allow her to play quietly nearby.

❧ As your toddler learns to eat independently, be patient with her messiness. If she begins to play or throw her food, let her know mealtime is over.

PINK AND BLUE HINT

Be a good role model. If you don't want your child to eat junk food, don't eat it yourself.

PINK AND BLUE HINT

Cut down on cleanup time by placing plastic sheeting or newspapers on the floor under the toddler's seating area. Also put a plastic place mat under her table setting.

❦ Use special child-sized plates, cups, and utensils to accommodate the child's little hands and fine motor skills. If she has a favorite selection of dishes, lure her to the table with them.

❦ If the toddler has difficulty mastering utensils, let her eat finger foods. Help her practice using a fork on foods such as soft fruit, cooked chicken, or pieces of cooked potato. She can practice using a spoon with her favorite yogurt or cooked cereal.

❦ Give the toddler or preschooler a small amount to drink with meals or snacks so she doesn't fill up with liquid and leave the solid food.

❦ Use a cup with a safety lid to eliminate spills and messiness. Remove the lid when your child becomes more proficient at using the cup.

❦ Involve your child with meal preparation by giving her simple tasks to perform, such as pouring, mixing, or making a sandwich. You can also let her help set or clear the table.

❦ Caregivers should follow your instructions for your child's daily healthful diet. Specify household rules regarding nutritious foods, snacks, and mealtime. Prepare a weekly meal and snack menu for the caregiver to observe.

❦ Don't be surprised if your child wants a particular "unwholesome" food because she has seen a television commercial or has seen other children eating this item. Rather than completely denying this food, permit an occasional treat to sate her desire.

❦ Limit sugary, high-fat items, and emphasize fruit or fruit-sweetened foods for dessert.

❦ As your child's social life expands, so will her exposure to candy, cake, and other sweets. A child is less likely to become obsessed with sweets if she is allowed to have them on special occasions and in moderation.

❦ Do not use food as a reward or bribe. A child's association with food should not be based on good or bad behavior. Receiving the wrong messages can create physical and emotional problems down the road.

❦ If you're concerned about your child's weight or if your family is predisposed to obesity, consult your pediatrician about the kind of diet and exercise regimen your child should follow.

❦ Teach your child to wash her hands before and after each meal.

PINK AND BLUE ALERT

 Due to choking hazards and tooth decay, certain candy treats to avoid are sugar lollipops, chewing gum, and any hard sucking or chewy candies.

The Picky Eater

It's not unusual for the feisty toddler to lose her appetite around the age of two. Food is not at the top of her list of things to do. Parents become anxious about their picky eater and worry she's getting insufficient nutrients. The child, who is experiencing newfound independence, senses this anxiety, and mealtime becomes a battle of the wills—with the parent often losing.

Forget about turning her into a connoisseur of fine delicacies for now, and concentrate on providing a healthful balance of whatever foods she'll eat. The following advice should calm your nerves and help fill the child's belly.

Time-Tested Advice

- ❤ Serve small portions with no more than three selections on the plate. Overloading a child's plate with too much food may turn her off.

- ❤ When possible, offer limited choices.

- ❤ Keep distractions to a minimum when feeding your child. Turn off the television, and don't allow playing with toys at the table. If necessary, allow her to bring a favorite transitional object to the table to keep her company, but not to play with.

- ❤ At mealtime serve the picky eater at least one food you know she enjoys, whether or not you're introducing a new food. Don't become a short-order cook if she refuses to eat the meal you have prepared.

- ❤ If your child is not eating at mealtime, reevaluate what time she snacks and how much she's consuming. Snack time may be too close to a meal, or the snack may be too large.

- ❤ Prepare foods in different shapes (use cookie cutters) and sizes to inspire the picky eater to eat.

- ❤ If your child cringes at the sight of one food touching another, use a plate with divided sections or use a small separate plate for each food served.

- ❤ If your child dislikes cooked vegetables, try serving them with a healthful dip. The activity of dipping will entertain her. Or disguise the vegetable by grating it and adding it to another food, such as zucchini or carrot bread or an omelet.

PINK AND BLUE ALERT

Don't use food as a reward or a bribe to get your child to eat. It will most likely backfire, with the child expecting something every time she's supposed to eat.

- For the preschooler who resists eating cooked vegetables, serve cut-up raw vegetables (parboiled carrots, zucchini, jicama, red or green pepper, cucumber without the seeds).

- Let the child participate in preparing her meal or snack. She'll be more interested in eating the food she has prepared.

- Serve food tepid, not too hot or too cold.

- Just because a child refuses a food one day doesn't mean it shouldn't be reintroduced a few times. Try cooking the food a different way to tempt her taste buds.

- If your child refuses to eat a certain food from a particular food group, substitute a food she likes from that same food group. For example, if she won't drink milk (dairy), try yogurt, cottage cheese, or any mild cheese. If she won't eat meat (protein), offer her poultry, mild-tasting filleted fish, eggs, tofu, or even peanut butter.

- Don't worry about your child's poor eating habits as long as the doctor advises you the child is growing normally for her age.

- If your child is not on a daily multivitamin and you're concerned she's not getting enough nutrients, speak to your pediatrician about prescribing one.

- If you feel as though your child didn't get any vegetables, fruit, or protein at a meal, then offer any of these items at another meal or snack time.

- Some children get stuck on a particular food and don't want to eat anything else. Don't overreact to

PINK AND BLUE ALERT

If your child refuses to eat anything from the essential food groups for more than two weeks, consult your pediatrician.

this constant choice. Continue to give the child her favorite food, but also offer a variety of foods that might entice her. Eventually she will get bored.

* If a child has a temper tantrum over food, it's best to ignore the behavior. Speak in a calm tone and let her know it is not all right to disturb the rest of the family's meal.

* If a child decides not to eat her meal after a reasonable amount of time, excuse her from the table. Do not offer her any other food until the next scheduled snack or meal. Be consistent, and eventually she and her stomach will get the message.

* Keep mealtime tension-free. It's an important family time to interact and bond, and subtly teaches social skills.

* Don't punish your child for not eating, and don't force her to eat something she doesn't want to eat. Forcing food can have a negative impact upon the child and could possibly create long-term eating disorders.

* A good book to read to your child is *D.W. the Picky Eater* by Marc Brown.

Meals and Snacks

Every child needs three healthful, well-balanced meals a day with at least two to three snacks in between in order for her body to perform at its optimum level. Breakfast, lunch, and dinner should be served at about the same time each day, since children thrive on routines and rituals. To ensure a child gets enough nutrients each day, serve meals and snacks that include a variety of foods from the basic food groups. When serving food to a toddler, be sure to cut it into bite-sized pieces.

Breakfast

The word *breakfast* literally means "break the fast." After a night's sleep, the body needs to be replenished. Breakfast is the most important meal of the day because it fuels the body and mind. Here are some suggested ideas:

★ Cooked cereal (oatmeal, Cream of Wheat, quinoa, toasted wheat, creamy oat bran) with low-fat milk
Sliced fresh fruit (banana, strawberries, pears, oranges)
Whole-grain toast or bagel

★ Waffles or pancakes with sliced fresh fruit
Low-fat milk

★ Scrambled or poached eggs
Bagel or whole-grain toast
Fresh orange juice

★ Dry cereal (such as brown rice, puffed rice, puffed wheat, yellow corn, red wheat) with low-fat milk
Toasted bagel or English muffin with peanut butter or almond butter
Sliced fruit (melon, kiwi, papaya)

★ Toasted cheese sandwich on whole-grain bread or tortilla
Fresh juice smoothie (orange juice blended with yogurt, strawberries, and banana)

PINK AND BLUE HINT

If your child is a picky eater, turn breakfast into a hands-on activity. Set up a simple buffet of low-fat yogurt (any flavor) and bowls of granola, uncooked rolled oats, and fresh fruits. Let her make her own yogurt sundae. Or if you have time for a hot meal, let the child help scramble eggs and select any cheese or shredded vegetable to add to the mixture.

Lunch

The child's lunch should include a fruit or vegetable (or both), protein, milk or a dairy product, and a grain. The following suggestions can be served at home or taken to day care or preschool (for more information, see Lunch Box Tips following the menu ideas):

* Turkey (or any protein filling) on whole-wheat pita bread
  Sliced apple
  Parboiled carrots
  Low-fat milk

* Chicken strips
  Fruit salad
  Zucchini bread
  Low-fat milk

* Pasta with tomato meat sauce sprinkled with Parmesan cheese
  Sliced Italian bread with butter
  Cooked broccoli
  Sliced seasonal fruit
  Low-fat milk

* Nut butter and jelly sandwich
  Sliced oranges
  Cut up jicama or cucumber (without seeds)
  Low-fat milk

Lunch Box Tips

When sending your child to day care or preschool, how you pack the food can make the difference between the lunch being eaten or tossed in the trash. Here are some simple ideas to follow:

❀ Take your child to the store and let her select a favorite lunch box.

❀ Keep food warm or cold by using an insulated lunch bag.

❀ To keep the lunch cold, pack a frozen 100 percent fruit juice box in a well-sealed plastic bag. As it thaws, it will keep the other items cool.

❀ To keep soup or pasta warm, pack it in a widemouthed thermos.

❀ Involve the child in food selections.

❀ A child is more likely to eat her lunch if she helps prepare and pack it. If things are too hectic at home in the morning, make lunch the night before.

❀ Pack small portions of several foods.

❀ To keep certain foods, such as lettuce or tomato, fresh and crisp, pack them separately.

❀ In warm weather, avoid sending foods that can spoil easily, such as dairy products and foods prepared with mayonnaise.

❀ Vary textures and tastes by including something smooth, crunchy, or chewy.

❀ Take advantage of healthful, prepackaged, convenience foods, such as string cheese, crackers and cheese, crackers and peanut butter, and 100 percent fruit juice boxes. Prewashed, precut vegetables are great for the older preschooler.

❀ Instead of regular whole-grain bread, substitute whole-grain rolls or buns, pita pockets, whole-wheat flat bread or corn tortillas (they make great roll-up sandwiches), rice cakes, or bagels.

☼ Be creative when preparing healthful alternatives that your child will eat. Try banana bread with low-fat cream cheese, bran muffin with pure fruit spread, or nut butter on sliced banana.

☼ Check your child's lunch box when she comes home from day care or preschool. Praise her for the foods she's eaten, and without being critical, ask her why she didn't eat certain foods that are now leftovers.

Dinner

Since it's more difficult for the entire family to eat breakfast and lunch together, make dinner a family ritual. It's great to be able to prepare elaborate meals; however, if you're pressed for time, cook meals on the weekends and freeze them until they're needed. The goal for dinner is to provide foods from the basic food groups, especially those that haven't been consumed during the day. Even though it is tempting and easier, avoid serving fast foods too often. If your schedule does not allow time for meal preparation, find food facilities that gear their menus toward healthful eating. Here are some dinner suggestions:

★ Roasted chicken
 Baked potato (white, red, sweet, or yam)
 Steamed spinach
 Applesauce

★ Grilled halibut
 Brown rice
 Baked squash
 Sliced melon

★ Pasta with meat sauce
  Bread with butter
  Steamed zucchini
  Fruit salad

★ Turkey hot dog on whole-grain bun
    (for a four-year-old and older)
  Mashed potatoes
  Asparagus tips
  Sliced oranges

★ Broiled lamb chops
  Peas and carrots
  Baked french fries
  Frozen low-fat yogurt

Snacks

Since the energetic toddler or preschooler has a tiny stomach and eats small portions, she gets hungry often and needs snacks to supplement her daily diet. A young child doesn't receive the essential nutrients and calories she needs in three meals a day, so it's important to offer healthful choices at snack time. Snack time is a good opportunity to fill in the missing foods from the basic food groups if she hasn't eaten them at an earlier meal. The toddler or preschooler requires two to three snacks each day at mid-morning, midafternoon, and occasionally an hour before bedtime.

Snacks should be spaced two hours between meals and kept on the light side. Remember not to allow your child to snack too often, or she'll lose her appetite and not eat well at meals. It's a parent's or caregiver's job to control what kind of snacks are given, when, and how much.

Here are some suggested nutritious snacks to tempt your budding connoisseur:

Grains

- ❊ Whole-grain bread or roll
- ❊ Rice cake
- ❊ Crackers
- ❊ Pita pocket
- ❊ Dry cereal
- ❊ Graham or animal crackers
- ❊ Whole-wheat flat bread
- ❊ Whole-grain fruit muffin
- ❊ English muffin
- ❊ Bagel
- ❊ Corn tortilla

Fruits

- ❊ Sliced, peeled, cut-up fresh fruit
- ❊ Fresh fruit juice or 100 percent fruit juice
- ❊ *Soft* dried fruit for preschoolers—apricots, raisins, pears, apples, pitted prunes

Vegetables

- ❊ Cold cooked vegetables for the toddler
- ❊ Raw cut-up vegetables for the preschooler
- ❊ Vegetable soup (served at room temperature)

※ Cooked dried beans (also a protein)—kidney beans, garbanzos (chickpeas), soybeans

Dairy

※ Low-fat milk

※ Cheese—sticks, cubes, shredded, or sliced

※ Yogurt—plain, fruit flavored, or frozen

※ Cottage cheese

Protein

※ Hard-boiled egg

※ Peanut butter and other nut butters

※ Tofu

Try the following food combinations for a healthful snack:

※ Nut butter on banana or peeled apple slices, peeled celery sticks (for the preschooler), whole-grain bread or crackers, minibagel, English muffin, or rice cake

※ Cheese on crackers, roll or bread, peeled apple or pear slices; melted cheese on bread, crackers, pita, or tortilla

※ Raw vegetables with a yogurt dip (for the preschooler)

※ Yogurt or cottage cheese and sliced fresh fruit

※ Soup and crackers

※ Cold cooked pasta shapes (bow ties, pinwheels, shells) with or without cooked vegetables

PINK AND BLUE HINT

Feeding a child too much pasta and bread may cause her to become overweight. There is nothing wrong with pasta and bread unless eaten in excess. It is better to alternate and serve a variety of starches, such as potatoes, rice, and couscous.

Time-Tested Advice

* A child should sit and eat snacks in the same place she has her meals.

* Do not let a child stand or walk around while eating. It not only is messy and dangerous, but also encourages poor eating behavior.

* Snack time, like mealtime, should have a time limit. If your child plays with her snack food, end the snack time immediately.

* If your child asks for snacks frequently, increase her portions at mealtime.

* Don't encourage late-night snacking, but if your child is hungry, it is a good time to provide any nourishment that she may have missed during the day. If she fell short in the dairy and protein group, offer peanut butter and crackers with a glass of milk to wash it down.

* High-fat, high-sugar foods should not be given as snacks routinely. Cakes, cookies, candy, chips, and other "junk foods" should be given sparingly. Studies prove that completely denying a child such items only increases their desire for the "forbidden" food.

The Juice Truth

The average toddler or preschooler could spend an entire day just drinking juice. However, parents beware! Juices often fill the child up, suppressing her mealtime appetite. It's important to choose a juice that's high in vitamin C and is 100 percent juice. The healthiest choice is fresh orange juice, because a six- to eight-ounce serving provides 100 percent of the daily value for vitamin C. Apple juice, often the most popular among young children, has the least amount of nutrients, unless it is fortified with vitamin C.

A toddler or a preschooler should drink four to eight ounces of juice daily, and it should never take the place of milk. Serve the juice in a cup, not in a bottle, to the toddler because sipping juice from the bottle will cause tooth decay.

Time-Tested Advice

* Juices made from fruits such as orange, grapefruit, strawberry, mango, papaya, pineapple, and apricot are high in C.

* If you give your child apple, cranberry, or grape juice, make sure it is fortified with minerals and vitamins, such as vitamin C and calcium.

* Avoid "fruit drinks" because they consist primarily of sugar and water.

* When purchasing fresh fruit juice (except citrus), make sure the label states the juice is pasteurized, a heating process that kills bacteria.

* Avoid juices with sulfites because they can cause a reaction similar to asthma.

* Drinking excessive amounts of juice can cause diarrhea. Apple, pear, and grape juice are the worst offenders.

* Since juice is high in calories, carefully monitor your child's juice intake to avoid unnecessary weight gain.

PINK AND BLUE HINT

Introduce one fruit juice at a time to be certain your child is not sensitive or allergic to that particular fruit. To monitor your child's sensitivity to a new juice, serve it for three consecutive days, during the day. The most common reactions are diarrhea and a skin rash.

PINK AND BLUE HINT

Make your child a delicious, nutritious smoothie drink by blending fruit with fresh juice, low-fat yogurt, or low-fat milk.

❧ Because fruit juice contains no fiber, do not substitute juice for whole fruits in your child's daily diet.

❧ Give the toddler watered-down juice.

Food Safety

Besides determining what foods are safe for the toddler and preschooler to eat, food safety involves how the food is handled and stored. Bacterial infection caused by contaminated food can be life threatening to young children, due to their immature immune system. A parent needs to be aware of the many culprits that produce these harmful germs and practice safe habits with food and its preparation.

It's very important that every parent and every caregiver take a CPR and first-aid class in order to learn the correct techniques to aid a choking or injured child. Check with your pediatrician, local YMCA, hospital, fire department, American Red Cross, or American Heart Association for classes in your area.

An Ounce of Prevention

A young child must be served foods that are safe for her to chew and swallow. Avoid small, hard foods, like a sucking candy, and small round foods, such as whole grapes, that can slip easily down the throat. Be careful of foods that are stringy and sticky, and items that swell when moist. Remove any pits or bones from food. Most common choking foods tend to get lodged in a young child's throat, obstruct the airway, and make it impossible to breathe. Serve the following foods with caution:

❀ *Apples and pears*—Cut up peeled apples, pears, and other firm fruits into small, bite-sized pieces. For a child under the age of four, it's best to cook these fruits until they are soft.

❦ *Carrots*—For the child four years old or younger, cook carrots until nearly mushy.

❦ *Celery*—Do not give raw celery to a child under the age of four. Remove the stringy outer layer with a peeler.

❦ *Cherries and grapes*—Serve quartered or halved pitted cherries or seedless, deskinned grapes to children under four years old.

❦ *Hot dogs*—Serve only to the preschooler. Remove the skin, and cut the hot dog into small pieces, lengthwise and crosswise.

❦ *Peanut butter*—Children under the age of four should never eat large clumps of peanut butter from a spoon or a finger. It's best to spread a thin layer on bread, crackers, or sliced fruit.

❦ *Raisins*—Do not give raisins to children under the age of four. Four-year-olds should eat only plump, moist raisins, preferably cooked in foods, such as breads and puddings.

PINK AND BLUE ALERT

Do not serve the following foods because they pose a potential choking hazard to young children: nuts, popcorn, pretzels, candy (especially hard and chewy), raw carrots or other hard raw vegetables, and whole hot dogs.

Time-Tested Advice

❦ Before eating, make sure your child washes her hands with warm water and soap.

❦ A child should always sit down when eating any food.

❦ An adult should be present when a child is eating.

❤ Do not encourage talking while your child is chewing her food. She can easily inhale and choke on the food.

❤ Never use glass or porcelain dishes when serving the young child.

❤ Do not serve food on a hot plate. If you heat something in a microwave oven, be sure not to serve it immediately, or change the dish.

❤ Teach your child not to run with food on a stick, such as sugarless lollipops and frozen fruit bars.

❤ Explain to your child not to eat food that has fallen to the ground because it is filled with invisible germs she cannot see.

❤ Teach your child not to take bites from another child's food. It's the easiest way for young children to spread germs to one another.

❤ Alert your child not to eat something that another child has sneezed or coughed on.

❤ Introduce new foods during the day. If there is an allergic reaction, it will manifest itself while the child is awake.

❤ Some foods cause allergic reactions, especially if there is a family history of allergies. Speak to your pediatrician and be careful of the following items:

    ◉ Artificial additives and preservatives

    ◉ Berries and citrus fruits

    ◉ Chocolate

    ◉ Cinnamon

- Dairy products

- Nuts and nut butters

- Pork products

- Shellfish (shrimp, crab, clams, lobster, scallops)

- Tomatoes and corn

- Wheat products

Safe Handling of Food

It is not unusual to hear today about children getting gravely ill from food contamination. Protecting your family against bacterial infection is a necessity. While the government has two watchdogs covering the safety of food, the U.S. Department of Agriculture (USDA) and the Food and Drug Administration (FDA), it is still virtually impossible to tightly control the many companies growing and distributing food within the United States. Even more difficult is the task of overseeing the produce from foreign countries, which is often riddled with bacteria. Therefore, it is imperative that you as a parent be diligent in reducing the risk of your family getting sick; to do this, practice safe habits when preparing, storing, and handling food.

Good sanitary habits must be at the top of everyone's list. Your efforts to protect your family must be consistent, whether you're cooking at home, shopping at the market, or dining out.

Adventures at the Supermarket

Trips to the supermarket with your child can be either a fun adventure or a nightmare. Timing is everything. It's a cardinal sin to take a hungry, tired child to the market and

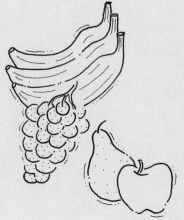

expect her to patiently behave in the shopping cart while you run up and down the aisles and then wait in a long checkout line. Going to the grocery store may not be your favorite errand, but if you handle it right, the excursion can be enjoyable and a learning experience for the young child.

Time-Tested Advice

❤ Be organized and bring a grocery list and coupons to cut down on time and money.

❤ Before entering the supermarket, establish rules with your child, such as keeping the safety belt buckled while sitting in the shopping cart, no yelling and screaming, and no grabbing food.

❤ Before arriving at the market, set limits on the kinds of food you'll purchase, to avoid in-market battles. It is not unusual for a child to want a particular food she has seen advertised on television.

❤ If your child begs for candy or any other unhealthful food, tell her no, and be firm and consistent in your response. Only on an occasional trip to the market should you allow the purchase of a sweet or high-fat treat, but establish this ahead of time.

❤ Bring along a toy to keep the child entertained.

❤ If the trip to the market coincides with snack time, either bring a snack with you or let your child pick out her snack at the market before you start your actual shopping. Limit the child to two healthful choices.

❦ The grocery store is a great learning center. Have your child identify foods as you place them in the shopping cart, and teach her which foods belong in the different basic food groups. You can practice counting numbers as you pick up certain items (e.g., "one, two, three apples"). Have her find a food item by color (e.g., green beans, red apples, and yellow bananas).

❦ Let the preschooler help you find items. Tell her to point out the item, and you'll remove it from the shelf.

❦ Praise your child for following rules and behaving well in the market.

Dining Out

Dining out with the young child can be an enjoyable experience, provided you plan ahead, keep realistic expectations, and maintain a sense of humor. Since more restaurants cater to young families than ever before, there are other options besides the usual fast-food chains. Pick a bright, noisy, child-friendly place that has a selection of foods your child likes or, even better, a child's menu. Save the fancy restaurant for a romantic night out alone.

Timing is critical when venturing out for a meal, so plan wisely. Don't take a tired, cranky youngster to dine and then expect her to behave. Being prepared and organized can make the difference between a successful meal and a total disaster. Parents should remember to take along plenty of patience. To survive the dining-out adventure, try the following tips.

Time-Tested Advice

❦ One of the best ways to get your child accustomed to eating out is by taking her first to a fast-food chain. This is a good starting point because fast-food chains are informal, have quick service, and familiarize your child to a public social setting.

❦ It is possible to keep a meal relatively nutritious at the fast-food chain restaurant by requesting ketchup or mustard instead of mayonnaise, removing the skin from chicken, and sharing an order of french fries. If your child has a high-fat meal when dining out, balance the rest of her diet that day with low-fat, low-sodium meals at home, such as chicken with fresh steamed or sautéed vegetables. Moderation is always the key.

❦ Teach your child good table manners by being a good role model. Simple table manners a young child should learn include no throwing food or utensils, sitting and not standing in her seat, no banging on the tabletop, putting a napkin on her lap and using it, no yelling, and using "please" and "thank you" when appropriate. For more information on manners, please see Chapter 7, "Behavior."

❦ Organize a Dining Out bag filled with an assortment of entertaining items, such as pop-up books, crayons and coloring books, small action figures or dolls, sticker books, or any favorite toy that isn't too large to tote. Also pack a few favorite food snacks, such as peanut butter on crackers, fresh cut-up fruit or vegetables, dry cereals, and boxed 100 percent fruit juice in case the service is slow or the meal is disappointing.

* For the preschooler, play simple paper and pencil games like tic-tac-toe, or help her practice writing her name and numbers.

* Give your child your undivided attention to keep her from getting restless and bored. This is a good time to engage her in conversation and teach her how to be social.

* When dining at nicer restaurants, make a reservation and request a seat by a window when possible. The view can keep the child amused. Call in advance to see whether booster seats are available; if not, bring your own.

* When a restaurant doesn't have a child's menu, order appetizer portions for your child. If there are other young children or siblings with you, let the children share a meal. Or share part of your meal and your spouse's meal with the child, especially if her appetite is small.

* Remind your child not to bother other people sitting nearby. If she's having difficulty sitting still, take turns walking outside the restaurant.

* If your child is uncooperative, let one parent eat while the other parent takes care of the child, then trade places.

* Praise your child for good behavior when dining out. Her reward will be a return visit to the restaurant.

PINK AND BLUE ALERT

 Never tell your child she is fat, and do not discuss her weight or size unless she talks about it.

The Overweight Child

If a child under the age of five appears to be overweight, it most likely is due to family genes. A young child with a family history of obesity needs help early in her life with dietary precautions. While heredity can play a major role in a child's tendency to gain too much weight, overeating and not enough exercise can also contribute to this condition. Since parents have control over the foods a toddler and preschooler are offered, it may be easier attacking this problem in the early developmental years. There are some things a parent can do to help the child either lose weight or slow down her weight gain.

Time-Tested Advice

- ❤ Your child should eat three well-balanced meals a day and never skip a meal.

- ❤ Do not make the portions large, and discourage requests for second helpings.

- ❤ Encourage your child to eat slowly and chew her food well.

- ❤ Serve your child no more than sixteen ounces of low-fat or non-fat milk per day.

- ❤ Keep juice consumption down to eight ounces of 100 percent fruit juice a day.

- ❤ Encourage drinking plenty of water, before each meal and throughout the day.

- ❤ Avoid serving fatty foods, such as bacon, sausage, eggs, butter, and fast foods. Prepare skinless chicken, and trim fat from meats. Instead of frying, bake, grill, broil, boil, or steam foods.

❀ Keep plenty of fresh fruits and vegetables on hand, and encourage them as snacks instead of potato chips, cookies, and other high-calorie snack foods.

❀ Your child should eat only two snacks a day. If she enjoys fresh fruits and cut-up vegetables, she can indulge a few more times a day; otherwise, discourage snacking (grazing) all day long.

❀ Encourage fresh fruit for dessert.

❀ Do not forbid sugar in your child's diet; just make sure it is eaten in moderation.

❀ Insist your child eat only in the kitchen or dining room, not in front of the television, while playing video games, or while riding in the car.

❀ Do not have your child eat alone.

❀ Avoid using food as a reward.

❀ Daily exercise can help reduce weight gain or keep weight down. A parent can help a young child exercise by doing it with her. For instance, take a walk each day in your neighborhood (if there's a family dog, put the emphasis on walking the dog), take the stairs instead of an elevator, jump rope, dance to lively music, or run and kick a soccer ball.

❀ Limit television viewing to no more than two hours a day so your child will not be sedentary for too long a period of time.

PINK AND BLUE HINT

A parent should not put a young child on a strict diet and deprive her of food when she says she's hungry. This could lead to eating disorders later in life.

PINK AND BLUE HINT

The finicky eater will more likely be hungry at mealtime if she has expended an abundance of energy at playtime.

A parent should discuss her child's weight problem with the pediatrician. If the doctor feels it is necessary, she may recommend a nutritionist to work with the parent.

Exercise

Exercise is an important element in a young child's life because it helps develop gross and fine motor skills. Daily physical activity builds muscular strength and stamina, improves coordination, contributes to bone density, and keeps weight under control. Exercise challenges the body and builds brainpower.

A young child requires plenty of calories for growth as well as activity. Sufficient exercise will increase the need for calories. An inactive body is more likely to store fat instead of burning it off. Experts recommend limiting television viewing because idleness at an early age can be a leading contributor to obesity. If your family has a history of being overweight, encourage plenty of activity and exercise to offset those family genes. When a child enjoys exercising at a young age, she may make it a lifelong habit to be physically active, especially if her parents are good role models and exercise regularly.

Sleep

Does this scenario sound familiar to you? It's 9:00 in the evening, and you can't wait to go to sleep. However, there's just one small problem: weighing in at twenty-eight pounds and ready to rumble, your two-and-a-half-year-old toddler. It doesn't seem possible, with his action-packed day, that he's not ready to throw in the towel and call it a night.

This is not atypical behavior for a young child. Sleep has different meanings to different children at different ages. It could represent separation from his loved ones or just separation from the pleasures of his new discoveries each day.

Instead of caving in to the nightly battles, set a bedtime plan, create a nightly ritual, and stick to it consistently. Even the busiest and most resistant child will drift off to sweet dreams.

From Crib to Bed

Most toddlers are ready to move from crib to bed between the ages of two and three. Don't rush this step. It's time to make this transition either when you're confronted with the safety of your toddler climbing out of the crib or when your child tells you he wants to sleep in a bed. The move to a "big bed" ignites all kinds of emotions for the child and parent alike. The toddler is bursting with pride and joy, and at the same time coping with a new set of anxieties. Parents, on the other hand, must be attentive to the child's newfound freedom.

PINK AND BLUE ALERT

While your toddler is still sleeping in a crib, put the mattress on the lowest rung. Always use the locked side rails to prevent him from falling out or wandering around the house.

Time-Tested Advice

❀ If your child is climbing out of the crib, it's time to put him in a bed.

❀ Before making the move from crib to bed, talk with your child about sleeping in a "big bed," just like mommy and daddy or an older sibling.

❀ Visit the local library or bookstore and select a few children books that tell a story about sleeping in a bed, such as *Alex's Bed* by Mary Dickinson, *Devin's New Bed* by Sally Freedman, and *Winifred's New Bed* by Lyn Howell.

❀ Consider how the timing of moving from crib to bed will affect your child. If a new baby is on the way, give your toddler a few months to get used to his new bed. Then he won't feel as if he's being forced to give up his crib for the baby. If his crib converts to a youth bed, make the necessary changes a few months before the baby's arrival.

❧ If your child is going through other transitions in his life, such as a new home, new day care, preschool, or divorce, delay the change until he has made a comfortable adjustment.

❧ When making the transition from crib to bed, there are two different approaches:

1. Go cold turkey and remove the crib immediately. Let your child help dismantle it and put it away.

2. If your child's bedroom is spacious enough, put the new bed in the room along with the crib. In this way you can take your time with the transition. Let him try the bed at nap time and read him his favorite bedtime story on his new bed.

❧ When you're ready to purchase the bed and mattress, first do some preliminary footwork without your child. Then take him with you so he is included in helping make the final selection. Have him spend a few minutes lying on two or three different mattresses. Buy a good-quality firm mattress with a warranty of at least five years.

❧ Let the toddler select new sheets, a small soft pillow, and a blanket or quilt to make his new bed extra special.

❧ Have your child pick out a new doll or stuffed animal to accompany him in his new bed (along with any other favorite things he slept with before).

❧ To protect the new mattress, buy a waterproof pad and mattress cover.

PINK AND BLUE ALERT

If your child is climbing out of his crib and you still haven't purchased a bed, remove bumper guards, stuffed animals, and any items he could use as "steps." Also, remove any hanging toys so he can't choke himself.

PINK AND BLUE HINT

Place the new mattress right on the floor until your child is comfortable in his new sleeping arrangement. This will also make it easier for him to get in and out of bed.

PINK AND BLUE ALERT

In case your child wanders out of bed, protect him by putting a securely locked safety gate at the top and bottom of the stairwell. As an extra precaution, put a gate at his bedroom door.

* Buy guardrails to protect your child from falling out of his new bed.

* When you set up the new bed, have your child assist you. He'll want to put his favorite stuffed animals and dolls on the bed, along with his new "pal" that you just purchased.

* In addition to the guardrails on the new bed, place pillows on the floor to cushion any falls.

* If possible, position the bed so the head and one side of the bed are against walls.

* Hold off buying bunk beds until your child is at least five years old.

* Be sure to continue regular bedtime routines when switching from crib to bed.

Bedtime Routines

While leading medical authorities have different opinions on sleep, the one theory they all agree on is the need for a bedtime ritual. A predictable routine provides a sense of comfort and security, especially for the toddler who may be anxious or resistant to nighttime separation. Create a relaxing and calm atmosphere before your child goes to bed.

Time-Tested Advice

* Keep bedtime at the same time every night.

* Be consistent and follow the same routine in the same order each evening.

❧ Assist your child in cleaning up his bedroom. To prevent accidents, make sure no toys or other objects are lying on the floor.

❧ Decide how much time is required to help settle down your child before bedtime. Allow fifteen minutes to thirty minutes (no more than that).

❧ Don't overexcite or roughhouse with your child before bedtime.

❧ Include quiet activities, such as the following:

  ◉ Read bedtime stories together—not scary ones.

  ◉ Give your child a bath.

  ◉ Play musical or story tapes or CDs, and keep the music mellow and the story upbeat.

  ◉ Cuddle and sing favorite songs.

  ◉ Let him put his toys, dolls, and stuffed animals to sleep.

  ◉ Make up a story that includes some of the activities your child participated in that day.

  ◉ Give your child a massage.

  ◉ Say prayers together.

❧ Be sure to say good night to everyone in the home. He might want to say good night to different objects he likes. Point out that everything rests at night, even machines.

❧ Don't try to rush the routine he's accustomed to; he'll feel cheated if you leave something out, and it may delay sleep even more.

PINK AND BLUE HINT

If you keep your child's bedroom door partially closed, tie a bell around the knob. Then you'll know when he's up and about.

PINK AND BLUE HINT

If a parent is out of town, make sure the child receives a good night phone call. If phoning is impossible, tape a message for your child so he can hear the parent's voice. This will be reassuring to him.

- If your child hasn't taken an evening bath, have him wash his face and hands before going to sleep.

- Be sure he brushes his teeth and goes to the bathroom (if he's toilet training or already toilet trained) before going to bed.

- Tuck your child in bed and give him a good night kiss.

- If you and your spouse are going out for the evening and won't be home for the bedtime ritual, teach your baby-sitter the exact routine. To allow for a smooth transition, request the sitter arrive at least one-half hour before your departure.

Bedtime Conflicts

Let's face it. Children don't like going to bed. Have you noticed how alert they become at bedtime or how many excuses they have for not going to sleep? Bedtime struggles usually develop as a result of your will ("time to go to sleep") over their manipulation ("just one more story, one more game"). To further complicate matters, the physical confinement of the crib is now replaced with the freedom of the "big bed" and a new sense of liberation.

While you can't force your child to fall asleep, you can demand that he remain in his bed in his room. As conflicts arise, be firm; if you give in, you're setting yourself up for future problems. Children are smart and learn really fast what behavior they can get away with. Set your guidelines, be consistent, and remember, *you're* in control. To assist you in solving bedtime battles, try the following tips.

Time-Tested Advice

- ❧ If you have been following the same bedtime ritual each evening and resistance to bedtime escalates, change the routine. If you haven't been reading a bedtime story, now is the time to try it. If your child likes music, play soft and soothing music to help him fall asleep.

- ❧ You and your spouse must agree on a plan together. Don't contradict each other in front of the child.

- ❧ If your child struggles with staying in his room, march him immediately back into his room with little conversation and as little close contact as possible. Keep repeating this process (as often as necessary) without getting angry or raising your voice. Make it a rule: Once it's bedtime, he must never leave his bedroom (unless he needs to go to the bathroom).

- ❧ A child must learn how to fall asleep on his own without parental interaction. If your child says he's not tired, give him a flashlight so he can look at a book or play quietly in his bed.

- ❧ Your child will probably stay in his bed in his room if you give him some control. He might want to sleep on the floor in a sleeping bag or prefer wearing his favorite superhero costume (without the cape) instead of pajamas. As long as it's not detrimental to his well-being, give it a try.

- ❧ If you know your child is OK and he is screaming for attention from his bedroom, close his door and tell him you'll reopen it when he calms down. You

PINK AND BLUE HINT

If your child has trouble settling down in the evening, use a kitchen timer and set a fifteen- to thirty-minute warning time before bedtime. When the bell rings, your child will know it's time for bed.

may need to repeat this procedure a few times until he gets the message. Be sure to open the door as soon as he quiets down.

- ❤ If he expresses fear of the dark, put a night-light in his room. (For more tips, see the section on Fear of the Dark, later in this chapter.)

- ❤ Alleviate constant requests for water by keeping a small sports water bottle with built-in plastic straw next to the bed for thirst-quenching sips. (If you're in the throes of nighttime toilet training, you might not want to do this.)

- ❤ Many children stall bedtime by making numerous visits to the bathroom. If you're certain it's a ploy, set a limit on how many trips your child can take.

- ❤ If your child is having difficulty separating from you, stay in his bedroom with him for a few minutes to help him settle down. Reassure him he's safe, and leave the room before he falls asleep. Letting him know you are in the house and not leaving will provide extra comfort.

- ❤ Teach your child a relaxation exercise by demonstrating the following: Tell him to lie on his back, close his eyes, and visualize each part of his body

PINK AND BLUE HINT

Put a chart in your child's bedroom, and reward him with a gold star for each night he cooperates and stays in his room. When he has five *consecutive* stars, take him to the store and let him pick out something special, or plan a fun activity, such as a visit to the zoo.

unwinding. Have him begin by relaxing his toes and feet, and slowly work his way up, releasing any tension in his body. At the same time, show him how to deep breathe, slowly inhaling and exhaling.

- It's not uncommon for a child to wake up in the middle of the night, but it's important that he learn how to fall back to sleep on his own. If he calls for you, go into his room, pat him on the back, and soothe him with your voice. If he comes to your room, as tired as you may be, do not invite him into your bed, or it may become a habit that's difficult to break. Take him back to his room, tuck him into bed, and tell him he may cuddle with you in the morning.

- Visit the local library or bookstore and ask for recommendations of books on bedtime conflicts. Some suggested books are *The Boy Who Wouldn't Go to Bed* by Helen Cooper, *Is It Time?* by Marilyn Janovitz, and *Can't Sleep* by Chris Raschka.

- If your child continues to resist bedtime, speak to your pediatrician.

Nighttime Fears

Beginning around the age of two, some children develop a variety of nighttime problems, such as fear of the dark, nightmares, fear of monsters, or night terrors. Often, changes in usual routines can disrupt sleep patterns. It's important to keep bedtime as calm as possible and avoid overstimulation, scary stories, frightening videos or television programs, and boisterous music.

Fear of the Dark

One of the most common phobias a young child develops is fear of the dark. And when you think about it, going into a dark room can be very intimidating, especially when you are two or three years old. Help him through this phase of insecurity by being patient and understanding. Encourage your child to talk about his fear so he can work through this problem and overcome it.

PINK AND BLUE HINT

 Put glow-in-the-dark stickers on the ceiling of your child's bedroom to distract his fear of the dark.

Time-Tested Advice

❧ Put a night-light or a lamp with a low-wattage bulb in the child's room.

❧ Give him a flashlight.

❧ Don't tease him about his fear.

❧ Praise him as he overcomes this fear.

❧ Go to the local library and get books to read to your child about fear of the dark. Try reading *Night and Day* by Margaret Wise Brown, *Franklin in the Dark* by Paulette Bourgeois, *It's Dark* by Karen Erickson, *Boo, Who Used to Be Scared of the Dark* by Munro Leaf, or *Lights On, Lights Off* by Anelise Taylor.

❧ Talk to your child's day care or preschool teacher about his fear. Since this is a common problem among children his age, the teachers will welcome the opportunity to discuss it with the class.

❧ If there's an older sibling, let the toddler sleep in his or her room, or vice versa.

Nightmares

Who hasn't awakened in the middle of the night sweating and shaking from a bad dream? Busy toddlers and preschoolers with big imaginations often relive their day's events in their sleep, which can trigger nightmares. Other factors that can contribute to nightmares are overstimulation before bedtime, inappropriate or frightening videos or television shows, scary stories, change (new home, new school, or new baby-sitter), illness, and stress (a separation, divorce, or death in the family).

When a child wakes up crying and upset, he may be experiencing a nightmare, which usually occurs during REM (rapid eye movement) sleep. Don't be surprised if he can tell you some of the bad dream he just had. Explain to him that he had a nightmare, and comfort him until he calms down. There's no need to discuss the nightmare the next day unless he brings it up.

PINK AND BLUE ALERT

 Be cognizant about what's on the television before your child's bedtime. Even if he is busy with some activity and not sitting and watching the television, something may still catch his attention and frighten him. For example, if the news is on and your child sees a fire (or any disturbing event), it can upset him. When he goes to sleep with these disturbing images, nightmares can occur.

Time-Tested Advice

❦ Reassure your child that he is OK with comforting words and a cuddle.

❦ Do not stay too long or encourage your child to come into bed with you, or this may become a habit.

❦ Acknowledge his frightening experience, but don't make too big an issue of it.

❦ Show your child he is safe by turning on the light. Then keep a night-light or lamp with low wattage on so he can feel secure, or offer him a flashlight.

- Tell him you are close by and if he needs you, you'll be right there.

- Keep bedroom doors open.

- If your child comes into your bedroom after you've already calmed him down, promptly escort him back to his room. Reassure him again.

- Offer a transitional object such as his favorite stuffed animal, doll, or blanket.

- Sing a favorite quiet song to him.

- Read *There's a Nightmare in My Closet* by Mercer Mayer.

If nightmares become worse and interfere with your child's daytime activities, speak to your pediatrician for other recommendations.

Fear of Monsters

Although monsters may seem silly to you, in some young children's minds, they really do exist. Exposure to television and videos make the unbelievable believable. And children's active imaginations can create pretty frightening characters. To ease their apprehensions, try these tips.

Time-Tested Advice

- Do a "monster search" at bedtime with your child. Open closets and drawers and look under and behind the bed to prove there are no monsters.

❀ Lock windows, and close shades, draperies, or shutters.

❀ Keep a night-light on.

❀ Give him a flashlight to check for monsters by himself.

❀ Make up some magical words together to scare away the monster.

❀ Have a transitional object such as a stuffed animal serve as the night watchman for the room. To make it seem official, put a toy sheriff's badge on the stuffed animal.

❀ Make a "Go Away Monster" sign with your child, and tape it on his bedroom door.

❀ To scare away the monster, make a "monster's potion" of water and vinegar (or anything you want to concoct), put it in a sealed plastic container, and let your child choose where to put it.

❀ Make a "disappear monster mist" using a plastic spray water bottle. Have the child spray the areas where he thinks the monster exists.

❀ Reassure your child that you are close by in case he needs you.

❀ Try reading books such as *Go Away Monsters, Lickety Split!* by Nancy Evans Cooney, *Bear Under the Stairs* by Helen Cooper, *Go Away, Big Green Monster* by Ed Emberley, *Dear Bear* by Joanne Harrison, and *There's an Alligator Under My Bed* by Mercer Mayer.

PINK AND BLUE HINT

When your child is watching television or a video in the evening, only allow him to watch upbeat programs.

Night Terrors

Unlike nightmares, where a child awakens and remembers his bad dream, a child with night terrors doesn't awaken and has no recollection of the incident. Night terrors usually occur about one to four hours after a child falls asleep, when he cycles out of the deepest stage of sleep. It is not uncommon for the child who is experiencing night terrors to display the following symptoms: bolt upright, cry inconsolably, thrash his body around, sweat, breathe rapidly, and have a trance-like stare. The child cannot be aroused or calmed down, and it may take anywhere from five to thirty minutes for him to get over the episode. For most children experiencing night terrors, comforting has no effect because the child is unaware of this event. For others, being held closely and comforted by the parent may help a little. Speak to your pediatrician if these disruptions become a regular occurrence.

Naps

Between the ages of two and three, your toddler will probably nap for approximately one hour. This is an important time for him to revitalize his energy. The typical nap time at this age is between noon and 2 P.M. The older your child gets, the less sleep he will require. By the age of four he will probably eliminate naps altogether. Parents are often surprised that their child will not nap for them at home but at school will go down without a whimper. The acceptance of a nap at school is largely due to a consistent school routine coupled with peer pressure (all the children must lie down).

If your child doesn't fall asleep at the usual nap time for several consecutive days and his schedule remains the same, chances are he no longer needs to sleep during the day. As a result of his shedding his daytime nap, you may find you have to put the child to bed earlier at night. Until naps are fleeting memories, follow these tips to minimize nap time struggles.

Time-Tested Advice

- 🌑 Establish a consistent nap time at the same time every day.

- 🌑 Plan a predictable soothing prenap routine, such as reading a story, singing songs, or giving a light massage.

- 🌑 If nap time comes right after lunch, a good routine to follow is a trip to the bathroom to use the toilet (or change the diaper), wash hands and face, and brush teeth.

- 🌑 Keep the routine pleasant and positive with kisses and cuddles; simple conversation about the morning's activities is also comforting.

- 🌑 Prepare the child's bedroom for nap time by shutting out any possible distractions, such as bright sunlight and noisy household machines.

- 🌑 If the child expresses separation anxiety, ease the transition with a favorite toy, blanket, or transitional object. Stay with your child for a few minutes if he insists, but leave the room before he falls asleep so he can learn how to sleep without your interaction.

- 🌑 Once naps have been eliminated, you can still insist on a quiet playtime in his room, which will give him a chance to recharge his batteries and give the

PINK AND BLUE HINT

 To avoid endless calls from your child or his wandering around the house during quiet time, set a kitchen timer. When the bell rings, he'll know it's OK to come out of his room.

parent a little respite. Even if it lasts only twenty or thirty minutes, everyone will feel a little better later on in the afternoon.

❀ Don't use a nap as a threat when disciplining the child because if you do, he'll consider nap time a punishment.

☙ 7 ☙

Behavior

Parenting is a lifelong journey. Along the road you and your
child will be confronted with many emotional roadblocks.
How you handle these detours in life can make all the difference in the world. Discipline is the key. It is the structure
a parent sets up for a child's life so she may experience the
real world happily and sensibly. To cultivate positive
behavior in a child, parents need to set appropriate limits,
establish clear boundaries, be consistent, and provide security and love. Children pattern their behavior after their
parents. Therefore, it is the parents' obligation to serve as
good role models.

Both parents must form a united front and agree upon
the same disciplinary measures in order to help your child
effectively. It's confusing to the child if one parent says one
thing and the other parent disagrees. Children are much

PINK AND BLUE HINT

Call the special time you spend with your child each day "[child's name] Time." This will identify the alone time the two of you have together. The parent must cease all other activities, such as phone calls and laundry. If possible and within reason, let the child select the activity.

more intelligent and perceptive than we give them credit for being. If you and your spouse have different opinions on methods of discipline, come to a mutual agreement that is comfortable for the two of you. If your points of view differ and you can't reach an amicable compromise, seek parenting counseling from a professional third party.

The role of parenting is to help a child become independent and self-reliant. A major part of that role is accomplished through discipline. By thoughtfully laying these disciplinary foundations, you will instill in your child self-control, self-discipline, and self-esteem.

Building Self-Esteem

Every child needs her parents' unconditional love and thrives on attentive caring and a loving attitude. Hearing the words *I love you* provides a sense of security and confidence. To build a child's self-esteem, parents must support and guide her. Love the child for who she is, not for how she behaves. When a child has a strong feeling of self-worth, she can attain and handle life's daily challenges, while also learning how to form and maintain healthy, gratifying relationships.

Time-Tested Advice

❦ Although parents have busy schedules, it's important to spend uninterrupted time with your child as part of your daily routine. This is essential for bonding.

❦ Show your child you're interested in her by giving your undivided attention. Get down to eye level to show you are really listening. It sends a positive message that nothing is more important than she is.

* Do soothing activities (e.g., reading to your child) and stimulating activities (e.g., building with blocks) with your child.

* Be careful not to overprotect your child. Allow her to master simple tasks, and encourage her to try new experiences so she can build self-confidence. Be focused on the process, not the outcome.

* Allow your child to take chances, as long as safety is not an issue, so she can learn from her mistakes. For example, if your toddler wants to try the slide, guide her through the process. Don't tell her not to do it because it is dangerous; instead, help her through the task by assisting her up the steps and down the slide. Praise her for her accomplishments.

* To give your child a sense of security and structure, set up daily routines she can count on. For example, meals and bedtime should be at the same time each day.

* Praise your child often. Be specific and descriptive when you praise her. Place the focus on the child's efforts and feelings of accomplishment to boost her self-esteem, rather than on the accomplishment itself.

* Praise the child for incremental changes in her behavior. For example, if your child is able to recover from a disappointment quicker than usual, acknowledge the change and commend her for the improvement.

* Teach your child to be responsible by giving her age-appropriate tasks to perform. Encourage her to

PINK AND BLUE ALERT

Never take away special time as a form of discipline for undesirable behavior. The message you send should be "No matter how you behave, I still want to be with you."

PINK AND BLUE HINT

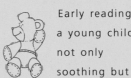

Early reading to a young child is not only soothing but also promotes cognitive development, including early literacy.

do things for herself, and guide her when necessary. Praise her for her efforts, putting less emphasis on the results.

♥ Acknowledge your child's feelings without judging, dismissing, or minimizing what she is saying. Validate her emotions by repeating her words so she learns to express herself. By listening to her feelings, you show her you value and care what she has to say. For example, say, "I hear your words when you say you had the doll first and then Joanna took it away. I see you feel angry with Joanna."

♥ Treat your child age appropriately. Do not have unrealistic expectations. A two-year-old shouldn't be expected to put her shoes on the correct feet by herself.

♥ To teach decision making, offer your child limited choices such as choosing between two different outfits. This will allow her to feel independent and give her a sense of control.

♥ Don't compare your child to other siblings, relatives, or friends.

Manners

Children aren't born with manners. Manners are a learned and imitated behavior, rituals a child learns through good role models. Most young children are not able to internalize manners because they are not developmentally ready. Toddlers and preschoolers are too young to understand, value, or appreciate how manners will help them later in life. It's the parents', teachers', and other caregivers' responsibility to model how to be polite, thoughtful, respectful, and considerate. Young children mimic the behavior surrounding them.

Don't expect a young child to be sociable and develop skills quickly. Sometimes she may want to say hello, and sometimes she may not. It's important not to get hung up on what other adults might think. Instead, keep in perspective that your child may not be developmentally ready to perform.

PINK AND BLUE HINT

If your child is not ready to use her manners, do not make it a power struggle.

Time-Tested Advice

❀ A toddler or preschooler can practice saying please, thank you, hello, and good-bye. Use these words consistently, so your child knows when and how to use them.

❀ A toddler or preschooler needs to be reminded frequently to use please and thank you because her memory is limited. Whenever a polite word is missing from her request, add the appropriate word to correct her.

❀ Take the pressure off your child if she doesn't use her manners in a social setting. For example, if someone says hello to your child and she doesn't respond, say, "Joanna is not ready to say hello today, but I'm sure she will learn."

❀ Praise your child when she uses polite words.

❀ Teach your child to be a good listener, by being a good listener yourself. When she speaks to you, make eye contact with her and remain silent until she finishes speaking.

PINK AND BLUE HINT

Use a kitchen timer when you must make an uninterrupted phone call. Since a young child does not have a sense of time, telling her to wait two minutes is meaningless. A ringing timer is a concrete concept she can understand. Keep a special box of toys only to be used when you must be on the telephone. Call it the "Telephone Toy Box."

❧ Be a good role model and set an example by always displaying good manners yourself. Respect and consideration are a two-way street. For example, when you park your car and the attendant hands you a ticket, be sure to say thank you so your child can see and hear how good manners are used.

❧ When you converse with your child (and other children), be sure to incorporate the same polite words you expect her to use.

❧ Be observant and point out other people's polite behavior. For instance, when someone holds the door open for the two of you, comment to the child how nice and polite the gesture was.

❧ A child wants attention when she interrupts an adult who is either talking on the phone, engaged in some activity, or speaking to another individual. If your child interrupts you, say, "Joanna, I'll be with you in a minute when I'm done talking to grandma." Remember, it is developmentally difficult to learn the concept of patience. When possible, avoid lengthy phone calls or involved projects until nap time or the designated quiet hour.

❧ Once the preschooler begins sitting at the table, encourage simple table manners, such as placing a napkin on her lap, chewing quietly, no talking with food in her mouth, and using the proper utensils. It's best to concentrate on one table manner at a time. Be realistic. A young child's memory is limited; therefore, expect this process to take time. She learns by example, so remember to be a good role model.

- ❤ The preschooler can be cooperative and lend a hand by taking her plate and utensils to the kitchen sink.

- ❤ Be considerate of others when you're taking your child out in public. Bring along toys and treats to keep your child from getting bored. A child should not be expected to behave like an adult.

- ❤ Show your child how to use a "quiet" voice when inside a public place.

- ❤ As your child gets older and develops peer relationships, show her how to be a good friend. For example, when a friend comes over to play, teach her to get along with others by having her share a toy.

Rewards and Incentives

Rewards are a form of praise to be used sparingly. A child needs to learn that her good intentions are rewards in themselves and that you value her good behavior. She shouldn't expect to receive something every time she cooperates and behaves well. After all, the best reward a child can receive is her parents' recognition and approval. However, an occasional reward, especially a spontaneous one, not only reinforces admirable behavior but also is fun. Rewards may range from stickers, small toys, books, coloring books, and crayons to a trip to the park, an extra story at bedtime, or lunch at a restaurant.

Sometimes rewards can't be given right away, and a child must learn to wait. She needs to understand that things don't always revolve around her. Explain to her that it's impossible to have the reward today (immediately), but that you'll do it tomorrow.

PINK AND BLUE HINT

 Go to the discount toy store (without your child) and purchase a few inexpensive toys or books your child would like. When she earns a reward, give her one of the surprises.

Rewards can be used as a positive incentive for the toddler or preschooler who is learning to master new skills. Sometimes, if you make the reward tangible, the child may be more motivated to accelerate her progress. For instance, if she stays dry through the night for five consecutive nights, she will accumulate five gold stars and earn a surprise.

Incentives and consequences motivate a child's behavior. They encourage a child to change or correct her conduct. Incentives and consequences should be discussed and determined ahead of time. For example, when you take your child to the supermarket, tell her that if she doesn't whine or grab things out of the shopping cart, she may select a treat. However, make it clear that if she doesn't listen to you, the consequence will be no treat. Always set consequences you can live with and carry out.

Bribes, on the other hand, are usually administered in a last ditch effort to resolve an ensuing crisis. Often parents fall into the trap of using bribes to elicit good behavior from their child. Bribes are a quick fix for the moment and are less effective than teaching incentives and consequences.

A final word on rewarding a young child: A hug, pat on the back, encouraging words, or even a smile is the sincerest form of praise your child can receive from you.

For more information on rewards, please see Chapter 2, "Toilet Training," and Chapter 6, "Sleep."

Misbehavior and Disciplinary Techniques

Toddlers and preschoolers are naturally curious, spontaneous, egocentric, unpredictable, and uninhibited. They display a full range of emotions and behaviors, including some not so desirable, and often in split seconds of each other. As social skills begin to develop around the age of two years, it's normal for the young child to have conflicts as she learns to interact with the world around her. She's a typical toddler or preschooler asserting her independence as her language skills expand. In addition, other factors may contribute to her misbehavior, including illness, hunger, exhaustion, boredom, or significant changes in the family's life.

When dealing with a young child, it's important to remember to separate the child from the act of misbehaving. Be clear that it's her actions you disapprove of, not her. She needs to learn from the beginning that every action has a consequence, which she may or may not like, but which she nonetheless must understand. Effective discipline is about being firm with and accepting of the child.

The Toddler

The toddler doesn't intend to misbehave or ignore a parent's request. When she's involved in an activity at this stage of development, she's not able to concentrate on more than one thing at a time. While the toddler does hear your voice, she's just not listening to your words. With good reason—she's too busy. On top of that, she's beginning to test her limits.

That's why it's imperative to establish clear boundaries and firm limits. When you see your child making bad choices, give a warning and follow it up with discipline if she doesn't listen to you. The consequence should be imposed immediately, or it will lose its effectiveness with the forgetful toddler. Be prepared to discipline your toddler several times a day, because she doesn't have good judgment and relies upon you to teach her acceptable behavior.

Learn to recognize your child's ploy to gain control. Her range of tactics can vary from passivity to hysteria and from sweetness to aggressive physical behavior. She's displaying the first signs of independence and wants to be in charge of

PINK AND BLUE ALERT

A parent should not criticize or undermine the other parent's disciplinary measure in front of the child. Solve these differences in another room, away from the child. If you cannot reach a compromise, consider seeking parenting help.

what she wears, what she eats, and what time she goes to bed. In other words, "I'm the boss of me!"

To help keep a balance between control and independence and to avert constant power struggles, follow these tips.

Time-Tested Advice

❤ When you need to get your toddler's attention, give short, simple verbal commands she can understand. Long-winded explanations fall on deaf ears.

❤ Speak in a quiet, controlled voice. A whisper is a very effective way to get a toddler's attention.

❤ Since toddlers have limited memories, reminding the child what she needs to do is an ongoing, repetitive process.

❤ When you're correcting negative behavior, speak face to face with your child, making direct eye contact. Yelling across the room is ineffective.

❤ If your child is ignoring your requests, take immediate action. For instance, if it's time to leave the park and she won't go, take her by the hand or pick her up and leave.

❤ Give plenty of fair warning when an activity needs to come to an end. A toddler needs time to make the transition from one activity to another. If the child resists, be sympathetic and then pick her up and leave. Tell her you know how hard it is to stop all the fun, but time is up, and you'll come back another day.

❧ When you want your toddler to do something, make a statement that doesn't require a choice or leave room for negotiations. Remember, "no" is always on the tip of a toddler's tongue. Instead of saying, "Do you want to take a bath?" say, "It's time to take a bath." Or think about using *yes* as in "Yes, you may have a cookie after you've eaten your dinner."

❧ Avoid using the word *no* too often because it dilutes the effectiveness of the word. If a child is tempted to play with a fragile object (your favorite vase), move it out of her reach. It beats saying no over and over.

❧ Turn a negative into a positive. Instead of saying, "Don't pull the dog's tail!" explain, "It hurts the dog."

❧ Save your nos for unsafe situations that compromise your child's well-being. To minimize threatening circumstances within the home, be diligent about child-proofing your home. (See Chapter 8, "Safety.")

❧ Give your child the opportunity to feel independent by allowing her to make limited choices. She needs decision-making practice, such as, choosing between two different outfits or two different breakfast cereals.

❧ It's OK to let your child make a mistake because she can learn from her error, as long as her safety is not threatened.

❧ Since it's difficult to hurry a toddler, plan ahead and allow *plenty* of time to get ready. There will be less tension getting out the door.

❧ If your child is unusually cranky, she could be getting sick.

PINK AND BLUE HINT

If your child responds well to a timer, take it along in your activity bag. When it's time to end an activity, give a warning and set the timer, just as you do at home.

PINK AND BLUE HINT

When two children fight over the same toy, give the toy a time-out. Then help the two toddlers come to a fair sharing solution. It is never too soon to teach young children how to compromise and work things out.

PINK AND BLUE HINT

Use a timer to demonstrate sharing a toy. Set the timer for five minutes and let one child play with the toy until the timer goes off. Then give the toy to the other child. Be sure the child without the special toy has some other diversion while waiting her turn. Praise the children for their cooperation.

* When your child is acting up, remove her and relocate her to a new setting before the situation gets out of hand. (For more detailed information, see Temper Tantrums later in this chapter.)

* Distraction is an excellent strategy. A young child will usually respond to a diversion, such as a new object or new location.

* Since a toddler has limited verbal skills, actions often take the place of words. When your child pushes another child, throws sand, or is physically aggressive, first use simple language to explain that this type of behavior is unacceptable and unsafe. If she continues to misbehave after the verbal warning, remove her from the situation temporarily with a time-out. (For more information, see Time-Out later in this chapter.) If the aggressive behavior persists, remove her permanently.

* Grabbing a toy from another child is very common at this age. If your child is the grabber, have her return the toy to its rightful owner, and distract her with another toy. To deal with future toy tugs-of-war, teach her to use her words so eventually she'll be able to express herself. This is an opportune time to teach her the concept of taking turns.

* Ignore minor misbehaviors. Pick and choose your battles.

The Preschooler

As your toddler moves into the next phase of her life, she is maturing intellectually, socially, and emotionally. She is beginning to comprehend the difference between right and wrong and to learn the consequences for unacceptable behavior. While no parent enjoys acting like an ogre, seeing a child cry, or being temporarily disliked, it's far more important to teach the child valuable lessons that will serve as the backbone for her entire life.

When enforcing discipline, a parent must consider the child's developmental abilities. For example, a three-year-old can't be expected to sit at a table in a restaurant as long as a four-year-old can. No matter how you approach the struggles that may ensue, don't expect perfection from the child or yourself. Continue to be firm and consistent on the issues most important to your family, and avoid threats if you are not prepared to follow through. Parents need to understand they have appropriate power to take control when necessary. Believe it or not, children need and crave effective discipline and structure.

It's important to remember that children do not all have the same temperaments. What works for one child may not work for another, so experiment with a few different techniques until you find one that works for you and your child. In addition to the Time-Tested Advice listed in the preceding section, The Toddler, here are more practical tips parents can employ on a regular basis.

Time-Tested Advice

❁ Since most preschoolers behave impulsively, yelling is a counterproductive method because it creates anger and humiliation. Speak calmly and firmly, and show her a more appropriate way to control herself.

❁ It's perfectly all right to discipline your child for out-of-control behavior, but don't shame her. First tell her to stop the unacceptable behavior ("Stop kicking") and then explain why ("Kicking hurts"). Remember to compliment your child when she listens to you.

- Avoid embarrassing your child in front of others. If she's displaying unacceptable behavior, pull her aside, explain what she's doing wrong, and offer a positive alternative.

- If you feel as if you're going to lose your temper, step back, take a deep breath, and count to ten. Another way to regain your composure is to leave the room for a few minutes and disengage from the conflict.

- If a child has a pattern of intentional acts of misbehavior, correct the misbehavior immediately. For example, if your child refuses to eat her lunch and throws it on the floor, make her clean up the mess, and do not offer any other food. Later on when she gets hungry, tell the child her tummy is talking because she didn't eat her lunch when she was supposed to.

- Ignore minor, but annoying, habits that draw negative attention. If your child whines and pouts, say, "I need to hear your big-girl voice." Praise her when she uses a normal tone of voice.

- Since preschoolers have selective memories, they constantly need to be reminded about rules. Take control of the situation, and walk her through what you want her to do. At the same time, acknowledge her feelings of discontentment. For example, if playtime needs to be over, say, "You need to stop playing now and follow mommy's rules. I know it's hard to stop when you're having fun."

PINK AND BLUE ALERT

Never shake a young child. It can cause serious neck and head injuries.

♥ If you're experiencing resistance getting your preschooler ready, play a game of "beat the clock." For example say, "I bet you can't get your pants on to the count of ten." She'll enjoy the challenge, and you'll subtly reinforce the exercise of counting.

♥ Sometimes it takes negative consequences to learn a lesson. For instance, if your child is on a play date and misbehaves, give her a warning. If she continues to act up, take her home.

♥ When a child dawdles, place your hand gently on her back and move her in the desired direction, distracting her with conversation about what she is going to do or see next.

♥ If you want your child to do something in particular, give her a positive incentive. For example, "When you're done putting your toys away, you may help bake cookies."

♥ When expressing your feelings to your child about her behavior, empathize with her struggle and acknowledge her feelings. For example, if you want her to put away her toys, use a supportive voice and say, "I know it's hard to put your toys away, but your job is to put them away when I ask you to."

♥ An adult apologizing to a child teaches humility and lets her know her feelings count.

♥ If you're experiencing repeated behavioral problems with your child, consult your pediatrician, parenting specialist, child psychologist, or director of a preschool.

PINK AND BLUE HINT

If you would like more information and help regarding your child's behavior, contact Parents Anonymous at (909) 621-6184 or on the Internet at www.parents anonymous-natl.org.

> ☀ Children are like parrots and repeat everything they hear. Be careful not to use foul language in their presence.

Temper Tantrums

Temper tantrums are normal regressive feelings of expression a young child may experience due to an inability to convey what is bothering her. She doesn't have the developmental skills for coping yet and therefore falls apart. The primary reason temper tantrums occur is that a child doesn't get her way and becomes frustrated when she doesn't receive immediate gratification. Other reasons for temper tantrums may be hunger, anger, fatigue, or even lack of attention. Temper tantrums can also be triggered by a child's frustration from following too many rules, not wanting to share or compromise, being jealous of a sibling, or not wanting to control her aggressive behavior (biting, hitting, kicking, throwing food, etc.). Tantrums also erupt when children are expected to sit still for too long. Young children need plenty of physical activity.

Tantrums can be curtailed if the parent keeps realistic, age-appropriate expectations of the child. To minimize tantrums, follow these tips.

Time-Tested Advice

> ☀ It is not unusual for a toddler or preschooler to be compulsive about what she wants and likes or dislikes. For example, she may not like one food touching another food on her plate and may refuse to eat. Reflect on her feelings by saying, "You sure don't like it when the peas touch the potatoes. Let's put each of them on a separate plate."

When a tantrum occurs, if possible, identify what triggered it so you can head off future tantrums. For example, if your child falls apart when running errands in the late afternoon, she most likely is tired and shouldn't be expected to be cooperative. Next time run fewer errands, or if possible, leave her at home with a sitter.

Stay calm so you don't make a bad situation worse. Yelling or hitting the child will only escalate the problem.

If your child is screaming and throwing a tantrum at home, don't respond to the behavior. As the tantrum winds down, praise her for better behavior.

If the tantrum is a result of your disciplining the child, hold your ground and do not give in. If she senses she can manipulate you, she will learn to throw tantrums to get what she wants.

If you're out in public and a tantrum takes place, don't let other people's reactions or judgments alter your position. Remove the child and tell her it is unacceptable to scream in public. For a parent's own comfort, it is perfectly appropriate to say to the other people being disturbed, "I'm sorry Jennifer is having a hard time controlling herself." There isn't a parent who has breezed through the toddler and preschool years without experiencing this kind of behavior.

To reinforce self-control when tempers flare, administer a time-out policy. (See the section on Time-Out for more specifics.) If the temper persists and the time-out is ineffective, it's better to put the

PINK AND BLUE HINT

To avert hunger tantrums when you are out and about with your toddler or preschooler, bring a few healthful snacks for her to munch on. Easy foods to take along are rice cakes, cut-up fruit, cereal, and crackers.

child in an unoccupied room. She'll learn that it's no fun to have a temper tantrum alone. Be sure the room you select is safe for her to be in alone, and leave the door ajar.

❁ When your child has a temper tantrum and is not listening, it is best for the parent to disengage from the conflict by telling the child that when she calms down, she will receive your attention. This will give the parent and child time to collect themselves.

❁ A tantrum can be reversed sometimes by distracting the child with an alternative choice of activity or toy.

Time-Out

For a toddler and preschooler a time-out is sometimes helpful and effective. A time-out isolates the child and gives her a chance to regroup and regain her self-control, making her realize she's going to have to help herself in order to return to the activities. It is an excellent way to correct misbehavior. It is important to explain why she is having a time-out, for how long, and what behavior is acceptable before she may rejoin the family or situation. Don't expect this method to work perfectly the first few times, but if you are consistent, your child will eventually learn to think before acting impulsively.

Time-Tested Advice

❁ Use a time-out only after you have clearly warned the child about her unacceptable behavior. Do not use a time-out for a first-time transgression. Request that your child heed your warning no more than once or twice, and be specific. For example, if you have asked your child more than once to stop kicking the chair and she doesn't listen, give her a time-out.

❧ A time-out should be imposed immediately if a child ignores your instruction and misbehaves after a fair repeated warning.

❧ Explain in short, specific words the reason for the time-out.

❧ The rule of thumb for the length of a time-out is one minute for each year of a child's age—for example, two minutes for a two-year-old.

❧ Choose a quiet uninteresting spot where your child can sit or stand. The location should be away from a television, window, door, bedroom, or any active area in the home.

❧ Do not put your child in the kitchen, bathroom, or any area that's not safe.

❧ Use a timer and start timing her as soon as she is in the designated location.

❧ The person who imposes the time-out should be the one to monitor and dismiss the child.

❧ Set rules for the time-out period:

   ◉ The child must stay in the designated time-out spot until the timer goes off.

   ◉ No toys or transitional objects are allowed.

PINK AND BLUE ALERT

If your child resists the time-out, firmly put her in the selected place. If she refuses to cooperate, stay with her and hold her until the timer goes off. Do not engage in conversation with her if you must physically restrain her. If she continues to act out, repeat the time-out period. Hold your ground so she understands who is in control.

⊚ Do not respond to what the child is doing to get your attention, short of hurting herself.

❦ When a time-out ends, give your child a hug. Don't discuss the problem anymore because you've already explained the reason for the time-out.

❦ Try to use the same set of time-out rules when misbehavior takes place outside the home. At the park, move her to a different location away from other children. In the car, if it is safe, pull over to the side of the road, turn off the engine, and do not engage in conversation. At a restaurant, take your child outside. When it is logistically difficult to use the time-out, go home and administer the time-out at home. This may be inconvenient, but it does get the point across.

❦ Do not overuse time-outs, or they will become ineffective.

Aggressive Behavior

Biting, hitting, kicking, pushing, pulling hair, and pinching are all as typical in a toddler or preschooler as a temper tantrum. These physically aggressive behaviors usually stem from the toddler's frustration of being unable to express her needs, due to limited language development. It is the toddler's way of getting her point across, as well as a way to simply make social contact. She is seeking immediate attention and reaction from those around her. In addition, if a parent does not put boundaries on overactive physical play, a child will think it's OK to behave that way. For example, some fathers stimulate aggressive behavior by playing too roughly with their young child, which can translate into aggressive play with other children.

Preschoolers tend to have better control over aggressive behavior, due in large part to their expanded verbal skills. However, preschoolers can occasionally revert to physical action, especially when the issue of delayed gratification arises. Their inability to be patient can cause a temper tantrum, leading to aggressive behavior. Don't let this kind of behavior slide; deal with it quickly and consistently. To deter this unacceptable behavior from escalating, try the following advice.

Time-Tested Advice

❀ Stop the physical aggression and intervene immediately. Comfort and attend to the hurt child first. Then hold or remove the aggressor from the situation and firmly but supportively tell her she may not behave that way. Tell the child the consequence will be she can't play with the other child.

❀ If a child is a biter, do not resort to putting bad-tasting foods or soap in her mouth or on her lips or biting her back as a solution to the problem. Say, "Biting hurts and is not OK." Remove the child from the situation, and tell her you won't make another play date as long as she bites others.

❀ A parent needs to observe what precipitated the inappropriate behavior. For example, your child doesn't want to share or is overtired.

❀ Divert the aggressive youngster's attention with another activity.

❀ Observe carefully before interacting with your child. Pay attention to when she is acting out of bounds.

Say, "I know you're upset, but try to get yourself under control."

❧ If your child has limited verbal skills when learning how to share, speak for her. Teach her how to express herself by giving her the words, such as "Please give me my doll."

❧ Help her learn to express her emotions by using words, not aggressive actions. If she's angry, teach her to say, "I'm angry."

❧ Acknowledge a child's feelings and let her know it's all right to be upset or angry but it's not all right to hit, bite, or kick.

❧ Don't try to teach the child a lesson by repeating the same aggressive behavior on her. For instance, if she pulls your hair, don't pull her hair back.

❧ Be sure to praise your child for correcting her aggressive behavior.

Fears

Fear in a toddler and a preschooler is a normal developmental struggle between reality and fantasy. A younger child is not cognizant of things around her and doesn't know to be afraid; fear is a learned behavior. However, insecurities often surface when the child starts feeling a certain sense of independence and separateness from the parent. Because of a child's small stature and lack of understanding of the world around her, everything seems bigger, and a feeling of vulnerability sets in. If a parent has unusual anxiety and is overly protective, he or she may inject fear into the child. Most of the time fear is a phase that disappears just as quickly as it develops, once the child learns to distinguish reality from fantasy. To help a child overcome a particular fear, visit your local library or bookstore and find books relating to her fear.

Time-Tested Advice

☀ Listen to the child carefully and acknowledge her fear. Don't dismiss her thoughts, even if they seem irrational to you. Make a simple statement: "I can see that's scary. Mommy and Daddy are here, and we can take care of you."

☀ Don't belittle, put down, or laugh at your child's fears. They are real to her.

☀ Demanding that a child confront her fear can have negative repercussions. If she's afraid of dogs, don't insist she pet the animal to get over it. Help her conquer the fear by getting some books and videos about dogs, especially humorous ones. Take her to a pet store, reassure the child that the dogs are safely locked up, and let her watch them. When she appears more comfortable, take her to the home of a friend with a small friendly dog or a bigger affectionate dog. Have the friend hold the dog, showing the child she has total control and won't let the dog go. If the child still appears scared, progress slowly and let her look at the dog from a distance. Continually praise the child and reinforce how well she's doing. Numerous visits to the friend's home should help alleviate the anxiety and build up her courage.

☀ If a parent acts fearful and anxious, a child will pick up on it and model the adult's behavior.

❦ Popular costumed characters can frighten a toddler or preschooler because a child is confronted with the natural struggle between reality and fantasy. In addition, if a child is used to seeing a character on television in small stature, and then sees this large character standing in front of her, it can be frightening. A child can feel overwhelmed and out of control, not knowing how to approach the large, partly human character.

❦ Clowns can be scary because of their gaudy makeup, loud voices, and unpredictable behavior. Don't push your child into befriending a clown if it makes her uncomfortable.

❦ Sometimes a simple explanation or demonstration can comfort a child's fear. For example, a toddler or preschooler may be frightened by the sound of an ambulance. Explain to the child that the loud noise alerts other cars and trucks on the road to move out of the way for the emergency vehicle. Say, "I know that noise must sound scary, but it's going to help someone."

❦ Visit your local library and find books relating to your child's particular fear.

For fear of the dark and monsters, please see Chapter 6, "Sleep." For fear of elimination, please see Chapter 2, "Toilet Training." For fear of bathing and shampooing the hair, please see Chapter 4, "Personal Hygiene."

❧ 8 ❧

Safety

You have been child-proofing your house since your child was born, and guess what, you've only just begun. The curious toddler or preschooler wants to see, taste, and discover everything new and different inside and outside the home. It's important to let him explore and develop a sense of independence without compromising his safety. However, a child this age tends to be naturally accident-prone, partly because he is so busy and absorbed in what he's doing that he doesn't pay attention, and partly because he doesn't understand what might be dangerous to him.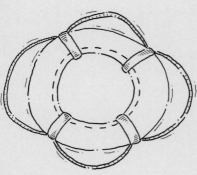

Be thorough in your efforts to protect your young child from suffering unnecessary calamities and mishaps. You can help avoid serious accidents by planning ahead and being organized. Never assume your child will know something is dangerous to touch, play with, or put in his mouth.

PINK AND BLUE HINT

If your child spends a lot of time at his grandparents' home, help them child-proof their residence in the same diligent manner that you have made your own home safe.

PINK AND BLUE HINT

Teach your child his first and last name, address, and telephone number. Practice it daily. Make up a song or simple rhyme to help your child memorize all the information.

To avoid using the word *no* frequently, remove any precious and fragile items from your child's reach.

One of the most important things parents and caregivers should do is take a first-aid class given through the local American Red Cross or YMCA and learn the technique of CPR (cardiopulmonary resuscitation). If you have taken a class but it's been a while, it's a good idea to take a refresher course. Another important safety precaution is posting emergency information by the most often used telephone in the home (see the next section, Emergency Information List, for specifics).

Never take anything for granted when it comes to your child's safety and well-being because it only takes a second for something to go wrong. It's important to keep a balance between becoming an overly anxious parent who hovers over the child, inhibiting his inquisitiveness, and a neglectful parent who does not pay careful attention to the active toddler and preschooler. An attentive parent recognizes the importance of keeping a constant watchful eye while maintaining a calm attitude.

Emergency Information List

Post emergency telephone numbers, addresses, and vital information by at least one phone in the house, where it will be visible to anyone handling an emergency. Here's the information you will need to post:

※ Children's names and birth dates

※ Home phone number

※ Father's and mother's work, pager, and mobile phone numbers

※ Home address, directions to the house, and nearest cross streets

❋ Pediatrician's name, telephone number, and address

❋ Neighbor's or relative's phone number and address

❋ Police and fire department (this includes paramedics)— 911

❋ Poison control center phone number

❋ Directions to nearest hospital emergency room

❋ Each child's allergies (if any), dietary restrictions (if any), and medication taken regularly

❋ Date of each child's last tetanus booster

❋ Medical history of serious illness or injury (if necessary)

❋ Health insurance carrier, including group number and ID number

❋ Pharmacy phone number and address

You should always leave a notarized letter of consent and authorization with the caregiver responsible for your child in your absence. This letter authorizes the caregiver to get medical treatment for your child. An additional letter should also be filed in your child's medical records at the pediatrician's office, authorizing the doctor to give medical care in your absence. If you will be traveling out of the country without your child, this notarized letter is very important.

Safety Inside the Home

The best way to determine potential hazards and dangers in your home is by seeing things from a child's perspective. That means getting on your hands and knees, just about a toddler's standing height, and looking at all the things around you. Have you been diligent in covering all electrical

PINK AND BLUE ALERT

If your child is taking medication, be sure to leave the caregiver specific instructions on dosage and what time to administer the medicine. Specify whether the medicine needs to be taken with food, what foods to avoid with this particular illness and medication, and whether the medicine needs to be refrigerated.

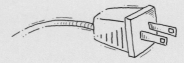

outlets, tying up dangling cords or electrical wires, covering sharp corners, and putting away all medicines, vitamins, cleaning agents, sharp tools and utensils, lighters, and matches? Have you removed poisonous plants within your child's reach and kept safety gates securely locked on the stairs? As your young child grows and becomes more mobile, new dangers can arise. He can reach things that are higher, climb on anything, and even open outside doors. Now it's time to child-proof your home again. Visit your local safety or juvenile store to purchase child-proofing hardware.

If you haven't already begun teaching basic safety rules to your child, start immediately. Teach him what is dangerous and can cause bodily harm to him. Some children, for whatever reasons, are more adventurous and take greater risks than others. If your child exhibits a "daredevil" disposition, take extra precautions and set stricter safety boundaries.

PINK AND BLUE HINT

To remember when it's time to replace the batteries in your smoke detectors, choose the same time every year—for example, when you change your clocks to daylight saving time in the spring or standard time in the fall.

Time-Tested Advice for Basic Home Safety

❦ Never leave your child alone in the house, condominium, apartment, or backyard.

❦ A first-aid kit is a necessity in every home. (Please see the section titled The Home Medicine Cabinet in Chapter 3, "Your Child's Health.")

❦ Equip your home with smoke detectors, flashlights, and at least one fire extinguisher (hung at an adult's height). Change the batteries in smoke detectors yearly, and keep extra flashlight batteries on hand.

❦ Lock up all medications, household cleaning products, aerosol cans, alcoholic beverages, and other dangerous substances, and keep them out of a child's reach. See the Poisons section in this chapter for more detailed information.

❧ Always keep doors leading to the outside of the house locked. If you know your child is particularly clever and has figured out how to unlock the door, add an extra bolt or lock above his reach. Put child-proof locks on all screen doors and sliding doors. Make sure a spare house key is readily available.

❧ For doors you don't want children to open, use doorknob guards; they are difficult for small hands to maneuver.

❧ Place colorful decals at your child's eye level on all glass doors, so he will see the glass.

❧ Either remove locks from interior doors or know how to unlock them if your child locks himself inside a room.

❧ Do not keep furniture or any item your child can climb on in front of a window.

❧ Make sure all windows have window guards, locks, and screens. In case of an emergency, all caregivers should know how to operate the window guards and locks.

❧ Windows should be opened from the top, not the bottom. Lock unopened windows.

❧ Never leave a child unattended in a room with an open window.

❧ Use cord shorteners or cord windups on all decorative window treatments, such as blinds, shades, and

PINK AND BLUE HINT

For peace of mind and extra protection, wire a ringing alarm to all outside doors. If your child opens the door, you'll be instantly alerted. Put a chime or a bell on his bedroom door if you're concerned about middle-of-the-night escapades.

PINK AND BLUE ALERT

Don't rely on window screens to protect your child because they can't support his weight.

draperies. A child can get tangled in a long cord, and strangulation can easily occur.

❧ Teach your child the meaning of words such as *hot*, *sharp*, and *dangerous* through constant verbal repetition and word/object association—for example, "hot stove," "sharp knife," "dangerous electrical outlet."

❧ If you own a freestanding purified water dispenser with hot and cold levers, keep your child away from it because he can burn himself on the hot water.

❧ Teach your child not to touch or play with anything electrical.

❧ If there are any frayed or worn electrical cords in your home, replace them immediately.

❧ Be sure to tie up all dangling electrical appliance wires so there is a short cord connecting the appliance to the electrical outlet. A child can easily pull on a long cord and have the heavy object (coffee pot, blender, or television) come crashing down on him.

❧ When unplugging an electrical appliance, first disconnect the cord from the electrical outlet, not from the appliance, to avoid electrical shock.

❧ If you live in an older home, make sure all electrical outlets are grounded in order to avoid electrical shock.

❧ Be careful of multiple-outlet power strips because not only are they easy for a child to pull out, they are also intriguing to a young child's curiosity.

❧ Beware of halogen lamps; they become very hot very quickly.

❦ Empty light sockets in lamps can be tempting to inquisitive little fingers, so be sure to fill all sockets with lightbulbs.

❦ Keep your child away from fans, electric wall heaters, floor heaters, and radiators.

❦ Be sure safety gates are always locked at the top and bottom of stairs.

❦ Never allow toys or playing on the stairs.

❦ Never leave a child alone on a balcony.

❦ Cover stair and balcony railings with Plexiglas or mesh netting. If you need assistance, consult your local child-proofing store or safety specialist.

❦ If there's an outside balcony, always lock the doors leading out to the balcony. Cover railings with Plexiglas or mesh netting.

❦ To avoid suffocation accidents, keep all plastic bags out of your child's reach in a safety-locked cabinet.

❦ Dry-cleaning plastic bags should be removed from clothing immediately and thrown away in a trash bin with a safety-locked lid.

❦ Place felt appliqués or corner guards on all corners and edges of furniture that your child can easily bump into.

❦ Keep the curious toddler away from open wastebaskets.

❦ Tablecloths are tempting for little hands to pull on and can be dangerous to a child's safety if heavy

PINK AND BLUE HINT

Safety outlet plugs with pliable prongs are easy for some young children to remove. Buy plugs that require turning or squeezing before removing from the outlet.

PINK AND BLUE ALERT

If you own a gun, it should have a trigger lock and be securely stored in a closet or cabinet that is inaccessible and cannot be opened by a child.

objects are placed on the cloth. To avoid accidents, use place mats instead.

❀ All fireplaces should be protected with safe, heavy screens that can't be moved or knocked over by a child. Keep children away from lit fireplaces.

❀ Do not leave newspapers or magazines near fireplaces, heating vents, or floor and wall heaters.

❀ Make sure all area rugs have nonskid pads to prevent slipping accidents.

❀ Don't allow your child to run in socks on hard floor surfaces in the house because he can easily slip and fall.

❀ Place jewelry items out of a child's reach; things that are small, shiny, and glittery attract a child's attention.

❀ Keep sewing, knitting, crocheting, and needlepoint supplies out of a child's reach.

Kitchen

Picture this: a hot stove, electrical appliances, sharp utensils, breakable china, a busy cook, and active young children scurrying about . . . a recipe for potential mishaps. Since the kitchen is the center of the household, here are the guidelines to reduce the risk of accidents.

Time-Tested Advice

❀ Your kitchen should be equipped with a smoke detector and fire extinguisher.

- Child-proof your kitchen with cabinet and drawer latches, oven locks, stove knob covers, and refrigerator locks (optional).

- Even when cabinets and drawers have childproof latches, some clever children figure out how to open them. For safety's sake, move sharp utensils, boxes with serrated edges, toothpicks, and any breakable items out of the child's reach.

- Do not store knives in a wooden block on the countertop, where your child could possibly reach them. Place sharp knives and forks in a safety-locked drawer.

- All cleaning products used in the kitchen must be stored in an inaccessible cabinet out of the child's reach. It's a good idea to double-latch the cabinet these cleaning items are stored in.

- Do not store cleaning products in empty food containers because anyone could mistake the hazardous product for something edible.

- Store all spices and aerosol cooking sprays out of a child's reach.

- While cooking, turn pot and pan handles toward the back of the stove. Fry and boil on back burners. Keep your child away from the stove so boiling water or hot oil doesn't splatter on him.

- Do not leave food cooking on the stove unattended.

- Make sure there are no oven mitts, dish towels, or wooden utensils close to the stove, toaster, or toaster oven when these appliances are in use.

PINK AND BLUE HINT

Select one accessible cabinet or drawer for your child to use while in the kitchen with you. Store plastic containers of various sizes, unbreakable bowls, wooden spoons, and toys in it. Your child can play while you cook, but be sure he's not too close to any hot appliances.

- ❧ Unplug small appliances from the electrical socket when not in use, and keep all electrical appliances out of reach to prevent them from toppling on your child. To avoid electrical shock, never leave the cord plugged into the outlet when it is not connected to the appliance.

- ❧ Move chairs, step stools, bar stools, and stepladders away from counters and appliances (including washer and dryer) so your child will not be tempted to climb.

- ❧ Do not allow your child to sit on a countertop because he can easily fall off the counter or put his little fingers into places that are unsafe. It also sends mixed messages that sometimes it's all right to climb on the counter.

- ❧ Since kitchen floors tend to be slick, clean up spills immediately so no one will slip.

- ❧ Clean up broken glass or dishes first with a vacuum or broom, then follow up with damp paper towels.

- ❧ Never hold your child when carrying any hot liquid.

- ❧ When removing hot dishes or pots and pans from the oven, stove, or microwave, keep children away and set these objects out of reach.

- ❧ Be careful not to put any hot item, such as a coffee cup, near the edge of a counter where a young child can easily grab it.

- ❧ It's best to keep garbage in a trash can under the kitchen sink behind childproof-locked cabinet doors. If this is impossible, then store the garbage in a trash can with a safety-locked lid out of your child's reach.

PINK AND BLUE HINT

Wrap all sharp objects, such as can lids, in newspaper before disposing of them in recycling bins.

❧ When loading the dishwasher, place knives and forks pointing downward in the silverware container to avoid puncturing accidents. Do not add dishwashing detergent until you're ready to turn on the dishwasher because a young child can easily reach the detergent, and it is harmful if swallowed.

❧ Do not pour water on a grease fire; instead smother the flame with baking soda or flour. If there's a small fire in the oven, turn off the heat and keep the oven door closed to extinguish the fire.

❧ Keep a young child away from the washer and dryer when in use. Always keep the doors to these appliances closed so a young child isn't tempted to climb inside.

❧ Laundry detergent, bleach, and fabric softener must be stored in a childproof-locked cabinet out of the child's reach.

Bathroom

The bathroom is another room that poses a threat to a young child if not child-proofed properly. The toilet, the water faucets, that big tub—they all attract the young child's curiosity. While it's an inconvenience to the adult to use a child-proofed bathroom, it's an absolute must!

Time-Tested Advice

❧ Never leave a child unattended in the bathroom.

❧ Lock up all medicines, over-the-counter medications, first-aid remedies, and vitamins. Do not use

PINK AND BLUE HINT

Recheck safety latches on all cabinet doors and drawers frequently. With constant use, latches can lose their locking effectiveness.

PINK AND BLUE HINT

To help your child distinguish the hot water from the cold water at the sink and tub, put a red rubber band around the hot water handle and a blue rubber band around the cold.

PINK AND BLUE ALERT

Before bathing your child, test the bathwater temperature to make sure it's not too hot. Always turn off the hot water first.

the medicine cabinet if it cannot be locked or safety-latched, because a young child could possibly use a step stool to climb up and help himself.

* Frequently check expiration dates on all medications. Flush expired medicines down the toilet.

* Keep all cleaning products, skin lotions, powder, hair products, shaving items (razors and blades), colognes, soaps, antiseptic mouthwashes, and cosmetics out of your child's reach.

* All types of air fresheners (aerosol cans and plug-ins) and potpourris should be kept out of a child's reach. Their sweet aromas are attractive to the young child's acute senses.

* If you are concerned about the hot water temperature in your house, lower the temperature on the water heater. (Normal temperature is 140 degrees Fahrenheit, so you may want to reduce the temperature to no less than 120 degrees Fahrenheit.)

* Put protective spout and knob covers on the bathtub to prevent a child from turning on the water and burning or bumping himself.

* Make sure the floor of the bathtub and shower has either a bath mat, nonskid strips, or appliqués to prevent slipping accidents.

* Place a nonskid, rubber-backed bath mat in front of the tub or shower to absorb water dripping off a wet body.

* Keep all toilet lids closed with a safety latch when not in use. A child can fall in and drown in a small amount of water. Open toilets are tempting to play

in and very dangerous, not to mention unsanitary. If your child is in the throes of toilet training, the safety latch is a nuisance but a necessary precaution.

* Each time your toilet-training child needs to go to the bathroom, an adult should accompany him.

* Do not use glass items in the bathroom because they are unsafe.

* Keep hair dryers and any other electrical items unplugged and out of a child's reach when not in use.

* Hot tubs, saunas, and steam showers are unsafe for young children.

* When a child uses a step stool, an adult must be by his side to prevent accidents or any other "typical toddler" mischievous behavior.

Garage

Trouble lurks in all areas of the garage, so it should be off-limits to young children. Pay special attention to the following tips.

Time-Tested Advice

* Lock all vehicles in the garage.

* If you keep tools in the garage, store and lock them out of your child's reach.

* Garden products, such as weed killers, insect and snail poisons, and fertilizers, are poisonous and

PINK AND BLUE ALERT

Never leave a child unattended in the bathtub. Drowning can occur, even in a small amount of water. If the doorbell rings while your child is in the tub, either take the child with you to the door or don't answer it. Turn on the telephone answering machine and return calls later.

should be locked up in a place that is inaccessible to your child.

- ♥ Car maintenance products, such as oil, gasoline, antifreeze, and brake and cleaning fluids, should be locked and stored high above a child's reach.

- ♥ If you have an automatic garage-door opener, mount the wall button at least six feet above the floor, where a child can't reach it. Store the remote in the glove compartment of your car.

- ♥ Don't operate the automatic garage-door opener when anyone is standing close by.

- ♥ If you have an unused refrigerator or freezer, either deadbolt the door shut or remove the door so a child will not use it as a hiding place, where he could easily suffocate. Better yet, get rid of the appliance.

- ♥ If you have exercise equipment in the garage, be sure the door leading from the house into the garage is always locked. A child can easily climb on a treadmill, push the buttons and injure himself. Free weights should be stored out of a child's reach.

- ♥ Adult-sized bicycles should be hung on bicycle hooks (available at bicycle stores) out of child's reach because a child may be tempted to climb on the big bike, and it could topple over and injure him.

PINK AND BLUE ALERT

If your automatic garage-door opener was installed before 1993, replace it with a newer model, or retrofit it with a backup safety device. The new mechanisms have an electric eye or edge sensor, which protect a child by stopping the door before it makes contact with anybody or anything.

Child-Proofing Your Pool and Backyard

Just as inside the home, there are inherent dangers in your very own backyard. Look around and see what is potentially hazardous to your young child, such as a swimming pool, a hot barbecue, poisonous plants, a broken fence, garden tools, and backyard play equipment. It's equally important to pay close attention to anyone else's backyard where your child plays. Outdoor play always requires an adult's watchful eye.

Time-Tested Advice for the Pool

❦ Never leave a child unattended in a backyard with a pool because drowning is a common childhood accident.

❦ Never allow a child in a pool without supervision by an adult who knows how to swim and knows CPR (cardiopulmonary resuscitation). Even if your child takes swimming lessons and knows how to swim, he is still not pool safe and must be watched by a responsible adult.

❦ Any adult watching a child in the pool should be in the pool or sitting by the edge of the pool and dressed in swimming attire.

❦ If there is a swimming pool (in the ground or above the ground) in your backyard, it must be surrounded by a fence at least four to five feet high on all sides of the pool with vertical slats less than four inches apart. In addition, the fence should have a self-closing and self-latching gate that opens outward and is always locked.

❦ A pool cover is not a substitute for a fence because children can slip under a loose-fitting cover.

❦ Move away any furniture that is close to the fence surrounding the pool, so a child can't use the furniture as a step to climb over the fence.

PINK AND BLUE ALERT

Regardless of what age your child begins to take lessons, just remember she is not pool safe and should never be left alone . . . not even for a second!

PINK AND BLUE ALERT

Never take your eyes off children in a swimming pool! Drowning accidents can occur in seconds.

PINK AND BLUE ALERT

At swimming parties make sure there is always *at least* one adult "designated pool watcher" supervising the children at all times.

❤ Be sure your pool (and any other pool your child swims in) is chlorinated properly. Do not allow children to go into the pool immediately after you have added the chlorine. It is not unusual for a young child to get diarrhea if he swallows too much pool water.

❤ Every pool owner must have rescue devices strategically placed around the pool, such as a safety pole (long enough to reach the middle of the pool), life preserver, and heavy plastic-coated ropes. These items are available at pool supply stores.

❤ Keep a portable phone by the pool in case of emergency.

❤ Do not rely upon water wings or other flotation devices to protect a child in the water. They can easily deflate and should not serve as baby-sitters.

❤ When swimming activities come to an end, remove all inflatable toys, floating mats or chairs, and anything else that might be alluring to a young, curious child.

❤ Along with taking all precautionary measures to safeguard your child from swimming accidents, it's still important to teach him never to go into a pool without adult supervision.

❤ Do not allow children to run or roughhouse around a pool.

❤ Young children can drown in a few inches of water, so be sure to empty wading pools after each use. Even though wading pools are small and shallow, adult supervision is necessary.

- If you have a hot tub or spa in your backyard, do not allow your child to go in it. Always keep it locked and covered securely with a heavy, sturdy cover that a child cannot remove.

- If you take your child to a public pool where there is a lifeguard on duty, don't expect him to watch only your child. Since the pool may be crowded, it's always safer to be in the water with your child.

- When thunderstorms strike, everyone must evacuate the water.

- If you're going to the beach with young children, be sure there is a lifeguard on duty; however, do not depend on him to watch your child since beaches tend to be crowded. Regardless of a child's age, never take your eyes off him, in or out of the water.

- Due to unpredictable ocean, lake, or river conditions, never leave your child alone in the water. You should always hold a toddler's hand in the water, and when watching a preschooler, stand next to him in the water. If the water looks too rough and warning flags are posted, do not allow your child in the water.

PINK AND BLUE HINT

As an extra precaution, put an alarm or loud bell on the pool gate so you will know when the gate is being opened. Or, install a motion-sensing alarm that is triggered if anything falls into the pool.

PINK AND BLUE ALERT

If drowning occurs, immediately begin administering CPR while someone else calls 911. There's a much better chance of recovery when CPR is given on the spot.

Time-Tested Advice for the Backyard

- Do not leave a toddler unattended in a backyard.

- Teach your child never to leave the backyard for any reason without an adult.

❀ Buy age-appropriate play equipment that is designed for two- to five-year-olds.

❀ Always follow manufacturer's directions carefully when assembling and anchoring equipment. Although grass appears to be a good foundation for hard landings, it's safer to put the equipment on wood chips, mulch, or pea gravel at least ten inches deep. This soft surface should be extended six feet on all sides; add extra feet for swings.

❀ Purchase swings with seats made of durable plastic or canvas since metal swings can be very dangerous and get too hot when exposed to the sun. For children under three, purchase swings with support on all sides and safety belts. Be sure swings are suspended from a heavy metal chain covered in plastic.

❀ Slides should be made of durable plastic.

❀ Make sure all equipment is firmly anchored and there are no weakened supports.

❀ Every year inspect your play equipment for loose nuts and bolts, rusty hardware, splintered and rotting wood, and protruding parts that could catch clothing or injure a child.

❀ Sandboxes should be refilled each year with new sand. To keep sand in good sanitary condition, always keep the sandbox covered when not in use.

❀ Follow these rules for play equipment safety:

  ꩜ An adult must always supervise children on all play equipment.

- A child must never walk in front of or behind a child on a swing.

- A child must not swing on his stomach because he could swing out of control and possibly hit another child swinging next to him.

- Only one child at a time may climb up the steps and go down the slide. To avoid accidents, be sure no other child is at the base of the slide.

- Your child must not wear loose-fitting clothing, items with drawstrings, loose belts, capes, mittens dangling from clips that hook to jacket sleeves, scarves, or mufflers. These can get caught on play equipment and cause strangulation.

- A child must never throw sand at others.

- Check for rocks and other debris before children play on equipment.

- If there are any holes in the ground in your backyard, fill them to protect your child from falling.

- Check all gates and fences to make sure they are secure and in good condition. Repair broken slats or rails, splintered wood, broken latches, and any protruding parts that could injure a child or catch on clothing.

- Make sure gate or fence doors are always locked.

- It's best to have children play in the backyard, not in the driveway; however, if you allow playing in the driveway, children must be supervised by an

PINK AND BLUE ALERT

To protect your child from strangulation, remove drawstrings from all clothing. Replace hood, neck, and waist drawstrings with Velcro, snaps, or buttons.

PINK AND BLUE ALERT

Teach your child never to run out into the street to retrieve his ball, tricycle, or any other toy.

adult. Park your car at the end of the driveway to block other cars from entering. The car will also serve as a barrier to the street. Set the emergency brake and lock the car. (When moving the car, either put the children in the car with you or make sure another adult is watching them.)

❤ It's important to introduce a bicycle helmet (approved by ANSI, ASTM, or Snell) with your child's first tricycle or riding toy so that he becomes accustomed to wearing one. When he graduates to a two-wheeler, the helmet will already be a habit. Make it a rule: No helmet, no bike riding.

❤ Never allow a child to stand on the back of the tricycle and use it as a scooter. Also, don't let him stand on the seat of the tricycle or any riding toy.

❤ Keep all garden tools (hoes, rakes, shovels, spades), any motorized tools, and all poisonous gardening supplies (weed killer, snail poisoning, pesticides) locked up and out of a child's reach.

❤ When spraying insecticide outdoors, keep your child inside until toxic fumes subside. Always follow the manufacturer's directions.

❤ When a lawn mower is in use, keep your child inside. If you have a ride-on lawn mower, never let your child sit or ride on it. Store the lawn mower in a location that is inaccessible to him.

❤ Since it's difficult to remove every single poisonous plant, tree, or flower your child comes in contact with, teach him not to put any plants, leaves, flowers, berries, or mushrooms into his mouth.

❤ Drowning can occur even in a small bucket, pail, flowerpot, or cooler. A curious child can easily topple into a bucket filled with rainwater (or any collection of water). To prevent this from happening, store these items upside down out of a child's reach.

❤ Keep children away from a hot barbecue. Charcoal lighter fluid and matches must be kept out of children's reach. If you own a gas barbecue, be sure gas lines are securely connected.

❤ If your home has a deck or porch, protect your child by blocking the steps with a safety gate. Railings or posts more than four inches apart should be covered with mesh netting or Plexiglas.

❤ Winter activities for young children require constant adult supervision. Follow these safety tips for fun in the cold:

  ◉ Use an age-appropriate sled with sides, back, and a safety belt. Do not use makeshift sleds and avoid hills or slopes that can pose a danger. For safety's sake, only an adult or much older child should be allowed to pull the sled.

  ◉ Never permit a young child to ride headfirst on a sled.

  ◉ Discourage your child from eating snow since the ground is full of contaminants.

  ◉ Don't let your toddler or preschooler play near older kids who may be roughhousing in the snow. In particular, tightly packed snowballs can be very dangerous.

⊚ Make sure your child is dressed appropriately for the cold weather, including waterproof jacket, mittens, and hat. If you see your child is cold or his clothing is wet, it's time to go indoors. Change him into dry clothing immediately.

⊚ Never leave a young child unattended in the snow, even in your own backyard.

Poisons

PINK AND BLUE ALERT

Never administer syrup of ipecac, which induces vomiting, without consulting your pediatrician or poison control center first. Check the expiration date periodically.

Toddlers and preschoolers are naturally curious and do not have the complete capacity (yet) to fully understand the elements of danger. At this developmental stage, they are very oral, putting anything and everything in their mouths. To protect them, parents must be extremely conscientious in placing all poisonous items and medicines (including nonprescriptions and vitamins) out of their reach. Be prepared by posting the phone number of the local poison control center by all telephones in your house and keeping syrup of ipecac locked in your medicine cabinet. Call the center for free phone stickers.

Most poisonings involve common household substances, such as cleaning products, lotions, shampoos, and detergents. If a child ingests a substance, never take for granted that it is nonpoisonous. When in doubt, do not hesitate to call the poison center. However, if the child is unconscious or has labored breathing, call 911 first, as time is of the essence. If you know what he ingested, read the ingredients on the container to the 911 operator so he can accurately advise the paramedics. If you must go to the hospital, take the container with you.

Here are some telltale signs of poisoning:

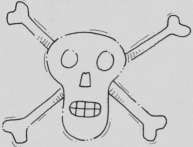

☙ Catching your child swallowing the poisonous substance

☙ Playing with or near an open container of medicine or household product

☙ An unusual odor on the child's breath

☙ A visible smear, stain, or burn around the mouth

☙ Vomiting

☙ Unusual sleepiness and difficulty focusing

☙ Labored breathing

If you think your child has ingested a poisonous substance, even if his behavior is normal, take him with you to the telephone and call the poison control center. Have the following information available:

☙ Child's age, weight, and general health condition

☙ The name of the product or medicine ingested, its ingredients, and the quantity consumed (if you know)

☙ The child's symptoms

☙ Your address, phone number, and closest hospital

Time-Tested Advice

❤ Keep cleaning products and other potentially hazardous products on a top shelf in childproofed cabinets.

❤ While cleaning the house, be careful not to leave out the products and rags you are using or to put them in a place your child can reach.

PINK AND BLUE HINT

Periodically clean out your medicine cabinet and flush expired medications down the toilet.

PINK AND BLUE ALERT

If your child visits his grandparents' home regularly, install childproof locks on medicine cabinets and cupboards used to store potentially harmful items. Remind them to keep medicines and all dangerous products locked up. In addition, if grandma carries medication in her purse, she must keep it out of your child's reach.

- When using noxious spray products, keep your child out of the room until the odor has dissipated.

- Lock up all prescription and nonprescription medicines, vitamins, and iron supplements in a childproofed medicine cabinet. This also includes children's medicines, especially ones your child might recognize having taken before.

- If you are pregnant, keep prenatal vitamins locked in a cabinet, out of your child's reach, because the iron content in these pills is poisonous to a young child.

- Many young children have been poisoned by iron pills because they are small and colorful, look like candy, and can be swallowed easily. Keep the pills stored in a locked medicine cabinet that a child cannot open.

- Don't take medicine or vitamins in front of your child because he may want to imitate you.

- Although some medicines and vitamins may be sweet and even pleasant to the child's palate, never refer to them as candy. It may tempt the child to take more.

- Always keep products and medicines in their original containers. Remind anyone working in your home to follow this rule.

- Shampoo, soap, perfume, colognes, and other personal care products used daily should be placed out of a child's reach.

- Buy child-resistant containers, but don't rely on them to be 100 percent childproof because clever little hands given enough unattended time can figure out how to open the containers. For safety's sake, keep them out of the child's reach.

- ❋ Never store cleaning products and food together on the same shelf. If possible, keep them in separate cabinets.

- ❋ A poison sticker on a package is no guarantee your child is protected against swallowing a dangerous substance since he may be too young to know or understand what the label means.

- ❋ When possible, purchase items that are labeled non-toxic, especially for arts and crafts projects that your child will be doing.

- ❋ Teach your child in simple language that poisonous items are dangerous and harmful to his health.

- ❋ Alcoholic beverages must be locked up or placed on a high shelf a child cannot reach. When serving alcoholic beverages to guests, remind them not to put their drink down where a child can easily pick it up.

Lead Poisoning

Lead poisoning is dangerous to a child's health because it can cause anemia, learning disabilities, hyperactivity, and aggressive behavioral problems. A child can get lead poisoning if he puts his hands in his mouth after playing with or on something, such as playground equipment, that has old chipped or flaking lead paint. If he picks at the leaded paint and ingests it or inhales paint dust, this too can cause a lead poisoning problem. (Intact lead paint doesn't pose the same problem.)

PINK AND BLUE ALERT
If you have visitors staying with you, remind them to keep any medicines, vitamins, and personal care products locked in their suitcases.

PINK AND BLUE HINT
You can purchase an easy lead-testing kit for your drinking water at your local hardware store. Follow the directions carefully.

PINK AND BLUE ALERT

If you purchase a home that was built before 1978 and has the original paint, protect your family from lead poisoning by repainting the entire house. If you're concerned about old lead pipes, have your water tested. Talk to your pediatrician about blood testing if you suspect your child has been exposed to lead.

Potentially Poisonous Items

The following items are potentially dangerous and should be kept out of a child's reach:

Acids
Alcoholic beverages
Ammonia
Antifreeze
Aspirin
Bleaches
Boric acid
Car maintenance products (oil, window-washing fluid, upholstery and tire cleaners)
Cleaning fluids, disinfectants, and powders
Cologne and perfume
Detergents (dishwasher and laundry)
Drain cleaners
Fertilizers
Furniture polish
Gardening chemicals
Gasoline
Glue
Hair products (shampoos, dyes, perms, straighteners)
Hydrogen peroxide
Insecticides
Iron supplements and pills
Kerosene
Lighter fluid
Medicines (prescription and nonprescription)
Metal polishes (silver, brass, and copper)
Mothballs
Mouthwash (with alcohol)
Nail polish and nail polish remover
Oven cleaner
Paint and paint thinner

Pesticides (animal and insect poisons)
Plants (see list below)
Rubbing alcohol
Tobacco (all kinds)
Turpentine
Vanilla and almond extracts
Vitamins

Poisonous Plants

While plants add decoration to a room or backyard, beware!
Many can cause severe reactions and should be avoided. The
following is a partial compilation the Los Angeles County
Arboretum has listed as poisonous if eaten:

Angel's trumpet	False hellebore
Autumn crocus	Foxglove
Azaleas	Glory lily
Baneberry	Hemp
Bleeding heart	Holly
Buttercup	Horse chestnuts
Boxwood	Hyacinths and bulbs
Bushman's poison	Hydrangea
Caladium	Iris and bulbs
Carolina jasmine	Ivy
Castor bean	Jamestown weed
Chinaberry tree	Jimson weed
Coral plant	Lantanas
Crown thorns	Lily of the valley
Daffodil	Locust
Daphne	Mescal bean
Delphinium	Milkweed
Dieffenbachia (dumbcane)	Mistletoe
Elderberry	Monk shoal
Elephant's ear	Morning glory
English laurel	Narcissus bulb

PINK AND BLUE HINT

Label all indoor plants with the botanical name. If your child eats a leaf or flower, you'll be able to quickly identify it for your pediatrician or poison control center.

Nettle
Night-blooming jasmine
Nutmeg
Oak
Oleander
Philodendron
Poinsettia
Poison ivy
Poison oak
Poison sumac
Pokeweed
Pothos

Primrose
Rattlebox
Rhododendron
Rosary pea
Skyflower
Sweet pea
Tomato plant leaves
Vicia faba
Virginia creeper
Water hemlock
Wisteria
Yew

For additional names of harmful plants, contact the poison control center or the local department of parks and recreation.

Safety Outside the Home

Whether you're off to the park or the shopping mall with your youngsters, it is never too early to educate them about safety away from the home. Begin with simple rules in simple language to get your point across. Make sure your preschooler knows his full name, address, and phone number with area code.

In this day and age, it is never too soon to teach your child what a stranger is: "someone you don't know." Identify strangers in your daily travels, and explain that they don't have to be dirty or weird-looking to be threatening to your child's well-being. It's also important to teach your child which parts of the body are private (using the proper names) and that he has the right to say no to unwanted touching, no matter who's doing it. By establishing an open rapport with your child, you can encourage him to feel comfortable telling you about intimate things that scare or bother him.

Make it a family rule that he should not hide any secrets, especially if someone has threatened or compromised him.

Time-Tested Advice

❦ Begin to teach your child to look both ways before crossing a street or alley, never to jaywalk, and to wait for the pedestrian signal at traffic lights. Point out the international Walk and Don't Walk signs so he'll learn to recognize what they mean. The parent or adult in charge should set a good example and follow pedestrian safety rules with the child.

❦ When taking your young child out of the car, be sure to hold his hand the minute he gets out of the car. Make sure little hands are out of the way when opening or closing car doors.

❦ Always hold your child's hand when walking across the street, in a parking lot, on a busy sidewalk, on a sidewalk near a busy street, in a store or mall, or in any crowded location.

❦ When you go to the mall with your child, never let him leave your side, even for a minute. If he's in a stroller and has fallen asleep, don't leave him unattended.

❦ To avoid unnecessary accidents on escalators, make sure your child faces forward, holds on to handrails, and doesn't play on the stairs. Be careful of untied shoelaces, scarves, and mittens that can get caught easily on the moving stairs.

❦ When you are using a stroller, it's safer to use the elevator and avoid the escalator.

PINK AND BLUE ALERT

Teach your child never to talk to strangers unless you are standing directly with him. Explain to him that he should never accept food or toys from strangers. If someone is bothering him, he should immediately tell you or the adult in charge.

PINK AND BLUE HINT

To discourage strangers from establishing contact with your child and pretending to act familiar, do not allow the child to wear clothing or a backpack with his name on it.

PINK AND BLUE HINT

When you go to the park with your child, keep him strapped in his car seat while you take his tricycle and other toys out of the car. This will ensure his safety while you are busy unloading his playthings. When leaving the park, strap your child in first before reloading the car.

* Memorize what your child is wearing so you can describe him if he gets separated from you.

* When driving in a parking lot or pulling in or out of a driveway, take these precautions (especially in a sports-utility vehicle):

  * Always look in your rearview and side-view mirrors, and continue checking as you pull out.

  * Before getting into your car and pulling out of the driveway, check to make sure no children are close by and no toys are in the way.

  * If your child is not accompanying you when you leave, make sure a responsible adult is watching him so he does not follow you to the car.

PINK AND BLUE ALERT

If a child receives a hard blow to the head and becomes unconscious, call 911 immediately. Keep the child still until help arrives. If bleeding occurs, apply pressure to the wound. If he begins to vomit, gently roll him on his side, carefully cradling his neck and head to prevent choking.

Playground and Park Safety

A playground or park is an exciting place for a young child to play and socialize, but it can also be dangerous. Choose a location that is clean and well maintained. Make sure an adult supervises play closely. Encourage young children to play on age-appropriate equipment that is sturdy and sits on soft surfaces, such as sand, wood chips, or mulch. Always check the area for potential dangers, such as broken glass, beer cans, rocks, sharp edges, unstable railings, loose or protruding nuts and bolts, rusty hardware, splintered and rotting wood, hot surfaces, peeling paint (can cause lead poisoning), and dog excrement.

It's very important to give your toddler or preschooler room to play and explore at the park or playground and not hover over him. However, you must keep him in direct eye contact at all times. When watching more than one child, keep the children in a small enough radius so that you can watch all of them at the same time. For safety rules to enforce at the playground or park, please refer to Time-Tested Advice for the Backyard, earlier in this chapter.

Car Safety

If there is one place where safety rules must never be compromised, it's in the car. Even if you're only going around the block, it is mandatory to put your child in a car safety seat and use the seat belts properly. Make it a rule: No car seat, no seat belt, no ride! If a child disobeys this rule and unbuckles the seat belt once the car is in motion, pull over to the side of the road and turn off the engine. Do not start the car again until the child is buckled in.

When purchasing a car safety seat, make sure the certification label states that it meets Federal Motor Vehicle Safety Standard 213. While the National Highway Traffic Safety Administration recommends every young child be restrained in a car safety seat, each state has different requirements on age and weight. In general, state laws advocate using a car seat until the child is four years old or weighs forty pounds.

For maximum protection, if there is a seat belt with a shoulder harness for the center seat, put the car seat in the center of the backseat facing forward. Always follow the manufacturer's directions when installing a safety seat, and be sure it sits tightly, with no room for movement. Make sure the seat is compatible with your car's seat belt system since some seats need special belt attachments or tethers (safety straps that secure the seat to an anchor metal plate that is bolted into the shelf area of the backseat).

When a child weighs more than forty pounds, you may transfer him to a booster seat, which must be placed on either side of the backseat in order to use the car's lap/shoulder restraint seat belts. Do not purchase a booster

PINK AND BLUE HINT
Always have your child wash his hands after playing on playground equipment. Since young children tend to put their hands in their mouths, this is the best way to control the spread of germs. Carry a small bottle of instant gel hand sanitizer with you for easy cleanup.

PINK AND BLUE ALERT
Never allow your child to sit on anyone's lap, even if you're only going around the block.

PINK AND BLUE HINT

When purchasing a car seat, be sure to drive to the store in the car you will be using to transport your child. Before you leave the store, make sure the car seat you select properly fits into your car. Fill out and mail the registration card for the car seat so that you will receive notification if there are any recalls.

PINK AND BLUE ALERT

Since there is so much controversy over automobile air bags, a child should always sit in the backseat of a car.

PINK AND BLUE ALERT

Never place a booster seat in the center of the car's backseat unless the center seat is equipped with a shoulder harness and safety belts.

seat with a shield. There is a new model of booster seat that has a five-point harness and rubber bar for your child's greater protection.

Your car should always be equipped with a flashlight, first-aid kit, jumper cables, flares, blanket, and a bottle of purified water. Regular maintenance on your car is essential for everyone's safety.

Time-Tested Advice

❀ Be a good role model and always wear a seat belt correctly.

❀ Never use a car seat that has been in a crash. Do not use a secondhand car seat if you don't know its history and have no proof it meets Federal Motor Vehicle Safety Standard 213.

❀ Do not allow a young child to eat in a moving car. If he chokes while you're driving, it will be very difficult to respond. However, if another adult is in the car with you, the child may eat if the adult sits next to him.

❀ Using a cell phone and driving at the same time can be very dangerous. If you must talk on the phone, pull over and park in a legally safe location.

❀ Never allow anyone to smoke in the car. Secondhand smoke is harmful to your child's health and can contribute to upper respiratory problems, as well as motion sickness.

❀ On hot days cover the car seat with a light-colored blanket or large towel so exposed metal or plastic parts don't burn your child's skin. The light color will keep it from retaining heat.

* Always lock power windows so little fingers don't get caught.

* Never take a child out of a car on the street/traffic side.

* Hold your child's hand when he gets out of the car, and never take your eyes off him.

* If an ashtray lighter is within your child's reach, remove it.

For more information on traveling in the car with your child, please see Traveling by Car in Chapter 14, "Travel."

Fire Safety

Safeguard your home from fire by being prepared at all times. Smoke detectors should be installed in hallways leading to bedrooms, in each bedroom, and at the top of the stairs in a two-story house. Equip your kitchen and garage with a smoke detector and a fire extinguisher. If you live in a two-story home, there should be a fire extinguisher on each floor. Check with your local fire department for additional recommendations. Also, make sure each fireplace in your home is protected with a sturdy fire screen to prevent sparks from escaping.

Although fire is a scary topic to discuss with your young child, it is important to educate him in fire safety rules. A child as young as three years old can be taught simple procedures. To introduce the concept of fire safety, take your child to the local fire station and meet the firefighters.

PINK AND BLUE HINT

If you carpool with other young children, be sure there is a car seat for each child or a booster seat for each child over forty pounds or four years old.

PINK AND BLUE ALERT

Never leave a child alone in the car, not even for a second!

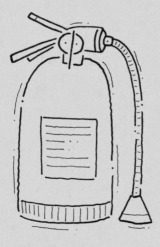

Time-Tested Advice

❦ Sound a smoke detector so your preschooler can become aware of the noise, and then teach him what to do if he hears the smoke detector ring.

❦ When a smoke detector beeps, the battery is running low and needs to be replaced.

❦ Since your child should never be home alone, instruct him to immediately call out for help to you or the supervising adult. Tell him never to hide anywhere, especially under the bed or in the closet.

❦ Check with your local fire department for decals to designate a child's bedroom so firefighters can quickly find and rescue a child.

❦ Practice fire drills periodically so everyone (including baby-sitters and relatives who visit frequently) in the house knows what the routine should be. Plan and practice a few different escape routes. Select a designated meeting spot, such as a big tree outside your house, so you can count heads.

❦ During drills, practice crawling on your hands and knees to the nearest exit because the air is safer close to the ground in a fire.

❦ In case of emergency, all doors and windows should always be kept free of obstructions.

❦ Periodically check the window guards and locks on all windows to be certain they can open properly.

❦ Teach your child the "stop, drop, and roll" method to extinguish flames from his clothing. The procedure is to cover the face with his hands, drop to the ground, and roll over and over until the fire is out.

🐾 Make sure a two-story home is equipped with at least one escape ladder.

🐾 In the event of a fire, do not try to extinguish the fire yourself, unless it is a small fire that can be contained easily.

🐾 At the first sign of smoke, everyone must evacuate the house. Call 911 for the fire department from a neighbor's phone.

🐾 Never reenter a smoke-filled house or building, not even to help rescue a person, pet, toy, or valuables. Tell the firefighters, and let them perform their duties.

🐾 Ask your local librarian or bookstore for age-appropriate book and video recommendations.

🐾 Make it a rule that there is no smoking inside your house.

🐾 Under no circumstances should young children play with or be around sparklers and firecrackers. For safety's sake, take your family to a public display of fireworks.

PINK AND BLUE ALERT

Keep matches, lighters, and lighter fluid out of a child's reach.

Pet Safety

Since you can never hold an animal accountable for its behavior, it is very important to teach your young child simple rules on how to be safe around pets. Toddlers and preschoolers love animals and tend to get overexcited when playing with a pet and do not realize it when they may have upset or physically harmed the animal (such as pulling its tail). Enforce the following simple rules to help educate your child in pet safety.

PINK AND BLUE ALERT

Never leave a young child unattended with any animal, even the family pet.

Time-Tested Advice

❀ A child should not approach any animal unless he has permission from you and the pet's owner.

❀ Once your child has been given permission to pet the animal, first let the pet sniff the back of your fist, and then allow your child to offer the back of his hand.

❀ A child should be taught to gently pat the animal on the back and never on the face. In addition, a child should never put his face into the animal's face.

❀ Teach your child not to touch or make eye contact with an unfamiliar animal. For example, if a dog is tied on a leash and the owner is not around, your child should stay away from this animal.

❀ No one should touch a dog that is barking, growling, or acting frightened.

❀ Teach your child to approach an animal calmly. He should not scare the animal by rushing up to it, waving his hands, or yelling.

❀ If an animal is eating, sleeping, or chewing a toy, teach your child not to bother it. Never grab a toy out of an animal's mouth.

❀ Keep a child away from dogs playing with each other because the dogs' behavior is unpredictable.

❦ When you feed your animal, watch your child carefully because he may want to taste the animal's food. If possible, put the animal and its food in an area away from the child.

❦ If you have a doggie door, be careful that your young child does not climb through it.

❦ If you own an animal that is kept in a cage (such as a rabbit or reptile), keep the cage door securely locked so a child cannot let the pet out without your permission.

❦ Keep a fish bowl out of the child's reach so he doesn't accidentally tip it over.

❦ Your child should get into the habit of washing his hands with either soap and water or instant gel hand sanitizer each time he touches an animal.

❦ Do not allow your child to play with a cat when it is in the litter box.

❦ An older pet may be less tolerant of a young child's antics. Even if the pet has been a part of the family for a long time, it's still a good idea to watch the animal carefully when it's around a young child.

❦ If you are considering buying or adopting a new pet, take it to the veterinarian for a complete checkup before making any final commitments. Make sure it has all the necessary immunizations.

❦ Teach your child not to disturb a mother animal and her babies.

๑๙๑

Transitions

First we teach a child how to drink from either the breast or the bottle, then without her understanding why, we switch her to the cup. Next, that wonderful crib she has spent countless hours in is traded for a bed. And then the young child is expected to relinquish those convenient diapers and become toilet trained. Talk about changes. What about the pacifier, a move to a new home, and that new baby? No wonder it's traumatic for a little person to deal with all these things.

The word *transition* is defined in the dictionary as a "change, or passage from one state, subject, or place to another." When your child is making a transition, try to choose a time when she is not dealing with new stresses or fears. Always talk with her before the impending transition so she is emotionally prepared for the change. If her language skills are strong enough, encourage her to discuss how she feels, as she learns to cope with each new situation. Reading books to the child on a particular subject also can ease the transition.

When a toddler, as opposed to a preschooler, goes through a particular transition, she may exhibit some behavioral problems due to a lack of language skills. Be patient as you teach her how to express her feelings. Make yourself available for extra cuddles and support, and stay consistent in your efforts to help her over each hump. Do not humiliate or punish the child if she is having a difficult time; instead, praise her endeavors.

Weaning from Bottle to Cup

If your child has not already given up her bottle, it's time. The longer you wait and the older the child, the more difficult it is to make the transition. In addition, prolonged bottle drinking can cause tooth decay. By now a toddler should be drinking from a cup daily, even though she may not be comfortable or satisfied drinking from it. Saying good-bye to the bottle can be traumatic for your child because she has become so attached to it. While your child goes through this withdrawal, be sure to give lots of hugs and encouragement. To ease the weaning process, follow these tips.

Time-Tested Advice

❦ Let your child select a few training cups with her favorite characters or colors.

♥ Make the bottle less appealing by putting water in it or diluting the juice or milk, and make the cup more enticing by filling it with full-strength beverages.

♥ Do not allow your child to carry a bottle around with her during the day or night, and limit its use to the house. When she insists upon drinking from a bottle, set boundaries by making her sit in a particular place that isn't necessarily fun. If you notice the child is dawdling while drinking from the bottle, set a time limit.

♥ Gradually cut back on bottle feedings by first eliminating the lunch bottle for two or three days, then the morning bottle, and finally the dinnertime one. Or elicit your child's help in this process by allowing her to choose the bottle-feeding time she's willing to give up. Replace each bottle feeding with a cup. If your toddler rejects the cup, do not give in to her. Eventually she will get thirsty and be forced to drink from the cup.

♥ Remove all bottles from her sight, and change the place you store them so she can't find them.

♥ If you think your child can handle it, go cold turkey. Tell her she's a big girl now and it's time to give up the baby bottles. Have her help you throw away all the bottles so she's involved in the process. Give the bottles a going-away party.

♥ Another weaning method to try is the cutting-the-nipple approach. Over a period of a week, do the following:

1. On the first day, enlarge the hole in the nipple with either a pin or the tip of a sharp knife. The fluid will flow much faster with little sucking.

2. On the second day, cut the tip of the nipple with a scissors, allowing the fluid to flow more rapidly.

3. Over the next few days, cut the nipple back more and more each day. Eventually your child will be drinking from the bottle instead of sucking from the bottle.

4. At this point offer her fluids from a sipper training cup or a boxed drink with a straw to satisfy her sucking urge.

5. Once your child has successfully completed this method, throw away any remaining bottles.

❋ Take advantage of a vacation and wean your child from the bottle away from home, where there are fewer reminders of a habit associated with the security of home. Bring along a sipper training cup to facilitate this transition.

❋ If there's a new baby in the house, talk to your toddler and remind her that bottles are for babies and she's a big girl, who drinks out of a cup like mommy and daddy. Do not allow her to manipulate you into giving her a bottle. Continually praise her for drinking out of a cup.

❋ Make a chart, and every time the child drinks successfully out of the cup, give her a sticker to put on the chart. When she has a predetermined number of stickers, reward her for her efforts.

❦ It is not unusual for a child who is weaning from the bottle to be particularly cranky and irritable.

❦ When children give up the bottle, it is common for them to temporarily refuse to drink milk. Supplement their diet with liquid or powdered calcium during this time.

❦ Ask your pediatrician to speak to your child about giving up the bottle. A few words of encouragement from the doctor can go a long way with little children.

❦ Visit the library or bookstore and ask for suggested books, such as *My Bye-Bye Bottle Book* by Jane Gelbard.

Adios to Pacifiers

A child's attachment to a pacifier is similar to her affinity for the bottle. If your child walks around sucking her pacifier all day long, it could be detrimental to her dental development and interfere with her communication skills. By the time a child reaches two or three years old, the need to suck is less important and more a habit. To kick the pacifier obsession, try the following advice.

Time-Tested Advice

❦ Only allow the use of a pacifier at home, and gradually limit its use each day. Set time limits (use a kitchen timer) and location boundaries. For example, your child can only have the pacifier for thirty minutes in the morning sitting in the kitchen and thirty minutes in the evening in her bedroom. Reduce the time allotment each day until there is no time left, and then have your toddler throw the pacifier away herself.

* Over a period of a week, reduce the number of pacifiers your child has until there's only one left. Throughout the week, talk with her and praise her for being a "big girl" and giving up the "baby" pacifier. When there is only one remaining pacifier, give a going-away party and have your child give the pacifier to the trash collector to throw away.

* Another approach is the cut-the-nipple method. Begin by cutting the tip of the pacifier with a scissors. Over a period of two or three days cut the nipple a little more each day until there's nothing left to suck on.

* For some families the cold turkey method works best. Explain to your child that she's a big girl now and it's time to give up the pacifier. Let her throw away the pacifier herself. She may whine for a few days, but do not give in.

* Or, when you're going on a vacation, plan to eliminate the pacifier by saying you forgot it and she's too old for you to buy another one. The different environment is a good distraction.

* Offer your child a reward as an incentive—for example, a new toy, doll, or stuffed animal of her choice. Give her a star or sticker to put on a chart for each day she doesn't use the pacifier. Once she

has accumulated five stars in a row, take her to the store and let her select the reward.

♥ If your child is having a difficult time giving up the pacifier, consult your pediatrician.

Transitional Objects

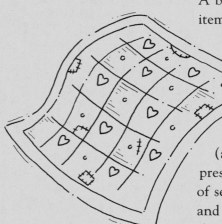

A blanket, stuffed animal, or doll can become an important item in a youngster's life, so much so that the child cannot be without it. This transitional object provides a tangible sense of security and comfort to the toddler or preschooler. It's usually something familiar she identifies as hers alone, such as a baby blanket. The object can be especially comforting if the child is faced with a fear or anxiety (afraid of the dark), a new situation (new day care or preschool), or a new transition (crib to bed). During periods of separation from parents, it also may remind her of them and the strong attachment to them. In the parents' absence, this object fills a void and helps her learn to soothe herself.

As long as the transitional object is not detrimental to your child's health or development, let her enjoy it, with certain restrictions. Keep limits on its use so she doesn't become obsessed with the object. For example, the item should be limited to inside the home, and she should be discouraged from taking it outside to the backyard. Allow your child to have it at bedtime but not during a meal. The only exception to these rules might be taking "blankie" on a trip if the destination is unfamiliar to your child and it can comfort her through this transition.

There are a few drawbacks to possessing one favorite object—mainly remembering where it is, maintaining its

PINK AND BLUE HINT

When your child is ready to give up her transitional object, give it a special place of retirement as a sign of respect for your child's attachment to it.

cleanliness, and eventually giving it up. Respect your child's attachment to this comforting tool, and remember she won't be walking down the aisle at her high school graduation with "blankie" in tow.

Moving

Although the move to a new home may be exciting for the parents, most children would prefer to stay where they are. The old home represents stability and familiarity, while the new home presents all sorts of unknowns to a young child. Be sure to share the news of the impending move with your child in advance. However, since a toddler or preschooler has no concept of time, tell her about two to three weeks before the move. If possible, show her the new house, her new bedroom, and the new neighborhood so she can actually see where she's going to live. If the move is out of town, photograph or videotape the new home for her to see.

As you anticipate and prepare for the move, stay calm and keep an optimistic attitude so your child will do the same. Talk to your child about the move, encouraging her to discuss how she feels, so you can help her adjust to the big change. To minimize the stress of relocating to a new home, try the following advice.

PINK AND BLUE HINT

Wash the transitional object when it is dirty and unsanitary, or your child may become attached to its particular odor and never want you to wash it. Use scent-free soaps and avoid softeners so the object's odor is not significantly altered.

Time-Tested Advice

❀ Make sure your child understands that everyone and everything are making the move.

❀ Circle the move date on a calendar, and mark off each day to help her understand exactly when you will be moving.

❧ Involve your child in the move so she feels a part of the experience. Give her crayons and stickers, let her decorate a box, and then have her put the toys in it a day or two before the move. If you have a pet, have her pack up the pet's bowls, toys, and food.

❧ Visit the library or bookstore and ask for suggested books about moving. Some books on this subject include *Goodbye House* by Frank Asch, *The Berenstain Bears' Moving Day* by Stan Berenstain, *M Is for Moving* by Velma Ilsley, *Moving* by Fred Rogers, and *Moving Day* by Tobi Tobias.

❧ Prepare your child for the move by helping her construct a new house with her building blocks. Or, if your child has a dollhouse, pretend to move in and out of that house. She will have the opportunity to express her feelings about the new move through role-playing.

❧ If it is logistically impossible to keep the same pediatrician, ask for recommendations for a new doctor before your move. Have your child's records sent to the new office. Locate the hospital and emergency room closest to your new home.

❧ Before your move, get recommendations for day care facilities or preschools in your new neighborhood. When you set up an interview, ask whether the school wants to meet your child at this meeting or at a later date. Please see Chapter 12, "Off to School," for more detailed information.

❧ Give your preschooler some decorating options, such as painting her room the same color as her old bedroom, choosing a new paint color, or selecting wallpaper or borders. Let her select a new item for her room, such as new sheets, a new table and chair set, or a new picture for the wall.

❤ With your preschooler's assistance, put together a photo album of favorite times in your old home, including pictures of her bedroom, the backyard, and friends and neighbors. It's a nice remembrance for her to look back on.

❤ On moving day, split up the responsibilities by having one parent watch the child while the other parent directs the movers. If this is not possible, have someone familiar with your child watch her as you orchestrate the move.

❤ If your child has a transitional object, do not pack it, so she can have it with her on moving day.

❤ Unpack your child's room first so she can become comfortable in her new surroundings as quickly as possible. If her room is organized, she will feel as though some sense of order is returning to her life. Be sure to tell the movers to put your child's boxes and furniture on the truck last so they will be the first things unloaded at the new house.

❤ If possible, arrange the furniture in her new bedroom the same way it was set up in the old house. The familiar layout will help ease the adjustment to her new bedroom in the new house. Or, if she has the language skills, ask her opinion on how she would like the furniture to be arranged in her new room.

❤ Maintain your child's daily routines and rituals to keep her life as normal as possible.

- ❧ Take a walk around the new neighborhood with your child, and introduce yourselves to the neighbors and their children. This will be a good time to find out about baby-sitters.

- ❧ Although you will be very busy organizing your family in the new house, it's important to put aside special time each day for you and your child to explore different areas in the new community, such as the playground, supermarket, library, and toy store.

- ❧ It isn't unusual for a toddler or preschooler to display regressive behavior after the move. Should she start having accidents after being toilet trained, suddenly have difficulty sleeping through the night, or ask for a bottle, just be patient. Talk with her about her feelings, fears, and anxieties, and read books about moving. Do not get into the habit of using rewards to get her back on track. Instead, employ the same methods you have always used to make any transition easier. If after a few months your child is still having trouble, contact your pediatrician.

New Sibling

PINK AND BLUE HINT

Constantly reassure your child you will still love her even after the baby is born.

A new addition to the family is exciting for everyone—well, almost everyone. It's no secret that many young children don't relish the idea of a baby coming along, taking the spotlight, and diminishing the attention and affection that have been showered upon them solely. Further complicating the matter is learning to share mommy and daddy with the new baby.

Sibling rivalry is normal behavior for a young child to display toward a new brother or sister. It is not unusual for the older child to feel anxiety, displeasure, jealousy, and anger about the new arrival in the family. In addition, she may even exhibit symptoms of regressive behavior, such as wanting to be held all the time, drinking from a bottle, clinging to a parent, thumb sucking, and asking to wear diapers or having accidents. If your toddler doesn't have the language skills to express her difficulty in adjusting to the new situation, she may revert to negative behavior, such as whining or throwing temper tantrums. A child may even exhibit aggressive behavior by hitting the baby or handling her too roughly. To help your toddler/preschooler resolve these emotional hurdles and accept her new role as a "big sister," try the following advice.

Time-Tested Advice During Pregnancy

❋ During your pregnancy, talk to your child about the new baby. Since young children have no concept of time, wait until you're four or five months pregnant (and showing) before you start the dialogue. Allow her to feel your stomach as the baby moves. Reassure her that the baby is an addition to the family, not a replacement for her. Encourage her to talk about her feelings, whether they are positive or negative.

❋ Take your child on at least one of your visits to the obstetrician, and let her listen to the baby's heartbeat. If you're having a sonogram, let her watch the screen to see the baby, and tell her she looked the same way in your stomach.

❦ Show your child pictures of her as a baby, and talk about milestones in her life.

❦ Read books to your youngster about pregnancy, babies, and becoming a sibling. Some suggested books are *When the Baby Comes, I'm Moving Out* by Martha G. Alexander, *Nobody Asked Me if I Wanted a Baby Sister* by Martha G. Alexander, *Along Came Eric* by Gus Clarke, *I'm a Big Sister* by Joanna Cole, *I'm a Big Brother* by Joanna Cole, *The Baby Sister* by Tomie DePaola, *Big Brother* by Robert Kraus, *A Baby for Max* by Kathryn Lasky, and *Getting Ready for New Baby* by Harriet Ziefert.

❦ Children are often misled to believe that a brand-new baby is going to be fun and an instant playmate. It's important to explain to your child that a new baby only sleeps, eats, and cries.

❦ Visit friends and relatives with newborns so your child can become familiar with babies and know what to expect.

❦ Do not push your child to learn new skills (e.g., toilet training) just before your baby's due date. You may have to wait until your child has adapted to the new baby.

❦ If you are moving your child to a different room or new bed, make the change a few months before the baby's arrival so your child will be comfortable with her new situation and not feel displaced by the new baby. Let her help decorate her new bedroom or pick out bedding for her new bed. Please see From Crib to Bed in Chapter 6, "Sleep," for more information on a new bed.

❦ Involve your child in preparing the new baby's room, such as helping set up the changing table and the crib. Take her shopping with you, and let her select various items for the baby, such as sleepwear, bibs, a stuffed animal, or a mobile.

❦ If the older sibling will be sharing her bedroom with the baby, specify that certain parts of the room are just for her. Be sure there is a separate place for her toys and clothing.

❦ Do not expect the older sibling to share her favorite stuffed animals, toys, or blanket with the baby. Respect those possessions most meaningful to her.

❦ Buy your child a baby doll, and have her practice holding it gently, feeding and burping the doll, changing diapers, and putting the doll down for a nap. This will help your child become familiar with the things you'll be doing to care for the baby.

❦ Toward the end of your pregnancy, take your child to the hospital so she knows where you will be when having the baby. Inquire about the hospital's policy on sibling visits.

Time-Tested Advice in the Hospital

❦ Plan who will care for your child during your hospital stay, since dad will be splitting his time between home and the hospital. Make sure it's someone your child is very comfortable with, such as grandparents or a relative, baby-sitter, housekeeper, or nanny.

PINK AND BLUE HINT

To reinforce your child's sense of security in your absence, make sure she keeps her same daily routines.

PINK AND BLUE HINT

Take a Polaroid photo of the baby and give it to your child so she can share the news about her new baby sister or brother at day care or preschool.

PINK AND BLUE HINT

It's a nice idea for the toddler or preschooler to draw a picture for the new baby. It will make her feel proud when you hang her artwork in the baby's room.

PINK AND BLUE ALERT

Never leave a young child unsupervised with an infant.

❀ Have your child visit you and the baby at the hospital. In addition, call her a few times a day, especially at bedtime. If you think it will be difficult for your child to visit the hospital and leave without mommy and the new baby, then have her come with daddy to pick you up.

❀ While you're in the hospital, dad should spend some special time with your child—for example, dinner at a favorite restaurant, an outing to the park, or a trip to the zoo or the children's museum.

Time-Tested Advice at Home

❀ When you first come home from the hospital, lavish attention on your toddler or preschooler, and let someone else hold the baby.

❀ When mom and the baby first enter the house, let the older sibling sit in a chair and hold the new baby. This is a perfect photo opportunity.

❀ When holding the baby, the older sibling should always sit and be supervised by an adult.

❀ When you talk about the newborn, always say "our" baby.

❀ When the older sibling is with the baby, point out how much the baby loves her and loves being with her. For instance, say, "Look at how our new baby smiles when she's with you." As the baby gets older, continue making positive comments so your child will grow to accept and love the baby.

- Encourage affectionate behavior between your older child and her new sibling, such as kisses (not on the mouth) and cuddles.

- Include your child in simple tasks to help you care for the baby, such as bringing you a diaper or helping at bath time. Remember to praise her for being such a good assistant.

- To make your older child feel included while you're feeding the baby, have her sit next to you and read a book or tell a story.

- While you're feeding the baby, your older child can give a bottle to her doll.

- Give your older child extra special love and attention during the first few months while she gets adjusted to the new baby. Put aside at least thirty minutes a day to spend "alone time" with the older sibling without the baby, and don't allow any interruptions. If you don't have a baby-sitter, then plan the alone time when baby is sleeping. Try reading, coloring, building with blocks, baking, playing with play dough, or any other interactive activity.

- Have a stash of toys wrapped and put away to bestow on your child when visitors arrive with gifts for only the baby. This will ease the resentment your child may harbor against the baby if she's forgotten by others. The gifts do not have to be elaborate or expensive, but they are thoughtful reminders that she is loved and just as important as the baby is.

- Ask your visitors to make a big deal over the "new big sister."

PINK AND BLUE HINT

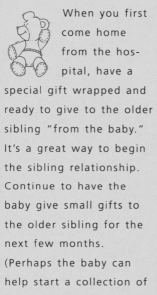 When you first come home from the hospital, have a special gift wrapped and ready to give to the older sibling "from the baby." It's a great way to begin the sibling relationship. Continue to have the baby give small gifts to the older sibling for the next few months. (Perhaps the baby can help start a collection of something, such as small stuffed animals, dolls, or miniature cars.)

PINK AND BLUE HINT

 Let your older child give the baby a bottle. If you are breast-feeding, express your milk into a bottle and let your child feed the baby. Make sure an adult is sitting close by supervising the feeding.

PINK AND BLUE ALERT

If your toddler or preschooler is aggressive and rambunctious, remove stools or chairs so she is not tempted to climb into the baby's crib or playpen without your knowledge.

♥ When the baby receives gifts, let your child unwrap the gifts for the baby. Tell her, "Since you're such a big girl, why don't you open these presents for baby because she is too little and can't open them."

♥ Do not insist that your child play quietly when the baby is sleeping. A baby should adapt to the many sounds in the household.

♥ Continue your child's normal routines and daily rituals, such as preschool, weekly gym class, afternoon snacks, bath time, and bedtime stories.

♥ If your toddler or preschooler displays aggressive behavior toward the baby, make it perfectly clear she may never hurt the baby, even if she is very angry. Encourage the older child to discuss any mixed feelings about the baby with you. Help her with suggestions for alternative behavior, such as coming to you for support when she is angry with the baby. A hug, kiss, and extra attention may be all she needs from you.

♥ While it is not unusual for a young child to act out negatively as the result of a new baby's arrival, do not dismiss or tolerate recurring misbehavior. Apply the disciplinary methods you would normally use, and reinforce how much you love her.

Divorce

When a divorce or separation occurs, it is never a happy experience for anyone, especially a child. Before the separation, be honest with your child, and tell her about the impending change, especially before she hears it from someone else. A toddler or preschooler at this stage in development is already struggling with her growing need for independence and her infantile need for protection. When one parent leaves the home, a real fear of abandonment can develop. After all, if one parent leaves, will the other leave her, too? The most important things your child needs to know are that both parents love her very much and that she is definitely not the cause of their divorce. Although the adults are no longer together, it is absolutely imperative to form a united front when it comes to the well-being of the child.

During this difficult period, a child can sense stress from the parents. She can suffer and feel the repercussions from the underlying tension in the home. If a child's behavior changes, it can be a sign she is troubled by the divorce or separation. Be cognizant of these behaviors: aggression, regression, withdrawal, clinging, or acting too perfectly (when she normally does not behave that way). There has to be some flexibility in your expectations of your child during this tough period. Each parent must be aware of the child and her feelings of sadness and disorientation. Some children do not show outward signs of difficulty, but it does not mean they are not experiencing any inner turmoil. Regardless of how your child reacts to the divorce, the change will significantly affect her life. Therefore, it is wise to seek professional counseling.

When a parent no longer lives in the same home with the child, it's necessary to stay in constant communication. For the child to maintain a close and secure relationship with both parents, try the following suggestions:

❀ If possible, minimize the stress by making as few changes as possible in your child's life, such as preschool, day care, or baby-sitter.

❋ If you can financially afford it, stay in the same neighborhood because your child will feel more secure living in familiar surroundings.

❋ To stay connected, the noncustodial parent should prearrange a time for daily phone calls to the child. Just hearing the parent's voice will be reassuring to the young child.

❋ Do not create unnecessary habits that will be difficult to break later, such as allowing the child to sleep in the parent's bed.

❋ Both parents should agree upon common discipline procedures. Consistency is important. Keep the same rules in both households so the toddler or preschooler won't feel any more confused than she already does by the divorce.

❋ Keep the same routines and rituals in both homes, such as bath time and bedtime story.

❋ Make sure both homes have the same amount of toys, stuffed animals, videos, books, and clothing. It's not appropriate for one parent to try to outdo the other. (This should not be a contest of trying to win the child's love through material gains.)

❋ Avoid verbal confrontations with your ex-spouse in your child's presence.

❋ Try not to talk negatively about the other parent in front of your child.

❋ The noncustodial parent should make every effort to keep promises made to the child. If you promise to go to a karate class, do not disappoint the child by failing to show up.

❧ Respect your child's scheduled visiting time with the noncustodial parent. Make every effort to be prompt for your child's sake.

❧ When the child returns from a visit with the noncustodial parent, don't put her on the spot and ask too many questions. Let her be the one to initiate conversation about the visit, and keep your comments positive. If she tells you something about the visit that bothers you, discuss it with your ex-spouse, in your child's absence, and not with your child.

❧ Visit the local library or bookstore, and select some recommended children's books that deal with the subject of divorce. Some books suggested are *Dinosaurs Divorce* by Laurene Krasny Brown and Marc Brown, *Two Homes for Lynn* by June Noble, *D Is for Divorce* by Lori Norris, *Let's Talk About It: Divorce* by Fred Rogers, and *Divorce Is a Grown Up Problem* by Janet Sinberg.

❧ Having a good laugh during stressful times is healthy for you and your child. Rent a funny video, read silly jokes from a joke book, sing out loud together, or play games.

Separation Anxiety

"Mommy, don't go, don't go-o-o-o-o-o!" How often does a parent of a toddler or preschooler hear these words? Typically, quite often. At some point it is perfectly normal for a toddler or preschooler to experience separation anxiety as she struggles between independence and dependence. Your child has become attached to you, the primary caregiver, and becomes upset when you leave her. She is used to being taken care of by you, so naturally when you leave her with someone else, her sense of security is shaken. The anxiety is accentuated if your child has never been exposed to other caregivers and has only been left in her parents' charge. Some toddlers do not experience clinging or separation anxiety, but when they reach the preschool years, they may encounter a delayed response to separating. In addition, a child who is shy or anxious may have more difficulty separating than an outgoing child.

Change and fear also may trigger separation anxiety. These feelings may occur when a child starts a new day care or preschool, a parent returns to work, a new baby-sitter is hired, the family moves, a new sibling arrives, parents separate or divorce, or the parents simply go out for the evening.

The good news about separation anxiety is that it doesn't last forever and it's a comforting sign that you and your child have a strong, loving bond. In the meanwhile, to ease the separations between you and your child, try the following tips.

PINK AND BLUE ALERT

Never sneak out on your child. Your deceit may give her a feeling of distrust whenever you leave her side.

Time-Tested Advice

❧ When separation anxiety occurs, reassure your child how much you love her by giving her lots of hugs and kisses. Remind her that whenever you leave her, you always come back to her.

❧ Just before your departure (from your house, day care, or preschool), give your child your undivided attention, focusing entirely on her.

❧ Always say good-bye to your child before leaving her. Make the parting short, sweet, and reassuring.

❧ Whether your child is going to school or day care, staying home with a baby-sitter, or going to grandma's house, always prepare her by telling her where you are going and when you will be returning.

- If you're going back to work and hiring a new caregiver, have that person spend time with your child in your home at least two weeks before your start date so your child gets to know her. Begin to leave your child alone with the caregiver for short periods of time when you're home, then progress to short spans when you're not home, eventually working up to the daylong separation.

- When your child clings to you, do not criticize or demean her. Instead, empathize and tell her you love her and will be back soon.

- If the parent shows signs of separation anxiety herself, the child will pick up on it and act anxiously, too. Stay calm and try not to lose your patience.

- One of the best ways to help your child with separation is to distract her with an engaging activity. She will be less likely to react to the separation if she's kept busy.

- If you will be leaving your child with a baby-sitter, be sure that person arrives before your child goes to sleep so she won't be startled if she wakes up and you're not there. Have the sitter spend time alone with your child while you're still home in order to make a smooth transition and avert an emotional meltdown when you leave.

- Expose your child to other adults and children so she learns to be comfortable with different people in new situations.

❧ Do not let your child's hysterical antics dissuade you from leaving. While you might feel bad that she's upset, also feel confident you have left her in good hands. Do not let her manipulate you.

For more information regarding baby-sitters, please refer to Time-Tested Advice for a Baby-Sitter, Housekeeper, or Nanny in Chapter 1, "The Caregivers."

❂ 10 ❂

Entertainment

The children's market for toys, books, music, and videos has become saturated with an abundance of products. Parents are asked to fork over significant dollars just to keep their children entertained. That's why it's important to select the right product that is not going to be a waste of your child's time or your money. Select toys, books, music, arts and crafts, and videos that will entertain, educate, challenge (but not frustrate), foster imagination and creativity, fit your child's developmental needs, and, of course, be safe. Through play a child develops and masters an array of learning skills, including coordination, language, and social interaction.

Pretend play and role-playing are an invaluable part of a young child's life because they give him the opportunity to use his imagination and learn to express himself. In addition, pretend play empowers a young child to have temporary

PINK AND BLUE HINT

While it is important to create a safe environment for your child to play in, it is equally important not to hover over him as he plays independently. Be an observer, and guide and direct him when he asks for your help.

control over his own little world where he makes up the rules and creates the characters. A toddler or preschooler loves to role-play by mimicking adults' actions and mannerisms and performing simple tasks just like those of grownups. By providing the child with his own props, such as child-sized household equipment, dolls, action figures, and dress-up clothing, you encourage this fantasy play.

Toys

For a young child, playing is not only fun and exciting but also very important work. While parents enjoy indulging their children with innumerable toys, be careful not to overdo it. A toddler or preschooler who has too many playthings can become not only unappreciative, but also distracted, having difficulty focusing on any one thing for more than a few seconds. Therefore, it is wise to provide your child with fewer toys and to rotate them regularly to help keep his interest and attention.

When purchasing a toy, consider how your child will play with it and whether you think it will hold his attention. It's best to invest in products that actively involve and challenge your child, as opposed to ones that are merely novelty items and fun for one time only. The three main things to consider for any toy are teaching power, durability, and lasting appeal.

Time-Tested Advice

❧ It is not necessary to spend a lot of money on playthings, because many items around the house are just as entertaining to a young child. For example, some junk mail can keep a child busy indefinitely, and so can plastic bowls and measuring cups filled with small amounts of water.

❀ Keep a separate supply of toys at the grandparents' home or any home your child visits frequently. Do not buy extra playthings, but take from your child's overflowing stock of toys.

❀ When a child is playing, the parent should resist the urge to take control or correct what the child is doing. It is far better to let him take the lead and have the parent follow along.

❀ Encourage pretend play by reversing roles with your child. Pretend you're the child and he is the parent.

❀ Be sure you put quality time aside each day and play with your child, giving him your undivided attention.

❀ Have your child sort through unwanted toys and donate them to a local charity. Make sure they are in good working order with no broken parts.

❀ Limit the number of toys you give your child so he doesn't become overwhelmed, overstimulated, or unappreciative.

❀ When possible, test a toy that is on display to be sure your child will enjoy the product and it meets your approval. Many video games, computer software, and riding toys are available for testing before purchase.

❀ If your preschooler has a toy or item that can be added to, help contribute to the collection at a gift-giving time. Some ideas include pots and pans for a kitchenette, action figures or dolls that go with an activity center, or even baseball cards.

❧ Stimulate your child's imagination with unstructured toys and open-ended activities such as puppets, dolls, blocks, and art materials.

❧ If your child seems uninterested in a toy that you think is still appropriate for him, put it on hiatus and bring it back in a month. It may rekindle his interest when he sees it again.

❧ For the older preschooler who has lost interest in a toy, try a temporary toy exchange with a friend or neighbor. If your child sees someone else having fun with the item, it may become appealing to him all over again.

❧ Change a toy's location. For example, if the toy is inside the house, take it outside for a change.

❧ Just because a toy is the latest sensation doesn't mean your child has to have it.

❧ When it comes to a special occasion, shop early in order to find the item you want to purchase. To save time, call ahead. If the toy is difficult to find in your city, ask a relative or friend in another city to help locate it for you.

Toddlers

If you've ever watched a windup toy that moves around in many directions or dances around and around, then you know what an active toddler looks like. Whether it is a button to push or a knob to pull, the inquisitive two-year-old wants to try it. His busy explorations through a variety of playthings will help encourage his physical and intellectual growth.

Sharing is a difficult concept for a toddler to grasp because he is possessive of his things and is used to solitary play. As he matures and begins to play interactively with other children, he will learn how to share. However, if you push the idea of sharing before he is ready, it will only be an exercise in futility.

Preschoolers

As a child gets older, pretend play becomes more important. By using his imagination and role-playing, the preschooler further develops his language and social skills. He also needs active play, like running and climbing, to use his big muscles for developing his coordination.

The preschooler begins to enjoy being more social and playing more cooperatively with others. While sharing is still not at the top of his list, be patient and understanding as he starts to learn the concept of give-and-take.

Toy Safety

Toys are an integral part of your child's life and should be chosen carefully. Not only do you want the toys to be fun and stimulating, but they must be safe, too. When making your purchases, pay close attention to the toy label's age recommendations and warnings. Select age-appropriate toys that are well suited for your child's abilities, skills, and interests. To protect your child and your wallet, follow these suggestions.

PINK AND BLUE HINT

 Check in your closet and ask grandparents to look in their closet for old clothing, shoes, scarves, hats, jewelry, and any other items that would be fun for a young child to dress up in.

Time-Tested Advice

- ❤ Do not give a young child a toy that has sharp points or edges.

- ❤ Avoid toys with projectile parts.

PINK AND BLUE ALERT

Since toddlers are known to put things in their mouths, purchase a "choke tube" at a toy or juvenile safety store. If a toy or any of its parts fit through the tube, do not give the toy to your toddler.

❦ Electrical toys with heating elements are inappropriate and dangerous for toddlers and preschoolers.

❦ Avoid toys with small removable parts for children under age three because of the risk of choking.

❦ Do not give a young child latex balloons because he can easily suffocate from deflated or broken pieces of balloons.

❦ Do not give your child toys with long strings or cords; they could cause strangulation.

❦ Buy sturdy, well-constructed toys that will not fall apart or break easily.

❦ Not only are noisy toys grating to an adult's ear, they can also damage a child's hearing. If the sound is too loud for you, then it will surely be too loud for your youngster.

❦ Toys must be decorated with nontoxic paint and constructed with nontoxic glue.

❦ Be sure an older sibling's toys are inaccessible to a younger child.

❦ Be careful of open seams on a rattle, doll, or stuffed (plush) toy that could release stuffing or pellets.

❦ Make sure a responsible adult is supervising your child when he is playing with his toys.

❦ Examine toys periodically, and discard ones that are broken and cannot be repaired.

❦ Always carefully follow toy manufacturers' assembly instructions.

- Do not leave toys near windows, counters, or any other place where a young child could use them as steps to climb on and possibly get into trouble.

- Do not buy a toy baby carriage, high chair, cradle, or any other item that a toddler thinks he can fit in. Wait until he is a little older and can understand the toy is strictly for play.

- To eliminate germs being spread, wash or wipe down your child's toys often.

- Show your child how to play with a toy safely.

Toy Storage

There isn't a home that doesn't wrestle with toy space logistics. To keep your home from being swallowed up by too many toys, use your available space practically and organize your children's toys to recapture domestic order. Not only will the result be aesthetically pleasing, but your child will have a much easier time choosing and finding things to play with.

Don't forget to clear out the objects your child has outgrown and doesn't play with anymore. If they are in good working order, donate the toys to a local hospital or children's charity. You can even teach your child a lesson in giving to others by having him select a few toys he doesn't want anymore and giving them to children less fortunate than himself.

Try the following storage ideas for your sake and the toys' preservation:

- Clear plastic containers with lids in a variety of sizes

- Stackable plastic bins (with or without rollers)

PINK AND BLUE HINT

Get your child into the habit of putting his toys away when done playing. This will teach him about the responsibility of taking care of things and help him avoid losing items.

PINK AND BLUE ALERT

Toy chests with attached lids are dangerous to use because the lid can fall down on a child's head or fingers. Purchase shallow chests that have removable tops and that a child can easily reach into by himself.

PINK AND BLUE HINT

Store toys according to category or group—for instance, doll and doll accessories in one plastic box, cars and trucks in another container, and puzzles on shelves.

PINK AND BLUE HINT

To help you and your child identify toy containers, either label the bin with the name of the toy, or glue a picture of the item on the outside of the container.

PINK AND BLUE HINT

Keep certain toys in one particular room, and don't allow them to be moved around the house; for example, bath toys stay in the bathroom. If the child wants to play with the toys, he must do so in the designated room.

❋ Wire mesh baskets (great at the bottom of a closet or hidden under the bed)

❋ Plastic laundry baskets (buy a few and sort the toys by category—blocks, cars and trucks, dolls, etc.)

❋ Sturdy open adjustable shelves, securely attached to the wall, at your child's reach (great for puzzles and books; use the highest shelf for items you don't want your child to get to without your assistance)

❋ A small suitcase or duffle bag

❋ Laundry bags that hang from easy-to-reach plastic hooks

❋ Mesh netting bags (great for water toys)

❋ Under an open staircase (good place to park indoor riding toys)

❋ Heavy cardboard cartons that your child can decorate with crayons, markers, and stickers (ask him to draw a picture of the items to be stored in that box)

❋ Medium-sized plastic garbage can with removable lid (available in different colors)

❋ Plastic dish drainers for standing books upright

Music and Art

Music and art are important because they teach the child to communicate and express himself in different ways. Early exposure to music and art promote skills such as problem solving, reading, and language development. In addition, a child can learn how to convey his feelings through art and music in an uninhibited way.

By incorporating art and music into your child's life, you encourage him to use his eyes, hands, ears, voice, and body as well. When a child hears music, he learns to listen. As he becomes familiar with the rhythm, notes, and words in a song, his memorizing skills are sharpened. The young artist learns about color, shape, size, and texture through different media such as crayon, paint, and clay.

Besides the music and art activities listed in Chapters 3, 11, and 13, here are some other suggestions for activities to do with your toddler and preschooler:

※ Take your child for a short visit to a local museum or art gallery that features large, colorful exhibits. Talk to your child about details he can recognize in the artwork, such as colors, shapes, texture, and subject matter.

※ Visit a local children's museum that encourages hands-on art and music experiences.

※ Designate a specific art area in your home for your child. Keep art supplies well stocked.

※ To add texture to your child's artwork, experiment with the following items:

   ◉ Old toothbrush

   ◉ Old comb

   ◉ String

   ◉ Salt or sugar

   ◉ Plastic wrap, aluminum foil, wax paper, paper towel, or bubble wrap (crumpled in pieces)

   ◉ Cheesecloth

   ◉ Flowers or leaves

※ Take your child to a children's symphony or family-oriented live musical performance.

※ Integrate music into your child's daily life by playing it at bedtime or bath time as a calming factor or at cleanup time as a motivator.

※ In addition to child-oriented music, play all types of music, from rock to country, folk to classical, so your child learns to appreciate and enjoy a variety of music. Listen and sing together.

※ Play upbeat music to get your child to exercise. It's a great way for him to move and express himself in an uninhibited manner.

※ If your child shows a particular interest in music, look into local music programs geared to the preschooler.

※ Young children love songs that are interactive or have repetitious verses, such as "Wheels on the Bus," "Old MacDonald," and "Itsy Bitsy Spider."

Books

One of the greatest gifts you can give your child is the joy of reading and love of books. According to the U.S. Department of Education, reading to your child regularly is one of the most important ingredients in reading and language development. For your child's future reading success, make reading time a daily pleasurable experience that you and he enjoy together so he learns to think of reading as a fun activity.

Time-Tested Advice

❧ Select books for toddlers that are bright, colorful, and cheerful. Nursery rhymes are very popular for this age, as are interactive books that let your child touch textures, smell scents, or lift flaps.

❧ For preschoolers look for picture books with easy-to-understand stories, captivating characters, and beginning concepts (e.g., alphabet and counting).

❧ Keep a variety of books in the house, such as board, pop-up, vinyl, sensory, and noisemaking books. Keep your child's books in one particular area that is accessible to him.

❧ Let your child select the book he wants to read. Giving him his choice encourages his taste and judgment. Don't be surprised if he wants you to read the same story over and over, because toddlers and preschoolers thrive on repetition and familiarity.

❧ To capture your child's attention, dramatize the book by speaking with expression or using different voices.

❧ Encourage your child to look at books on his own as well as with you.

❧ Visit the library and local bookstore for storytelling hour.

❧ Be a good role model and let your child see you enjoy reading.

❧ Choose a well-lit, comfortable, cozy area for reading. Children love to curl up on mommy's or daddy's lap at story time.

❀ If your child is restless and seems uninterested in a book, rather than forcing the issue, make up a quick ending to the story and try again later.

❀ Select books on subject matters that interest your child.

❀ Engage your child in the story by asking him to point out or find different colors or items on the page. As you read, stop every once in a while to discuss the story or enlist his personal commentary. Encourage questions.

❀ After you have read a book to your preschooler, ask him to draw a picture about the story.

❀ In your everyday travels with your child, point out words, such as *Stop* or *Slow* on street signs, *Exit* on buildings, and *Men* and *Women* on bathroom doors.

Computers

Since computers are definitely the way of the world, more and more parents are eager to introduce their toddlers and preschoolers to this technology. Computers make learning fun and enjoyable. There's no limit to what children can learn and do with the software that has been specifically designed for their age. It is not necessary to invest a large sum of money in a computer; it's the software that is most important. However, it's best to purchase a computer with lots of speed, a CD-ROM, and a color monitor. Look for software programs that will grab your child's attention and excite him. As you enter the world of computers with your child, here are some suggestions to keep in mind.

Time-Tested Advice

- ❤ Sit with your child when he's at the computer so you can help him and give him feedback and encouragement.

- ❤ It may take your child a while to learn how to manipulate the mouse. Show him how it moves, but then let him experiment with it.

- ❤ Before your child uses a new software program, review it so you are familiar with the information.

- ❤ Don't take control of your child's computer experience. Instead, be the observer. Guide and direct him when he asks for your help.

- ❤ Set time limits on the computer. Twenty minutes is sufficient for a preschooler.

- ❤ If you want to go on the Internet with your child, first preview the sites alone and note which ones you think are appropriate for your child. Then when you explore the Web with him, you can give him a choice from the sites you have already visited.

- ❤ To whet your child's computer appetite, look for age-appropriate interactive games, as well as programs with familiar characters.

- ❤ Do not substitute computer time for reading time.

- ❤ If you do not own a computer, visit the local library or computer center where children's software is available.

PINK AND BLUE HINT

Do not push a toddler into spending time on the computer. At this age, he is more likely to learn from building with blocks, dressing up, and playing in the sandbox.

Excursions

To your child, his family and home are his whole world. When you take him out and about, you broaden his view of the world and enhance his life experiences. As he meets new people and visits new places, his horizons expand intellectually and socially. Excursions may simply be errands close to home or may include lengthier jaunts, such as a day at the zoo or children's museum.

To make an excursion a success, it should be fun. Follow your child's lead, and let him tell you what interests him. Do not rush your toddler or preschooler if he is fascinated with a particular exhibit. You may not cover as much ground as you would like, but remember the experience is for your child's benefit, not yours. Keep in mind little legs get tired quickly, so make rest stops along the way. Here are some outings to do with your child:

※ *Children's museum* with hands-on exhibits—Avoid going to the museum during holidays, when it tends to be more crowded.

※ *Science museum* with dinosaur exhibits—Dinosaurs are mesmerizing to a young child. Tap into his interest by asking questions that inspire his imagination.

◉ If your child has plastic toy dinosaurs, plan an archeological dig in his sandbox or backyard, and let him find the buried items.

※ *Art museum* with large, colorful exhibits—When you come home from the art museum, plan an art activity.

※ *Aquarium*

※ *Library or bookstore*—Take your child to story time.

※ *Zoo and petting zoo*—Let your child linger at exhibits that really capture his attention. Bring along instant hand sanitizer to clean your child's hands after petting the animals in the petting zoo.

- On your ride to and from the zoo, play games in the car such as I'm Thinking of an Animal. Describe the animal and let your child guess what it is. Or make up a story together about your child's favorite animal, and have him draw a picture when he gets home.

- Play Animal Charades at home.

- *Botanical gardens*

- *Plant or flower nursery*

- *Nature centers*—Call ahead and find out what programs are available, such as hiking trails or visiting wildlife displays. On sunny days, remember to cover your child's skin with sunscreen and insect repellent, bring a hat, and carry a bottle of water.

- *Fire station*—Call ahead of time to see when you can visit the station.

- *Airport or train station*

- *Boat, train, or bus ride* for a short distance

- *Historical landmarks*—Call ahead for hours of operation and tour information.

- *The top of an observation tower*—Always hold your child's hand and keep a close eye on him.

- *Street fairs*—Hold your child's hand, because he can easily get lost in the crowd.

- *Amusement park* with a young children's section—Don't force your child to go on rides that seem scary to him. When possible, go on the ride with him. If you're not

PINK AND BLUE ALERT

While you want to give your child room to explore, it's very important to keep a close eye on your toddler or preschooler at all times.

riding with your child, stand close by where he can see you.

☀ *Beach or any waterfront area*—Always go to the beach prepared with sunscreen, hat, extra towels, blanket, sun umbrella (optional), cold drinks, snacks, and beach toys. (Please see Chapters 8, "Safety," and 14, "Travel," for more information.)

  ◉ Start a seashell or rock collection. Each time you visit the beach, your child will be kept busy looking for these items.

☀ *Fishing* at a local pond, lake, or trout farm (activity for a four-year-old)—Go to a local tackle shop and ask what kind of fishing rods with safe hooks are recommended for young children and what kind of bait to use. Ask if they have fiberglass rods with a push-button reel for your child's easy handling. If possible, rent equipment the first few times. Remember to purchase a fishing license at the tackle store.

  ◉ Teach your child how to cast off carefully so no one around him gets hurt.

  ◉ Stand next to your child when he's fishing, and put the bait on the hook for him.

  ◉ To remove any disappointments or expectations, explain to the child that most people don't catch something every time they go fishing.

  ◉ Remember to bring insect repellent, sunscreen, and a hat.

  ◉ Keep the outing short; a half day is usually long enough.

- ✹ If you don't plan to clean and cook the fish, then throw it back into the water. This is a good way to teach a young child to be a responsible, ecologically minded fisher.

- ✹ *The park or local playground*

- ✹ *Pet store*

- ✹ *Child-oriented concert or performance*—Possibilities include a circus, ice-skating show, magic show, or puppet show.

- ✹ *Sporting events*

- ✹ *Hikes*—Don't go on too long a hike, unless you are prepared to eventually carry your child. If you enjoy taking hikes frequently, you might want to invest in a child carrier that will hold a child up to forty pounds.

  - ✹ Dress appropriately for hikes. Make sure everyone wears comfortable shoes. For more detailed information, see Time-Tested Advice for Camping in Chapter 14, "Travel."

  - ✹ Do not wander off trails.

  - ✹ Take along water.

  - ✹ Teach your child what poison oak or poison ivy looks like and to stay away from it.

  - ✹ Play games along the way, such as finding things in a particular color, picking up leaves or stones, or following the leader (change the walking pattern by skipping, jumping, hopping, or marching).

- ✹ *Movies for children*—Many movies are inappropriate for very young children, so be sure the movie is OK for toddlers and preschoolers. Take your child's booster seat into the theater so he can see the screen better.

☀ *The mall*—Hold your child's hand, and don't plan too much time for shopping. Play a scavenger hunt game by looking for a certain item or color in the store windows.

☀ *Errands*—Take your child with you to the supermarket, bakery, post office, dry cleaner, car wash, veterinarian, and bank. Please see Running Errands, also in Chapter 14.

☀ *Restaurants*—Please see Dining Out in Chapter 5, "Food, Nutrition, and Exercise."

❧ 11 ❧

Home Sweet Home

Home is the place where your child should feel most safe
and secure. Moreover, it's important for each member of the
family to have his or her own personal space, even if you
live in tight quarters. A child needs a special place that is
fun and functional. Include daily activities at home to entertain and enrich your child's life.

Home should be the place where you establish routines
that provide a sense of continuity and rituals that teach the
child values. Rituals give a toddler or preschooler a feeling
of reassurance through repetition. Breakfast with the family,
walking the dog together, Sunday at the park, and good-
night kisses all give the child something to look forward to
and expect in her daily home life. She finds comfort in
familiar routines like brushing her teeth each morning and

evening, taking a bath after dinner, and getting ready for bed with a bedtime story.

Enlisting your child's help with simple chores around the house can make her feel useful and encourage cooperation. This will also boost her self-esteem and make her feel appreciated, no matter how small the accomplishment may be. While it may be more time-consuming for the parent to oversee the child's chores, the investment will pay off later when your child can do things for herself and the rest of the family.

Chores

It's never too early to begin to teach a young child a sense of order and responsibility. Even a two-year-old can be taught to put her toys away in a convenient toy bin when playtime is over. Young children are eager to help around the house doing grown-up chores because to them, the line dividing play from help is virtually nonexistent. To a toddler, it's just as much fun to wash the car as it is to do a puzzle; for the preschooler, helping pull weeds in the garden is an exciting activity. Initiating her help with a simple task provides a feeling of pride, independence, and accomplishment.

While it may be faster and easier to just do the chore yourself, it's important to be patient and take advantage of your child's interest in assisting you in a task. In the beginning, help her with the chore, and then gradually back off as she masters it. Be consistent and don't let her off the hook, or she will think it is not necessary to fulfill her responsibilities, as small as they may be. If you develop a routine with chores at a young age, it will eventually lead the child to perform the chore without coaxing, as part of her obligation to the household.

If a parent conveys an enthusiastic attitude toward the job she is performing, it will most likely rub off on the child as well. Keep realistic expectations of what your child can and can't do, so struggles will be avoided and no one becomes disappointed and disillusioned.

Chores for Toddlers

Here are some chores a toddler can do:

- ❀ Put toys away

- ❀ Undress and place dirty clothes into a hamper

- ❀ Dress herself with easy pull-on pants or skirt

- ❀ Bring in the mail or newspaper

- ❀ Help fill the pet bowls

- ❀ Assist in household cleaning chores, such as sweeping and mopping, using child-sized equipment

Chores for Preschoolers

In addition to the list for toddlers, here are more chores a preschooler can do:

- ❀ Sort laundry or help fold her clothes

- ❀ Dress herself unassisted but leave the buttons, laces, and zippers for you

- ❀ Help set the table with place mats, napkins, and silverware

- ❀ Clear her unbreakable dishes and silverware from the table

- ❀ Help wash vegetables and fruit

- ❀ Pour her cereal into a bowl

PINK AND BLUE HINT

Give your child her own household items to work and play with, such as a child-sized broom, dust pan, mop, apron with pockets (can hold a spray bottle filled with water), carpet sweeper, and sturdy plastic gardening tools.

PINK AND BLUE ALERT

Do not let children lick a bowl or spoon used in a recipe containing raw egg.

❧ Help bake cookies, prepare sandwiches, and stir cold mixtures (do not allow anyone to lick a spoon or bowl that has raw eggs)

❧ Assist parent when changing younger sibling's diaper, or help fetch a bottle, blanket, or toy

❧ Help in the garden by pulling weeds, turning the dirt over, and watering flowers with a hose or watering can

❧ Help parent wash the car or wash her plastic riding toy

Time-Tested Advice

❧ Begin by giving your child small jobs to do with you, so she feels successful.

❧ Show your child exactly what you want her to do, explaining it in simple words. For example, when she is done playing with a puzzle, put it on the shelf and say, "This is where the puzzle goes when you're finished playing." Then it will be easier for her to follow your directions. You may have to repeat this process and dialogue a few times before your child fully understands it.

❧ Be sure the chore fits her capabilities. Do not give a young child jobs that are too time-consuming and difficult.

❧ Praise the child for a job well done, and tell her how much you appreciate her efforts. Do not criticize her if her performance falls short of your expectations.

- When a child asks to help with a chore, do not discourage or dismiss her offer. As long as it doesn't compromise her safety, encourage her enthusiasm and put her to work.

- Toddlers love to mimic grown-ups. When a child wants to help you clean the house, let her assist in a simple task. For example, if you are dusting furniture, hand her a clean rag and enlist her help.

- Teach your toddler to take off her wet diaper and put it in the diaper pail. This will help her learn to become responsible for her own self and at the same time subtly introduces her to toilet training.

- Make cleanup of toys less overwhelming by organizing them in containers by category (e.g., blocks, puzzles, dolls, and accessories). Put them in easy-to-reach bins.

- Sing special songs together as you clean up, or play lively, upbeat music to get things moving. Toddlers love to pitch in and help put things away to *Barney's* cleanup song.

- If a task is particularly messy and the child seems overwhelmed, it's OK for an adult to help, as long as that person doesn't take over and complete the job without the child's help.

- Although timing a child can motivate her to get a chore done, speed should not always be the goal for a young child. Completing the task properly is far more important than getting it done quickly.

- If there are siblings in the household, encourage teamwork. It's more fun working with someone else and gets the job done faster.

PINK AND BLUE HINT

When you want your child to put her toys away, try a humorous approach by letting a puppet or favorite stuffed animal announce cleanup time. Or have her wear a construction helmet when putting away blocks. Whatever tactic you take, remember that young children respond well to silliness.

PINK AND BLUE ALERT

Avoid leaving the news on when your child is in the room, since so much violence is reported daily.

PINK AND BLUE HINT

If you're buying a new television, consider purchasing one with the V-Chip, which allows you to block out channels you don't want your child to watch.

* Make a chart of your child's chores to be done, and when she has completed them, let her select a sticker to put on the chart. It's a great motivator!

* Do not bribe or offer rewards as an incentive to get your child to perform a chore. And never use work as a punishment, or you'll spoil a child's enthusiasm for lending a hand.

Television

Television can be an excellent learning tool for a toddler and preschooler, as long as the viewing time is limited and monitored. Young children need to use their physical resources for healthy growth and development, and sitting in front of the television for a long while will not stimulate the child's body or mind. Many parents get into the bad habit of using the television as a baby-sitter. Instead, the television should be used to educate the child and foster her imagination. For your child to receive the greatest benefits from television viewing, watch TV with her. Use it as a point of reference to discuss what you have seen together.

As the parent, you have the power to decide what kinds of programs your child will watch. In addition to regular television programming you find suitable for your child, videos are a great alternative. Select interactive videos designed to get your child to participate with the people and characters on the cassette by singing, dancing, clapping hands, exercising, or following simple directions. Or if you have a video camera, replay home videos. Do not allow your toddler or preschooler to watch scary shows that can frighten her and leave a negative impression.

At-Home Activities

Whether the sun is shining or it's raining cats and dogs, your toddler or preschooler needs to be stimulated with age-appropriate activities when hanging around the house. A child loves to be busy with fun things at home in the comfort of her familiar surroundings. It is the parent's responsibility to organize interesting, imaginative pastimes that encourage and strengthen gross and fine motor skills and develop the child's senses.

Arts and Crafts

Keep a well-stocked supply of arts and crafts items in your home. Here are some basic supplies to get started with:

※ Large colored crayons

※ Washable colored markers

※ Washable paints (including finger paints)

※ Paintbrushes (with rounded handles)

※ Egg cartons, empty yogurt cups, or small plastic margarine containers (to use as paint holders . . . no glass, please!)

※ Colored chalk

※ Construction paper, tagboard, cardboard, plain white paper, and finger painting paper or freezer wrap (use shiny side)

※ Nontoxic, washable glue or glue stick

※ Old buttons and beads (for the preschooler)

※ Doilies

※ Blunt child-sized scissors ("lefty" scissors for the left-handed child)

PINK AND BLUE HINT

 Keep your arts and crafts supplies stored in either a large box or a plastic bin out of the child's reach. Tape a checklist to the outside of the container, and when you're running low, you'll know to restock.

PINK AND BLUE HINT

Choose one area in your home as the designated arts and crafts area, so your child knows this is the only place where these activities are allowed. The kitchen or the laundry room is the best location for "messy creativity."

PINK AND BLUE HINT

Before starting messy activities, lay a plastic covering on the floor to cut down on cleanup time.

PINK AND BLUE HINT

Coloring and paint books are restrictive for young children and stifle creativity. It's better to let children paint and draw free-form.

With these items on hand, any of the following activities will be easy to set up for your child. In addition to the ideas offered here, please see Activities for the Sick Toddler or Preschooler in Chapter 3, "Your Child's Health," for more at-home suggestions, which can be done whether your child is sick or healthy.

Drawing and Painting

✻ In addition to the standard paintbrush, try painting with sponges (cut up a new clean one), cotton swabs, cotton balls, plastic bottle tops, or string.

✻ Vegetables, such as a carved potato, carrot, turnip, or broccoli, are different painting tools children enjoy experimenting with. Just be sure she doesn't put the paint-coated vegetables in her mouth.

✻ Draw a picture of a turkey by tracing your child's hand with the thumb fully extended away from the other fingers, which are close together. The thumb is the head of the bird, and the four fingers represent the feathers. Let your child color and decorate her turkey. This is also a good Thanksgiving activity.

✻ Make little insects or animals using the child's fingerprints as the body. For best results, use washable nontoxic ink pads in various colors. Allow the prints to dry, and then draw on legs, antennae, beak, tail, eyes, etc.

✻ Buy soap finger paints to use in the bathtub, or make your own by adding a few drops of food coloring to a mild liquid soap that is safe for your child. If your child resists taking a bath, this is a great enticement.

You can buy finger paints or make your own:

FINGER PAINT

½ cup cornstarch
¼ cup facial cream
¼ cup water
A few drops of food coloring

Combine all the ingredients. (They should have pastelike texture.) Store in a well-sealed plastic container.

This paint washes off with soap and water, but it can stain clothing, so your child should wear either a smock or an adult's old shirt. When working with finger paint, cover the floor with a plastic or vinyl tarp. If you don't have a child-sized easel, tape the paper to the covered floor or cover the refrigerator door first, then tape the paper to it. Finger painting requires constant adult supervision!

Play Dough

Children love to help make play dough. It's economical and smells better than the store-bought kind. Try this recipe for hours of fun:

PLAY DOUGH

1 cup flour
1 cup water
½ cup salt
1 teaspoon cream of tartar
1 tablespoon cooking oil
Food coloring (10–20 drops, depending on the degree
   of color you want)

Mix all the ingredients in a saucepan, and cook over medium-low heat until mixture pulls away from sides of pan and becomes very thick.

Transfer to a cutting board or countertop, and knead until cool. Keeps three months in an airtight container or sealed plastic bag at room temperature.

Use cookie cutters, rolling pin, garlic press, potato ricer, plastic spoon or dull-edged plastic knife, and plastic bottle tops to create anything imaginative.

Homemade Musical Instruments

If you are interested in making your own musical instruments and you're able to handle the "musical noise," try making one or more of the following instruments with your youngster:

☀ Make a *drum* from an empty coffee can with plastic lid. Use plastic or wooden spoons as the drumsticks, or have her use her hands the way you play a bongo drum. Either end of the can will create a sound.

☀ *Shakers* can be made from a few different things:

  ☺ Take an empty, washed out soda can, fill it with dried beans or pennies, and then tape the tab opening shut.

  ☺ Fill a coffee can with dried beans, then tape the plastic lid closed.

  ☺ Fill an empty plastic milk container halfway and seal it shut with the bottle top.

  ☺ Let your child decorate paper plates with crayons or markers. Staple two paper plates together. Before putting the last few staples in, fill with beans.

☀ For the crashing sound of *cymbals* give her two metal pot lids to bang together.

☀ *Rhythm blocks* can be easily made from two wooden building blocks and sandpaper. Tape one side of each block with sandpaper.

☀ For a real *grating* sound, give your child a plastic grater and wooden spoon.

In addition, young children love to blow store-bought whistles and to ring bells, but these can get annoying very quickly.

Backyard Activities

Going outside and playing in the backyard allows your child the opportunity to run around and expend her pent-up energy. Whether she's on her riding toy, throwing a ball, or going on the swings, an adult should always be outside supervising the child. For complete information on safety in the backyard, please refer to the section titled Child-Proofing Your Pool and Backyard in Chapter 8, "Safety." Here are some things for your toddler or preschooler to do outside the house:

☀ Your child will be happily occupied playing in a sandbox with pails, shovels, molds, strainers, trucks, and cars. To keep the sandbox clean and free of fleas, always cover it when not in use. It's a good idea to change the sand once a year.

☀ Investing in backyard equipment will provide years of entertainment for your child. Please see Time-Tested Advice for the Backyard in Chapter 8 for tips and safety information.

☀ Teach your child how to ride a tricycle. It is imperative she wear a helmet. When she graduates to a two-wheeler, putting on a helmet will be automatic.

PINK AND BLUE HINT

Learning the skills of pedaling and steering a tricycle help an energetic preschooler work on his coordination and balance. When purchasing a tricycle, select one that is the right size for your child with adjustable seat, wheels, and pedals. In addition, look for a tricycle with good sturdy construction in either plastic or metal with chip-resistant paint.

PINK AND BLUE ALERT

When a child is riding any wheeled vehicle, there must be adult supervision.

PINK AND BLUE ALERT

Never allow a toddler or preschooler to ride a wheeled vehicle in the street.

※ Water play can be mesmerizing for a young child. She can bathe her doll, measure water in containers and cups, or help water the flowers. When the weather is warm, it's easier being barefoot.

※ If you have a grassy area in your backyard, connect a store-bought sprinkler and let your child run through it. If you have automatic sprinklers, be sure your child sees the sprinkler heads and doesn't trip over them.

※ Have a picnic lunch in the backyard. Lay out a blanket, and don't forget the sunscreen.

※ Play a game of catch with a ball, or practice kicking one.

※ Set up a tent or let your child make one from a couple of chairs, large boxes, or small table covered with a sheet or old blanket.

※ Play hide-and-seek.

※ Plan a treasure hunt by placing things around the backyard, or tell her to find as many green things as she can. Don't make it too difficult for the child to find things, or she may get frustrated and not want to play.

※ Plant a garden together. Give your child her own tools to use, and have her help cultivate what she has planted.

※ When the weather is warm, wading pools provide hours of fun in the backyard. For more information about swimming pools, please see Time-Tested Advice for the Pool in Chapter 8.

※ Buy washable colored chalk and draw hopscotch on the cement, or just let the child draw pictures with the chalk.

☀ In the summertime, sit outside and watch the sunset. Listen to the sounds of the crickets and birds, and smell the sweet fragrances of summer.

☀ Sit under a tree and read a book together.

Family Pets

There probably isn't a family that hasn't owned some kind of pet at one time or another. Pets are fun for children and teach them important lessons for life, including responsibility and kindness. Not all pets are right for every family. You should consider certain criteria, such as size of pet, the amount of care required, space limitations inside and outside your home, cost of pet, upkeep expenses (food, veterinary care, grooming, training, and toys), and age of children. From goldfish to a hamster to a dog, each pet has its pros and cons. Take the time to make a choice your entire family can live with.

For information on pet safety, please see the Pet Safety section in Chapter 8, "Safety."

PINK AND BLUE ALERT

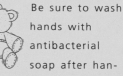

Be sure to wash hands with antibacterial soap after handling, petting, or playing with a pet.

๑ 12 ๑

Off to School

Socializing with other young children is an important part of your child's growth. Your toddler or preschooler may have already participated in a "Mommy and Me" program with you. Or he may be playing with other young children in your neighborhood or in a play group.

By the age of three or four, many parents opt to send their children to preschool to provide them with additional stimulation outside the home. There are pros and cons to sending a child to preschool, whether part-time or full-time. It is a personal choice.

If you decide to send your child to preschool, do your homework well. Choosing a preschool for your child is a big decision. Look for a program that suits your child's needs in an enriching and stimulating environment that provides an uplifting and positive experience. Even if your child is flour-ishing at home, he still needs daily interaction with children his same age in a program that develops social, physical, educational, and creative skills. The goal of any preschool should be to help a child gain independence, feel confident about himself, learn to make decisions and follow directions, stimulate his intellectual needs, foster his creativity, encourage cooperative interaction with his peers and teachers, and be happy in the school setting.

Choosing a Preschool

While you're not sending your child off to college just yet, selecting the right preschool for your child is very important. First and foremost, you must do your homework and not rely solely on recommendations from other people. In many parts of the country, you have to start this process a year or more in advance. Check listings for preschools in your community, call them in advance, and ask to schedule a visit without your child.

When searching for a preschool, there are certain basic considerations to keep in mind, such as location, hours of operation, days per week, full day versus half day, and cost. While it is important to take note of the physical structure of the school and its amenities (play equipment, variety of toys, books, and arts and crafts), your focus should be on the people who run the program and who will care for your child. Look for a preschool that incorporates symbolic, imag-inary, and dramatic play, along with an early literacy program to foster your child's emotional and intellectual growth. It is also important that the school has a diverse population. The following questions should help you select the right preschool for your child:

❁ Is the school licensed by the city, county, or state or accredited by the National Association for the Education of Young Children (NAEYC)?

❁ Do the director of the school and the teachers have college degrees in early-childhood education? Often, only the director and head teachers have college diplomas and certification in early-childhood education. However, the assistant teachers should have a minimum of twelve hours of continuing education and on-the-job training in this area.

❁ What is the entrance policy? Do they interview only the parents? Do they want to meet your child?

❁ Ask to observe the teachers who will be teaching your child's age group. Do they speak respectfully to the children, using eye contact at the children's level? Do you like the way the teachers interact with the children? Are they focusing on the children and listening to them? Do they have a pleasant disposition toward the children? Do the teachers have a sense of humor? Are the teachers dressed in comfortable clothing so they can sit on the floor, play in the sandbox, or participate in outdoor activities?

❁ What is the teacher-child ratio? While there is no national standard, a toddler program should have one teacher for every six children, and in a preschool program, the NAEYC recommends there be one teacher for every seven to ten children.

❁ Are the children grouped according to age or in a mixed-age grouping?

❄ Is there enough personal space for each child? Make sure the room is not overcrowded and the children have plenty of space to move around in.

❄ Are there enough books, toys, arts and crafts materials, etc. for all the children? Are the toys easy for the children to reach?

❄ Does the school incorporate an early-childhood literacy program into its curriculum? The NAEYC encourages integrating this program into preschools.

❄ Are the classrooms and outdoor area clean, safe, and well lit? Wall sockets should be covered, and there shouldn't be exposed electrical wires or cords dangling from window treatments. Make sure the play equipment is stable and well maintained with no protruding parts, such as nails and splinters.

❄ What are the school's emergency procedures in case of an accident involving your child or in case of a natural disaster, such as a hurricane, tornado, or earthquake?

❄ Does the school have a kitchen, and does it provide healthful, safe meals and snacks? Is the kitchen clean? If your child brings his own lunch and snacks, what is the policy toward "junk" food? Most schools prohibit candy, gum, and sodas.

❄ What is the school's philosophy toward discipline? How does it handle temper tantrums and conflicts between children?

❄ Will the school admit your child if he is not toilet trained? What is its approach, and will the staff be supportive of your child's efforts?

❄ Does the school encourage parental involvement? Is it a requirement to volunteer your time and work in the classroom? If so, is your schedule flexible enough to accommodate this commitment?

❊ How does the school handle the child separating from the parent? Can you stay with him until he is comfortable separating from you?

❊ How often does the school inform you of your child's progress? Do teachers keep a daily log on each child?

❊ How will your child fit into this particular school's surroundings? If you have a quiet, shy child, you may want to choose a school with small classes so he will not be intimidated.

❊ Are the children happy and having fun?

Preschool Programs

The layout of the classroom will reveal to you what skills the preschool emphasizes. A well-organized, spacious classroom should be arranged with a variety of activity centers, such as the following:

❊ A cozy, inviting book corner filled with lots of age-appropriate, diverse books

❊ An arts and crafts area supplied with paints, easels, modeling clay and accessories, crayons, markers, scissors, and other materials

❊ A block area to inspire creativity and gross motor skills

❊ A dress-up area with plenty of clothing and child-sized items (e.g., stove, pots and pans, plastic food, stroller, dolls) for imaginary and dramatic play

❊ A puzzle and game area

- ❦ A science area with a class pet, such as a hamster, a guinea pig, or a rabbit

- ❦ A math area to introduce counting and measuring skills—for example, a sand, water, or pasta table with measuring items

- ❦ A writing area supplied with paper, thick pencils, and crayons

- ❦ A computer area with interactive games

A classroom does not need all these activities at one time. Some areas, such as blocks, the book corner, the dress-up area, the classroom pet, and the computer, are constants. Other activity centers need to be rotated daily to keep the children interested and challenged. For example, the math, science, and writing areas can be alternated, and in the art area the materials should be changed daily.

The outdoor area is just as important as the classroom because the preschooler needs to exercise his gross motor skills and expend his pent-up energy. In addition to swings, climbing structures, and a sandbox play area, there should be tricycles, child-sized table and chairs, and enough space for the children to play. The equipment and outdoor area must be safe and well maintained. While the teachers oversee the playtime outside, they should remain more in the background and allow the children time to roam and play freely (within the perimeter of the area) in an unintrusive way. If conflicts arise, the teachers are there to help the children resolve their problems.

Preschool Jitters

Once you have selected the preschool your child will attend, it's a good idea to drive by the school frequently and point out the building to him. Most schools arrange a get-together before the actual start date so children can meet each other and the teachers and become familiar with the school layout. However, if your child tends to be anxious about changes, ask if you may bring him to visit the school a few weeks before it begins and, if possible, meet the teachers one-on-one to make the experience less overwhelming.

To make the transition for your child as smooth as possible, before school begins talk to him about what he will be doing at preschool and the new friends he will be making. It's also important to create and maintain a routine and to take it slowly during the first few weeks.

The first day of school is always the toughest for the child, as well as the parent. The idea of separating from you may be traumatic and produce lots of tears. Separation anxiety is common among young children. Preschools are sensitive to this issue and will work with you to gradually help your child overcome this problem. Often this fear arises from not knowing whether you will come back for him, so reassure him that whenever you (or the caretaker) leave him, you (or the caretaker) will always return for him. Your child may also be reacting to your ambivalence and emotions of letting go. Whether or not *you* are ready to say good-bye, it's imperative you display an enthusiastic, positive attitude.

Sometimes a child may think that while he's at school he is missing out on something fun the parent is doing without him. Reassure him you are running errands and doing other chores, such as going to the dry cleaner and cleaning the house, which are not fun. Or if there is a baby at home, he may think the baby is getting lots of attention while he's away. Explain to your child that he'll have a better time at school, and describe some of the activities he will be doing.

To help your child make a successful transition into the new preschool, try the following tips.

Time-Tested Advice

❤ To prepare your child for school, especially if he expresses any preschool jitters, get age-appropriate books and videos on this subject matter. Some suggested books are *Curious Kids Go to Preschool* by Heloise Antoine, *Chatter Box Jamie* by Nancy Evans Cooney, *We Go to School* by Elizabeth Hathon, *Katherine Goes to Nursery School* by Jill Krementz, *Going to My Nursery School* by Susan Kuklin, and *Nursery School* by Harold Roth.

❤ Before school begins, take your child to the store and let him pick out a new lunch box and backpack. Don't forget to put his name on them with indelible ink. This is a good way for him to start recognizing his name in print.

❤ Use labels with your child's name on backpacks and clothing to identify his belongings.

❤ Create school-related rituals to help your child get used to the new routine. For instance, let him pick out his outfit and help pack his lunch box the night before.

❤ Be sure your child wears clothing and shoes that are appropriate for school and play.

❤ If your child is having a hard time separating from you, give him a photograph of you to comfort him. If he has a favorite transitional object, suggest he take it with him to school but leave it in his cubby for safekeeping. Remind him not to carry the transitional object around unless he's willing to share it with others.

PINK AND BLUE HINT

Surprise your child by putting something special, such as an "I Love You" note or a kiss imprinted on a napkin, into his lunch box.

- On the first day of school, arrive as early as possible to help your child settle in and become comfortable in his new surroundings before the other children get there.

- It's a good idea for both parents to alternate dropping off the child at school.

- Always get your child to school on time.

- If your child shows signs of preschool jitters, acknowledge his fear. Say, "I remember feeling scared my first day of school, too. I'm here with you, and we'll go into school together." Do not dismiss or criticize his fear.

- Never sneak out without saying a short good-bye to your child, or he will not trust you.

- Before you say good-bye and leave, make sure your child is involved in an activity that will help him make a comfortable transition into the classroom.

- Since a young child does not have a concept of time, give him a concrete idea of when you will return, such as "right after story time."

- Always be on time when picking your child up from school. If you're running late, notify the school so they can prepare your child for the delay.

- If your child expresses a feeling of being left out while he's at school and you are at home with his new baby brother or sister, tell him you will spend time alone with him when you pick him up from school.

PINK AND BLUE ALERT

If someone other than you or your spouse is picking up your child from school, give the school a note stating who has permission to pick him up.

❀ If your child is enrolled in a part-time program and is confused about what days he is attending school, use a calendar and have him place stickers on the corresponding days he goes to school.

❀ When you pick up your child from school, don't ask too many questions. Let him tell you about his day when he's ready. If you share with him what you did while he was in school, it may encourage him to talk about his day.

❀ If your child is having difficulty adjusting to school, invite a classmate to your home for a play date. If your child doesn't talk about anyone in particular, ask the teacher to recommend someone.

PINK AND BLUE ALERT

 Make sure the preschool has all the necessary emergency information regarding your child.

෧ 13 ෧

Birthdays and Holidays

The celebration of birthdays and holidays is an excellent way to teach your child about family traditions and accentuate happy times together. The ritual of feasting at Thanksgiving or blowing out candles on the birthday cake becomes an important part of your child's life. Birthdays mark off milestones and developmental highlights in your child's past year. Young children love festive occasions and eagerly anticipate them with great enthusiasm. They come to expect fanfare, whether it is a small, intimate party or a big get-together.

Along with the celebration of birthdays and holidays comes the tradition of gift giving. Whether the present is big or small, it is never too soon to teach a child to express her gratitude for the gifts she has received. However, the typical toddler or preschooler is only thinking of one person: herself! This is normal behavior, so do not fret, but reinforce the "thank you" at the appropriate time. Eventually she will have the good manners to say it on her own, without being coaxed by her parents.

Birthdays

The main ingredient for a birthday party is nonstop fun. And when it comes to entertaining toddlers and preschoolers, you can never have too many activities planned. Since young children have short attention spans, it's wise to be flexible and plan numerous games, as well as arts and crafts. Don't try to do the party alone; instead, enlist the help of grandparents, relatives, and friends, or ask older siblings or children in your neighborhood (ages nine to seventeen years) to be party helpers. They can direct activities, assist in arts and crafts, help serve food and drinks, pitch in with cleanup, take photographs at the party, and be an additional set of eyes.

While your child's birthday is an important day to share with friends and relatives, it's better to have fewer guests. Some parents suggest that the number of children invited to the party should be no more than double the birthday child's age. If you're throwing a big party, the National Safe Kids Campaign recommends you have one adult supervising every five children ages two to three, and one adult for every nine children ages four and up.

Children can handle only so much excitement, so be sure to include a starting and ending time on the invitation. Toddlers do best at a party lasting one hour to one and a half hours and preschoolers can last no more than two hours. Beyond that time, you'll be a glutton for punishment! Plan the party around your child's nap schedule, so that she won't be too tired or cranky to enjoy the festivities.

PINK AND BLUE HINT
Take your child to a plant nursery and let her select a small tree that you can plant in honor of her birthday. The entire family will enjoy watching it grow as she grows.

PINK AND BLUE HINT

If the birthday child has an older sibling, give the sibling specific responsibilities at the party, such as greeting guests, collecting the birthday gifts, and taking snapshots of the party. Including the sibling in the birthday festivities will make her feel important, too.

PINK AND BLUE HINT

If you are inviting many children to the party, instead of renting small tables and chairs, spread plastic tablecloths on the ground, as for a picnic.

Your party will be more successful if you plan it in advance. Keep in perspective your child's age and temperament, as well as what things your child enjoys. For instance, does she have a special interest in something, love to play a certain game, or have a favorite superhero? Select a theme (let your preschooler help choose), and plan the party around it, including invitations, paper goods, decorations, goody bags, and activities. Popular themes to consider are animals, favorite cartoon characters, circus, sports, cars and trucks, dinosaurs, and seasons. You don't have to spend lots of money to ensure a fun time. Just plan more activities than you think you'll need, so you're not caught short in case one activity doesn't work out.

If you want to avoid the headache of a party at home, consider throwing it at a child-oriented restaurant, such as a pizza parlor or an old-fashioned ice cream shop. Be sure to ask what type of party packages the place has and what the price includes. You will still need to plan activities to keep the children from running wild around the restaurant. Other alternatives to an at-home party could be your favorite children's gym, the local YMCA, or a nearby park. If you select the park, you will definitely need additional help watching all the children, and you must still be well organized with plenty of activities.

You don't have to throw an elaborate extravaganza for the party to be a success. The key is keep it short and simple. The following party pointers will help pave the way for a smooth celebration.

Time-Tested Advice

♥ Be sure the party area is carefully child-proofed. Remove any breakable, valuable, or dangerous items.

Tape down electrical wires, and place gates by any stairways.

❧ Always have first-aid supplies available in case any accidents occur. Basic items to have on hand are antibacterial soap, hydrogen peroxide, antibiotic ointment, bandages, gauze pads, and an ice pack.

❧ If a parent is not present with her child, be sure you have a phone or pager number in case of an emergency.

❧ Choose one area that can be cleared of furniture to allow safe active playing.

❧ Have everything set up before party time. Make sure your video camera battery pack has been recharged sufficiently and there's plenty of film for the camera.

❧ If you plan to decorate with balloons, use Mylar because those balloons don't burst into small pieces. Throw away any broken balloon pieces immediately, so children can't put them in their mouths.

❧ Be ready with something for the early arrivals to do, such as coloring with crayons, decorating the cement with colorful chalk, chasing bubbles, or playing with a beach ball.

❧ As your young guests arrive, have a plain tablecloth laid on the floor, and ask each child to help decorate it like a mural. This will be a wonderful keepsake for your child to remember her party.

❧ Many parents hire clowns or other dressed-up characters as entertainment. For young children, these characters can be intimidating and even

PINK AND BLUE ALERT

 Do not let young children inflate regular (latex) balloons, as this can become a choking hazard.

frightening. Never force a child to go near the characters if it makes her uncomfortable.

- If you have a petting zoo, make sure there are plenty of adults to supervise in addition to the people who bring the animals.

- Make sure goody bags (party favors) are filled with safe, age-appropriate items and are all the same. This will avoid the hysteria if a child sees something that she didn't get but wants. Hand them out at the end of the party as each child leaves.

- Do not open gifts during the party. Not only is it difficult for young children to sit still and not be entertained, it is also hard for the birthday child to share her new toys with her guests.

- Plan a quiet activity when the party is winding down, such as storytelling or a simple puppet show.

- Have extras of everything on hand in case you miscalculated or someone brings an uninvited guest.

Food

Make your life easier by keeping the menu simple. There's no need to prepare lots of food because going to a party is exciting for young children, and they tend to be less interested in eating. Pizza is popular with children and easy to serve. If you want to be creative, you can use cookie cutters to make sandwiches. Some favorite fillings are peanut butter and jelly, egg salad, tuna fish, cheese, or cream cheese. Other easy food ideas include fresh fruit, rice cakes, cheese and crackers, individual boxes of cold cereal, miniature waffles, muffins, and bagels. Juice boxes (serve 100 percent fruit juice for health reasons) are the easiest drinks to serve to young children; just make sure you have plenty on hand.

Of course, no birthday party would be complete without the cake. Most children want only a few bites, so keep that in mind whether you're baking it yourself or ordering from the bakery. An ice cream cake is always popular. It eliminates the extra time to scoop and is less wasteful. Or you can have another activity by prebaking plain cupcakes or sugar cookies and letting each child decorate one, using prepared frostings, colorful sprinkles, and easy-to-chew candies.

Since parents of young children usually stay at the party, don't forget to have coffee, cold drinks, and some nibbles for them, too. Be sure hot coffee is kept out of children's reach.

Time-Tested Advice

* Serve safe foods when planning your menu. The following foods should not be given to young children: nuts, raisins, popcorn, hard candies, raw vegetables, grapes, and hot dogs.

* Be sure enough adults are supervising when the children are eating.

* Children should remain seated while eating. If they run around, they may not chew the food well and may choke.

* When serving the birthday cake, only an adult should light the candles and handle the knife. Don't let youngsters lean over the flames, and hold back longer hair when your child is blowing out the candles. Remove matches, lighters, and cake knives immediately after use, out of the children's reach.

Games

Getting everyone involved in something is always the best-laid plan. Games bring children together and encourage everybody to participate in a mutual activity. It's a great way to involve the shy, clingy child and an opportunity to introduce any new friends. To avoid tears and meltdowns, do not play games in which there are winners and losers. Play simple games that don't have too many rules, and avoid games that require blindfolding (most young children don't like to have their eyes covered). Here are some games to play:

※ Treasure hunts are fun and keep children busy. You can hide small, inexpensive gift-wrapped items, candies, pennies, seashells, or colored hard-boiled eggs in the backyard or around the house (tell the children what rooms they may look in). Make sure the items used in the hunt are age appropriate.

※ Games with music are an easy way to get children to participate. Musical Chairs and Freeze Dance require the children listen and move to the music. When you stop the music, the children must stop.

※ Musical circle dances such as the "Hokey Pokey," "Bunny Hop," and "London Bridge" get the kids in a party mood.

※ Other all-time favorites are Simon Says; Red Light, Green Light; and Duck, Duck, Goose.

※ Play Hot Potato to music, using a real potato or small rubber ball. When the music stops, the child holding the potato must sit in the center of the circle. The game ends when everyone is in the middle and there's no longer a circle.

※ Play Limbo, using a broomstick with an adult holding each end. This can be played with or without music.

❀ Sing-along tapes or CDs are fun for everyone, including the adults. Sit in a circle and sing together.

❀ Play a game of storytelling. The adult begins the story, and each child adds a line or two. Have another adult write the story as it's being told, and then read it back when the last child has had her turn.

❀ If the party is not too large, play hide-and-seek.

❀ Animal Charades is lots of fun for the preschooler. Let each child pick a piece of paper with the name of an animal from a hat, and then act out her selection while the others guess.

❀ If you can stand the noise, hand out a variety of child-sized musical instruments and have a parade.

Holidays

Holidays and the observance of family traditions are a wonderful time for your child to enjoy. Since a toddler or preschooler cannot be expected to remember past holiday celebrations, refresh her memory with pictures taken in the previous year. Talk about the upcoming holiday (not too far in advance), and expose her to whatever is important to you and your family.

In all likelihood, she will not be able to sit or partake in ceremonies at the dinner table for a long period of time, so whether it's Thanksgiving, Christmas, Hanukkah, Easter, or Passover, be realistic. Don't expect your young child to have the patience to sit and wait. Keep her routines and rituals the same, so she won't feel overwhelmed or confused. To help ensure happy holidays, follow these tips.

PINK AND BLUE HINT

When birthdays and holidays fall simultaneously, a child often feels cheated because the holiday festivities seem to overshadow the birthday. It's a good idea not to combine both celebrations. If possible, plan the birthday party earlier in the month, when dates are not conflicting, and be sure to give gifts for each occasion.

Time-Tested Advice

❧ Adults are accustomed to celebrating the holidays and know what to expect during those times. However, a young child needs to be taught what the holiday is, its significance to your family and to the rest of the world, and how it is celebrated. Check with the local librarian or bookstore for recommended books on specific holidays.

❧ Explain to your child what the guidelines and safety precautions are for each holiday. For example, on Halloween after you go trick-or-treating, the candy has to be checked before the child can enjoy a piece.

❧ Include your child in the celebration by giving her a simple task to perform. For example, when it's Thanksgiving, let her help fold the napkins and assist in decorating the house.

❧ For the toddler, it's important to discuss the holiday festivities and her schedule for that particular day, especially if it is going to be different from her usual routine. If it's Christmas or Hanukkah, tell your child when she is going to open the presents.

❧ Your child may get hungry and restless waiting for the big meal of the day, so give her a little food to keep her satisfied until mealtime.

❧ Toddlers and preschoolers get very excited about holidays and need to expend their energy. If possible, let your child play outside for a little while before the celebration.

❧ Seat your child next to you, her favorite family member, or a child who can help her during the meal and enjoy her company.

❧ To help instill a sense of tradition, bring out the same familiar holiday decorations year after year. For example, use the same Christmas ornaments for the tree or the same menorah for Hanukkah each year.

❧ Don't forget to keep a camera ready to capture family moments together. Children love to look at photographs.

❧ It's a nice idea to play a family game, such as charades, to bring everyone together. Little children can participate in this game, too.

❧ Amidst all the holiday excitement and preparation, parents become stressed and preoccupied with the details of the holiday celebrations. Do not forget to put aside time each day for your little child, who needs your love and attention.

Hanukkah and Christmas

If you celebrate Hanukkah or Christmas, this is a wonderful but hectic time to spend with your family. It's a time to reflect on how fortunate you are and what you can do to contribute to others less fortunate. Children can get very caught up in the gift-receiving season. It's never too soon to teach your young child that the emphasis should be on giving, not receiving. Ask your preschooler to go through her toys and decide which ones she would like to give away.

There are many activities to keep your child engrossed in the celebrations. A preschooler will enjoy watching live performances, such as an ice-skating show or a holiday concert for young children. Check your local newspaper for listings of special child-oriented holiday entertainment.

Children enjoy making their own gifts and giving them away. Here are some gift-giving ideas for you and your child to do together:

❁ Wrap gifts in your child's artwork, or have your child make her own gift-wrapping paper by coloring and decorating pictures on construction paper.

❁ Grandparents love to receive gifts that young children make. Make an imprint of your child's hand using play dough or baking clay, and carve her name and date onto it.

❁ Let your child decorate and color a cardboard picture frame. Insert a family photo and give to relatives.

❁ Make a pen or pencil holder from a clean can. To avoid sharp edges, cover the rim with masking tape. Decorate the outside of the can in one of the following ways:

  ◉ Glue on pastas of different shapes, and then paint the pasta.

  ◉ Paint the can and add stickers.

  ◉ Glue magazine cutouts on the can, creating a collage. Pick a theme, such as cars or sports.

  ◉ Scan or photocopy a photograph of your child, and glue the picture on the can.

❁ Make Hanukkah or Christmas cards from colorful construction paper, and let your child decorate the card with crayon drawings, stickers, glitter, etc.

Hanukkah

Since there are eight days of Hanukkah, the child should not expect to receive expensive or elaborate gifts each night. Little, simple presents brightly gift-wrapped will satisfy a toddler or preschooler. If you have a Hanukkah party, do a grab bag and decide what dollar amount each family will spend. Keep the toy neutral for either a boy or a girl. To keep your child safe, please refer to Time-Tested Advice for Hanukkah and Christmas in the Holiday Safety section of this chapter.

Here are some fun activities to do for Hanukkah:

❧ Create your own play dough menorah using a cookie cutter in the shape of a star. Have the child make nine stars, arrange them on a plate, and then place a candle in each of the stars. Or make a rectangular base about ten inches long and one and a half inches thick. Place nine evenly spaced holes in the base to hold dripless candles. Use the candle to make the impressions.

❧ Make a menorah out of felt, and use wooden ice cream spoons as the candles. Cut a simple menorah design out of felt. Glue it to a large rectangular piece of felt or cardboard. Each night, have your child put spoons in the correct number of slots.

❧ Instead of the traditional menorah with candles, substitute cupcakes or healthy minimuffins to represent each night of celebration. Insert one candle per cupcake or muffin for each night. Make another activity out of baking the cupcakes or muffins with your preschooler's help.

❄ Let your preschooler help you make cookie dough and then use special Hanukkah cookie cutters in the shape of dreidels and stars. She can decorate the cookies with blue or white icing and other edible decorations.

Christmas

Everyone loves to get into the spirit of the Christmas holiday. Let your youngster partake in the festivities of decorating the house and Christmas tree. If you have a Christmas party, do a grab bag and decide what dollar amount each family will spend. Keep the toy neutral for either a boy or girl. To keep your child safe, please refer to Time-Tested Advice for Hanukkah and Christmas in the Holiday Safety section of this chapter.

Here are some fun activities to do for Christmas:

❄ The preschooler can make a Santa Claus face from construction paper or cardboard and use cotton for the beard, large buttons for his eyes, red licorice for the mouth, and red felt for the hat.

❄ Let your child make her own personal Christmas stocking from one of Dad's old socks. Try gluing glitter, sequins, beads, buttons, and pieces of cutout fabric onto it, and label the stocking with your child's name in brightly colored indelible ink. Keep this activity age appropriate.

❄ Make Christmas tree ornaments out of baking clay. Let the child use cookie cutters for different shapes and then paint and decorate as she wishes. Remember to poke a hole into the top of each ornament before baking. Hang these ornaments on the top section of the tree so a child cannot reach them and won't have the chance to mistake the ornaments for food.

Holiday Safety

Keeping your child safe during the holidays can be a challenge, so it's important to take extra precautions. From pumpkins and costumes to menorahs and Christmas trees, the holidays bring both joy and danger. The following tips will help you and your child enjoy holidays more safely.

Time-Tested Advice for Halloween

* When buying or making Halloween costumes, always purchase flame-resistant products.

* Do not dress your child in long, full skirts or flowing capes that can brush up against lit jack-o'-lanterns or candles and catch fire.

* To prevent tripping and falls, make sure hemlines and cuffs are above the ankle.

* Props that can poke or stab someone should be made of flexible material, such as poster board or aluminum foil.

* Since covering a young child's face with a mask can be dangerous and difficult for her to see and hear out of, consider using hypoallergenic face paints or nontoxic makeup instead.

* Place strips of reflective tape on your child's costume and treat bag to make her more visible and safer in the dark.

* Make sure your child wears comfortable nonskid shoes to avoid spills.

PINK AND BLUE HINT

Test the face paint or makeup on a small area of your child's face a few days before Halloween to check for any possible allergic reaction, such as a rash or irritated red skin.

PINK AND BLUE HINT

If your child insists upon wearing a mask, have her take it off when walking between houses so she can see where she's going.

❧ Go trick-or-treating with your toddler in the late afternoon while it's still light out.

❧ Either you or another responsible adult should accompany your child trick-or-treating. Carry a flashlight and avoid "scary" decorated houses. It's best to visit familiar, well-lit homes.

❧ Another option for young families is trick-or-treating at the local mall. Be sure to keep a close watch on your child, and do not allow her to go anywhere alone.

❧ Inspect all treats before letting your child indulge. Throw away all torn wrappers, unwrapped candies, and baked treats (unless you know who made them).

❧ Children under four should not eat nuts, pretzels, raisins, chewy candy with nuts or caramel, hard candies, or jelly beans.

❧ When carving a pumpkin, keep knives and other sharp utensils out of the child's reach.

❧ For safety's sake, use light sticks (available at markets, hardware stores, party shops) instead of burning candles inside the jack-o'-lantern.

Time-Tested Advice for Hanukkah and Christmas

❧ Typical decorative holiday plants that are poisonous and must be kept out of a young child's reach are crown thorns, poinsettias, Christmas cactus, holly, and mistletoe.

❦ Keep lit candles out of child's reach and away from curtains, Christmas trees, and other flammable materials. Always blow out candles before leaving a room.

❦ Don't put candles on tablecloths because they can topple over if a child pulls on the cloth.

❦ Never let a young child participate in ceremonial candle lighting of the menorah without adult supervision.

❦ Throw away plastic bags and bubble wrap after opening presents, to avoid suffocation.

❦ Foil and colored wrapping paper may contain lead, so be sure to discard them immediately in a safety-locked trash can. Do not burn the paper, as it can release toxic fumes.

❦ Ribbon and string can cause strangulation, so throw them away immediately in a safety-locked trash can.

❦ Everyone loves Christmas trees, but they can be hazardous. Protect your family during the holidays by following these tips:

  ◉ If you purchase a fresh tree, make sure the needles are firmly attached, to avoid fire hazards.

  ◉ Set up the tree in a well-balanced, sturdy stand that cannot topple over.

  ◉ Trim low branches so they won't poke a small child in the eyes.

- Vacuum fallen needles daily so a young child cannot swallow the needles, which can irritate or become lodged in her throat.

- Don't use decorations or ornaments that look like food.

- Hang decorations out of a young child's reach. Decorations within reach must be unbreakable with no small detachable parts.

- Attach ornaments securely so they can't fall and break.

- If you must have tinsel, buy nonleaded, non-flammable tinsel, and hang it out of the child's reach.

- Use only UL (Underwriter's Laboratory)–approved indoor lights. Inspect them carefully and throw out any with old, frayed wires, loose connections, or broken plugs.

- Do not use more than three strings of lights on one extension cord.

- Place the tree away from any heat sources, such as fireplaces and wall or floor heaters.

- Always unplug the lights before leaving the house or going to bed.

- Do not burn pine needles in the fireplace because they can easily spark.

- When visiting friends and family during the holiday, keep a watchful eye on your young child because others may not take the same precautions as you.

- When going to holiday parties with your child, be aware of foods that may be unsafe for her, such as nuts, hard candies, foil-covered gelt, cocktail hot dogs, spiked eggnog, mulled wine, and alcoholic fruit punch.

- If you're at a party with your family and see unattended glasses filled with alcoholic beverages or hot drinks, move them out of children's reach.

- When baking, keep vanilla and almond extracts tightly closed and out of a child's reach. These products have a high enough alcohol content to poison a child.

⊚ 14 ⊚

Travel

Traveling with a toddler or preschooler can be a daunting experience for any parent. Whether you're running an errand or taking a trip on an airplane, the secret lies in being organized and prepared. While you may not be ready to travel around the world with your young child in tow, rest assured that the travel industry recognizes the need to serve even the tiniest customer. There are many resorts and vacation packages catering to the young family today at reasonable prices. Even the Internet can entice you to take off and explore with your family. Perhaps a week on a sandy beach fits your bill, or camping and hiking sounds like fun.

Wherever you go, to ensure a successful vacation with your toddler or preschooler, set up a realistic, well-planned itinerary, allowing flexibility for those unpredictable situations. No trip is ever going to be 100 percent smooth sailing, so it's better to be prepared for the unexpected. It is advisable to limit the first few trips to one destination. Once the child becomes a cooperative traveler, you can venture to more than one location.

Remember how easy it used to be to plan a weekend getaway at the spur of the moment before you became a family? All you had to do was throw a few things in the suitcase and go. Now that you have a child, you must plan more carefully. Forget about traveling light; the adage "less is more" definitely does not apply here! You'll actually need more things to accommodate and pacify the little traveler. Since traveling away from home can be both exciting and frightening for the young child, remember to take plenty of patience as well.

Packing Your Suitcase for All Modes of Travel

Since packing for any trip is time-consuming and requires organization, begin packing a few days before your trip. List all the things you'll need, and check them off as you place them in the suitcase. Check the local weather report for your destination so that you pack the appropriate clothing. Put any medication for your child or other family members in your purse or carry-on baggage so it is easily accessible and available in case you arrive before your luggage. In addition to the clothing you pack for yourself and your child, include the fol-lowing items:

❋ Child's toiletries: hypoallergenic soap, shampoo, and body lotion; bath bonnet (if necessary); favorite toothbrush and toothpaste; sunscreen

꙰ Extra disposable diapers (and diapering toiletries) or underwear, depending upon your child's toilet training stage

꙰ Safety plugs for exposed electrical outlets

꙰ A night-light that plugs into an electrical outlet

꙰ A travel alarm clock

꙰ A flashlight and extra batteries

꙰ A large bag for dirty laundry

꙰ Age-appropriate toys

꙰ A personalized first-aid and medical kit with aceta-minophen, antihistamine, cough medicine, thermometer, antibiotic ointment, bandage strips, sterile gauze pads, alcohol pads, insect repellent for children, and calamine lotion (using your pediatrician's recommendations for over-the-counter medications)

꙰ A transitional object, if your child has one (Your child may want to carry this item with him; just make sure he doesn't lose it, or everyone will suffer.)

꙰ A camera and film

In addition to the items packed in your suitcase, it's also a good idea to include in your purse a copy of your child's medical records, health insurance information, and your pediatrician's telephone number. If your child gets sick or needs to go to the emergency room, you'll have all the following vital information at hand:

꙰ Exact weight

꙰ Any chronic conditions

PINK AND BLUE HINT

If your child is prone to ear infections or other respiratory ailments, ask your pediatrician to prescribe medication for you to take on the trip. Call the doctor before administering the medicine.

PINK AND BLUE HINT

If you're going to a destination for an extended period of time, consider shipping bulky or heavy items ahead of time. It will leave you with less luggage to track down and carry around the airport or train station.

❧ Any prescription and nonprescription medicines currently being taken

❧ Any allergies

❧ Date of last tetanus shot

Traveling by Plane

The mere thought of traveling on an airplane with a toddler or preschooler can make some parents break out in a sweat. The image of being confined to a seat in a small area with a child who wants to spread his own wings and fly can be intimidating. However, with the right preparation and timing, you can create a seasoned flier. Anticipate the unexpected hassles that may occur by allowing enough time to check in, walk through the terminal, and get to the designated gate without being frantic. There's nothing worse than running to the plane with a toddler and carry-on bags in tow, so get there early enough to give your child time to run around a quiet gate area or play in the special children's play area, to release excessive toddler or preschooler energy. Even standing close to the viewing window and watching planes take off and land is exciting for little children.

All airlines require a child over the age of two to have a reservation and be ticketed for his own seat. When you book the trip, be sure to tell the airline reservation agent or travel agent your child's age, to ensure sitting together. When possible, choose nonstop day flights during the week, when the planes are less crowded. If your child still naps, select a flight that corresponds to his nap routine. Choose a time that is the least disruptive to his daily rituals.

Request bulkhead seats because they have the most legroom and you can make a play area on the floor in front of you. However, there's no storage under the seats, and all items must be placed in the overhead compartments. When your child takes a nap, be sure to put him in his seat with the belt securely buckled. If your child is playing on the floor and the plane experiences turbulence, immediately put him in his seat with the seat belt fastened securely. If the bulkhead is not available, request an aisle seat for better mobility and a window seat so your child can look outside the plane.

When you book your reservation, order a child's meal. You can order a special meal up to forty-eight hours before departure. However, don't rely on the airline for food or drinks because the serving schedule for the flight may not coincide with your child's eating schedule, and he may not like the food that is served.

Keep in mind that even a child can experience jet lag and have difficulty traveling to different time zones. When you arrive at your destination, put your child on the new time and follow his daily routine as closely as possible, to help him adjust and feel comfortable in his new surroundings. It may take a day or two for his body clock to get adjusted to the new schedule.

For hassle-free flying, follow these tips.

PINK AND BLUE ALERT

If your child is sick or shows any sign of illness, call your pediatrician. Make sure it's OK to fly.

PINK AND BLUE HINT

If you're investing in new luggage, purchase suitcases on wheels for easy handling, or buy portable luggage racks on wheels to transport your existing luggage.

Time-Tested Advice

* Prepare a well-organized carry-on bag. It should include the following items:

  ◉ Food and beverages you know your child likes

  ◉ A drinking cup with lid to avoid messy spills or juice boxes with straws

  ◉ Extra clothing, including a sweater or sweatshirt for the plane

- ◉ Disposable diapers and accessories for a toddler who is not toilet trained (figure one diaper per hour)

- ◉ Extra underwear for the toilet training toddler or preschooler

- ◉ Child wipes and hand sanitizer gel

- ◉ Medication your child might be taking

- ◉ Plenty of toys and books for entertainment

- ❀ Take advantage of curbside check-in. If unavailable, spring for a skycap to transport your bags while you assist the children. Don't forget to tip; the rule of thumb is at least one dollar per bag.

- ❀ Use your toddler or preschooler's stroller to save time and energy getting through the busy terminal. It's convenient to use if you're changing planes. Once you board the plane, store the stroller in either the hanging closet or overhead bin, if possible. If, however, your stroller is large, the airline personnel will check it (and give you a ticket stub) as you enter the plane, and return it to you when you deplane. A stroller is considered carry-on baggage, and since you've paid for your child's seat, he is allowed two pieces of carry-on, just like you. Another option is to leave the stroller (with luggage tag) with the gate attendant as you board and pick it up as you deplane. Be sure the gate attendant gives you an airline luggage receipt to retrieve the stroller.

- ❀ If your toddler or preschooler weighs less than forty pounds or will be more comfortable sitting in his

PINK AND BLUE HINT

Before boarding the plane, avoid giving your child sugary foods, because sugar can be an unwanted energy booster.

PINK AND BLUE ALERT

Listen carefully to the flight attendant's safety instructions, especially regarding young children, before takeoff.

PINK AND BLUE HINT

If your child has a cold and your doctor has advised you it's OK to fly, give the child the recommended dosage of decongestant before boarding the plane.

PINK AND BLUE HINT

Surprise your child with a few new toys he can unwrap on the plane, such as sticker books, mini play dough kits, activity game books, puzzles, pipe cleaners, age-appropriate electronic games, or small action figures or dolls. Save a few of these surprises for the return flight.

car seat, take it on the plane. It must be FAA (Federal Aviation Administration) approved. It won't count as carry-on baggage. The FAA does not allow a booster seat in place of a car seat.

❤ Take advantage of preboarding. If there are two adults traveling with the child, one can preboard and put things away, while the other person can remain at the gate for a few minutes longer, giving the child freedom to run around until the final boarding call.

❤ Sometimes preboarding has its drawbacks. If you board too early and your child gets antsy, it may make the flight seem longer. On the other hand, if you're traveling alone with your child, preboarding gives you the opportunity to get settled and organized in your seats before everyone else boards.

❤ Explain procedures for boarding and deplaning to your child. In addition, go over rules for acceptable behavior on an airplane. Don't let your child run up and down the aisle and disturb other passengers. Always hold his hand and remind him to speak in a quiet voice. Consideration of others is imperative, particularly in a confining situation like a plane.

❤ Once you're on the plane, make sure you grab a pillow and blanket from the overhead bin for everyone traveling in your party. If you can't find enough, ask the flight attendant for help.

❤ Bring along something for your child to chew or suck on during takeoff and landing to alleviate pressure in his ears.

❤ Pack a few bottles of purified water to carry with you on the plane because drinking plenty of water helps prevent dehydration.

❤ Let the preschooler pack his own backpack with a few of his favorite toys and books for the plane ride. Gauge the number of toys to take by the length of the flight. Don't let the child overload the backpack, making it too heavy for him to carry.

❤ Visit your local toy, book, or travel store for new travel entertainment ideas for your child.

❤ If you're toilet training your child, be sure to take him to the bathroom before he gets on the plane and before landing. Explain that there are only a few toilets on the plane and they are always busy, so he needs to tell you when the urge strikes. Help him out with frequent bathroom reminders.

❤ If you or your preschooler has a small tape or CD recorder with headphones, pack them for the flight. Bring your child's favorite music and books on tape to listen to.

❤ Be careful with hot beverages on the plane. A fidgety child can easily knock over the drink and burn the two of you.

❤ It's easier and less stressful to be the last ones off the plane, giving you the opportunity to take your time and collect all your items. Plus, when you arrive at the baggage claim area, there will be less waiting time.

❤ If you need a rental car when you arrive at your destination, reserve it in advance and get a

PINK AND BLUE HINT

Avoid taking toys that have pieces that can be easily lost. However, if a toy has a few parts, store them together in a self-sealing plastic bag.

PINK AND BLUE HINT

If your child experiences motion sickness, take along soda crackers, sugar-free gingersnaps, or brewed ginger tea in a thermos. Ginger helps sooth motion sickness.

confirmation number. Make certain your child's car seat will fit safely in the car. If your budget can handle it, go for the minivan. It has more room, more luggage space, and a bigger fuel tank than standard sedans.

Traveling by Car

Sometimes running a few errands in the car with your toddler or preschooler is just as exhausting as taking an extended trip. As soon as you buckle your child into his car seat and pull out of the driveway, he's asking, "Are we there yet?"

Regardless of the length of the car trip, it is mandatory for your child to be restrained in either a car seat or a booster seat, depending upon age and weight. In addition, always be a good role model and wear your seat belt—it's the law! The car rule should always be, No car seat, no seat belt, no ride! Keep in mind that the leading cause of death in young children is car accidents, especially within a few miles of home. For more information on safe traveling in the car, please see Car Safety in Chapter 8, "Safety."

Running Errands

Be organized with a list of things to do before leaving the house, and be realistic about how many errands you can complete with your youngster in tow. Try planning your errands around your child's schedule so you can accomplish more. If he falls asleep in the car when you are driving, you must wake him up when you arrive at your destination. *Never* leave him alone in the car, even if the car is locked. At every stop, take him with you.

Time-Tested Advice

❀ Check your tires (including the spare tire), oil, and water periodically to make sure the car is in good shape. Get regular tune-ups.

❀ If an ashtray is within your child's reach, keep it closed and remove the lighter.

❀ Always keep door and window buttons locked.

❀ If you're in the midst of toilet training, keep a potty and toilet paper in the car. Be considerate of others when disposing of the waste.

❀ If your child throws a temper tantrum or fights with another child while you're driving, pull over to the side of the road and calm him or them down. It's difficult to concentrate on driving and effectively deal with upset children.

❀ No smoking in the car. Not only is secondhand smoke harmful to your child's health, it also contributes to motion sickness.

❀ If you're the only adult in the car, do not allow your child to eat while you're driving because if he chokes, you can't help him immediately.

❀ While the car is in motion, do not give your child foods on a stick, such as lollipops or frozen bars.

PINK AND BLUE HINT

During the hot summer months, keep a blanket or large towel in the car to cover the car seat when not in use. This will protect your child's sensitive skin from burns or blisters.

PINK AND BLUE ALERT

While your child is eating, always park the car so you can assist him.

Long Trips

Thoughtful planning for extended car trips will make the ride more pleasurable. As a preventive measure and to ensure car safety, take your car to a reliable mechanic and have the car completely serviced. Before you embark on your excursion, carefully plan and organize each traveling day, allowing time for meals and rest stops. Do not plan an elaborate itinerary for your family's first extended road trip. Save multiple destinations for future trips.

In addition to the information in Running Errands, follow these suggestions for a successful road trip.

Time-Tested Advice

* If you don't already belong to a local automobile club, now is a good time to join one. Its staff can help you plan your trip, provide you with maps, make reservations at motels (usually at a discount), and assist you with roadside emergencies.

* Always reserve rooms in advance and request smoke-free rooms. Don't count on finding a place for the night along the way because if there are no vacancies, you'll really be stuck. Sleeping in the car is dangerous and uncomfortable, and you won't be well rested for the next day's drive.

* For easy trunk storage, duffel bags are more flexible than standard suitcases.

* To encourage napping, take pillows and blankets for each child.

* If your child is in the midst of toilet training and prefers either a portable potty seat or toilet seat attachment, take it with you. Don't forget the toilet paper and a disinfectant spray.

PINK AND BLUE ALERT

Don't hamper your visibility by overpacking your car.

❧ Let the preschooler pack his backpack with his favorite few toys and books. Keep it handy in the car to keep him entertained.

❧ Make a surprise bag filled with gift-wrapped small games, toys, and books specifically for the car ride. Dole out one or two items per day, making sure the gifts last the entire trip, coming and going. Some suggestions are small dolls or action figures, hand puppets, sticker books, pipe cleaners, and age-appropriate electronic games.

❧ Visit your local toy, book, or travel store and look for new travel entertainment games.

❧ Take some of your child's favorite music and story tapes or CDs to listen to in the car. Or, if the child has his own portable tape or CD player with headphones, take it along.

❧ Don't forget to take a camera with plenty of rolls of film for the trip, or buy disposable cameras.

❧ Occupy time by playing interactive games, such as counting red cars or animals; looking for shapes, numbers, and letters; singing together out loud; or playing Car Bingo, Simon Says, or a simplified version of charades. Remember to keep distractions down to a minimum for the driver.

❧ It's a good idea to start your travel day early enough to avoid the morning rush hours.

❧ Take frequent rest stops along the way so everyone can stretch, go to the bathroom, and grab some fresh air. This is especially important for the driver.

PINK AND BLUE HINT

If your family enjoys iced water in the car, fill water bottles three-quarters of the way and freeze them. When you're ready to go, add a little water to help them thaw. The melting ice provides cold water on the go.

- Look for stops that have play areas for your child to expend his energy, or take along a ball to throw or kick around.

- If there's more than one driver, be sure to take turns so one can rest while the other person drives.

- Take advantage of interesting stops along the way, such as a historical point, famous diner, or well-known specialty shop.

- Stop early enough in the day so the family can unwind at the pool, take a walk through the local mall, or play at the playground before dinner and bedtime.

- Driving at night is not recommended because it is too easy for the driver to fall asleep at the wheel.

- If your child experiences motion sickness, try these ideas:

  - Carry gingersnaps, saltine crackers, or pretzels for temporary relief.

  - Prepare ginger or chamomile tea, and keep it warm (not hot) in a thermos.

  - Avoid heavy meals and/or greasy foods before and during travel. A light snack frequently is a better solution.

  - Acidic fruits and juices tend to upset the stomach. Offer small sips of water or stop for frozen ices when possible.

  - Let the child sit next to an open window so he can breathe the fresh air.

- Pull over to the side of the road and let your child walk around.

- Carry a small plastic pail, self-sealing plastic bags, or towels for unpredictable upchucks.

- Apply a cold, wet washcloth to the child's forehead.

- To reduce symptoms, discourage reading and looking down, and encourage looking straight ahead.

Traveling by Train

If riding the rails sounds fun to you and your family, then "All aboard!" Amtrak is the nation's leading railroad service, covering the entire United States, in conjunction with smaller subsidiary lines. When planning a train trip, you still have to do thoughtful organizing ahead of time. Call your travel agent or Amtrak for its planner brochure, which gives a rundown of schedules and ticket prices. Young children require tickets, but the cost of the ticket is half price.

Book your reservations in advance so you have the tickets in hand when you arrive at the train station, avoiding the hassles of long lines. Arrive early for your departure so your child can have some freedom to run around before boarding the train. This will also give you a chance to board early enough to get seats together. If you're traveling overnight, book a sleeper compartment that includes beds and food, and offers more privacy.

When planning a trip by train, keep in mind the length of the trip and the ages of your children. Train travel is as confining as an airplane trip, and it takes longer to get to the destination. Unlike car travel, which allows you to stop when and where you want, trains run on a specific timetable.

Time-Tested Advice

❦ If you plan on traveling overnight, book a late afternoon or early evening train so everyone can sleep on the train.

❦ If sleeper compartments are unavailable or too costly, purchase a coach ticket and take along blankets for everyone. Pillows are provided.

❦ When you book the reservations, ask whether children's meals are available; if so, place an order. Cover your bases by taking along extra food, snacks, and drinks just in case your child doesn't like the food or gets hungry when the dining car is closed.

❦ Check your baggage and take a carry-on on the train. Pack the same kind of carry-on as for plane travel (see Traveling by Plane). If you're traveling overnight, add pajamas, a change of clothing, and simple toiletries to refresh yourselves in the morning.

❦ To keep your child entertained on the train, please refer to Traveling by Plane and Traveling by Car for suggestions.

❦ Let your child sit by the window to observe the scenery.

❦ If you know there will be a long layover at a particular stop, find out in advance what you and your family can do for entertainment, such as sightseeing or visiting the local zoo or playground.

* Trains do not have seat belts, so keep a watchful eye on your child at all times. To avoid accidents, insist your child sit when the train is moving.

* For safety's sake, always hold your child's hand when walking through the train.

Family Vacations

Taking the entire family on a vacation is more enticing than ever before, due in large part to companies that offer attractive packages targeted toward families. The key is selecting the right place that caters to children, as well as adults. First you have to decide what kind of vacation your family wants to take. Do you want to go to the beach, the lake, the slopes, or a dude ranch? Or does visiting theme parks or camping out sound more attractive to you? Once you know the kind of trip you want to take, then consider where you'll want to stay. Your choices range from self-contained resorts to hotels and motels, condominiums, house rentals, and recreational vehicles.

As you plan your vacation, remember that the most important ingredient is fun. You don't have to do a lot for the trip to be a success, but you do want to enjoy each day with your family. When you research the types of vacations available, consider budget, length of time, and location. Always ask for family rates and any other perks available. If you can plan far enough in advance, your options will be greater and more cost-effective.

PINK AND BLUE HINT

Don't cram too many activities into one day for your young child. You'll have a cranky kid and, in turn, a cranky parent.

PINK AND BLUE HINT

If your vacation takes you outdoors, whether it be the beach or the ski slopes, bring plenty of sunscreen for the entire family. Be diligent and reapply the sunscreen often throughout the day because it wears off and becomes less effective.

Safety Alerts for Your "Home Away from Home"

❋ Pack these safety items in your suitcase: electrical outlet safety covers, a plug-in night-light, safety latch for each toilet lid, and a few doorknob covers to keep bathroom and hallway doors off-limits.

❋ If your toddler is still sleeping in a crib, call to make sure the rental crib meets Consumer Product Safety Commission standards.

❋ Move all furniture away from windows, so children can't climb out.

❋ Keep windows and doors (especially balcony doors) securely locked.

❋ Tie loose electrical cords and any hanging drapery cords out of the child's reach to avoid strangulation.

❋ Remove small objects, toiletries, and any breakable items out of the child's reach.

Time-Tested Advice for Resorts, Hotels, and Motels

❤ Choose a location that is easy to get to. It's not a good idea to change planes and then drive a long distance to your destination.

❤ If your toddler still sleeps in a crib, reserve one in advance.

❤ Restaurants should be conveniently located on the premises and offer children's menus. Twenty-four-hour room service can be a necessity.

* On-site entertainment is a must. Look for a kiddy swimming pool, playground, game room, and sufficient grounds for running around.

* Check to see whether programs or camps are available for children aged three and older.

* Find out whether certified and bonded child care is available. The baby-sitters should be CPR trained. Ask the baby-sitter to arrive at least an hour before you go out, so you can spend some time reviewing your child's rules and routines. Be sure to leave a telephone number where you will be.

* Inquire about a hotel physician or a medical facility near where you are staying.

* Make sure your room has a small refrigerator. When you check in, ask them to empty the mini bar.

* Talk to the hotel regarding age-appropriate entertainment nearby, such as zoos, theme parks, water parks, playgrounds, or movie theaters.

* Ask whether the rooms have VCRs or in-room movie rentals and games for children. If a VCR is available, you may want to bring some of your child's favorite videos with you.

* Ask whether coin-operated washers and dryers are available on the premises. Hotel laundry services tend to be expensive.

* If your family is taking a ski vacation and you don't want to invest in ski clothing, borrow items from relatives or friends or rent from a ski shop.

🐾 It's a good idea to rent ski equipment at your ski destination. If there are problems or adjustments, they can be taken care of right away. Call ahead and reserve the equipment you know you'll need for everyone.

🐾 Call ahead and inquire about ski school instruction for the preschooler. You may need to reserve a space before your arrival, especially if it's holiday time.

Time-Tested Advice for Beach or Pool Vacations

🐾 If you're taking your child to a beach or pool, don't forget to use sunscreen often, especially after each time in the water, even if the sunscreen is water-resistant. A young child's skin is very sensitive and should be protected sufficiently. Take a hat along for him, too, and insist he wear it when playing in the sun for extended periods of time.

🐾 Mark all beach and pool toys with your child's name since many toys look alike. Keep them in a mesh bag that you can immerse in water and clean off at the end of a day's play.

🐾 Take a large beach bag to carry all your things down to the pool or beach.

🐾 Buy your child water shoes to wear in the ocean, lake, or pool to protect his feet from scraping or burning on the hot sand or pavement.

PINK AND BLUE ALERT

Never leave your child alone or unattended near a pool, ocean, or lake, even if he is water safe.

- If your child uses inflatable arm floaters or an inner tube for swimming, take them along. These devices do not keep children water safe, however, so never leave the child unattended in or near the water.

Time-Tested Advice for Camping

- If you're a first-time camper, visit a specialty camping store to purchase or rent camping gear. The store can suggest the best camping books for your particular trip and tell you about favorite campsites.

- For additional campsite suggestions, call your state or county parks department, the National Park Service, or conservation or natural resource agencies in your community.

- Whether you're sleeping in a recreational vehicle, in a tent, or out under the stars, be sure to reserve a campsite. When making the reservation, ask about facilities, such as toilets, showers, drinking water, electricity, and trailer hookups.

- For additional camping information, consult your local automobile club. The club can assist you with your reservations, whether they are state or private campgrounds.

- Campgrounds vary in what they have to offer. Base your selection on the kind of activities available, such as swimming, fishing, hiking, or biking.

PINK AND BLUE ALERT

When hiking in tall-grassy or woody areas, dress to protect against deer ticks, which can cause Lyme disease. Wear long pants and tuck them into your socks. Also, wear long-sleeved shirts with tightly fitted necklines. When removing clothing, double-check for hidden ticks. For more information on Lyme disease, please see Insect Bites in Chapter 3, "Your Child's Health."

- If you visit state or national parks, inquire about ranger-led programs and tours.

- Bring a sufficient supply of food and drinks and a well-stocked first-aid kit (including insect repellent and calamine lotion).

- Ask whether there is a market on the campgrounds or close by, in case you forget or run out of something, such as food or firewood.

- Be sure to know the campground's general rules and regulations on conservation, recycling, and quiet hours.

- If you plan on hiking, take along a child carrier to carry your toddler on your back.

- Don't forget to cover everyone's skin well with sunscreen and insect repellent. Reapply the insect repellent at nighttime.

- Know what poison ivy and poison oak look like so you and your family can avoid touching them and becoming infected.

- Have a backup plan in case of inclement weather. Check out the hotels and motels in the vicinity.

Traveling Abroad

When you are traveling out of the country, each member of your family is required to have proper documentation. If you're traveling to Canada or Mexico, each person needs an official birth certificate or a passport. All other foreign countries require a passport. If you are traveling alone with your child outside the United States, you are required to have a notarized letter from the other parent authorizing you to leave the country with your child.

When booking transportation reservations, ask about discounted fares for children.

Speak to your pediatrician about which prescribed and over-the-counter medicines you should take with you, in case your child gets sick. Fill the prescriptions before you depart. If a certain medication requires refrigeration, get it in powdered form; mix it with bottled water only when you need to use it. Be sure your child's immunizations are current. Ask your travel consultant, as well as your pediatrician, whether any additional vaccinations are recommended for your particular destination.

PINK AND BLUE HINT

In each city you visit, check with the American consulate for a recommended doctor and hospital nearby.

Vacations Without the Children

All parents need a break and time alone without the children to rekindle their romance. While it's exciting to go away, there's always some anxiety about leaving the children behind. Planning will ease the separation and smooth the transition. For peace of mind, carefully select a competent, trustworthy, and thoughtful caregiver. Grandparents may be an excellent choice. In most cases, you know your child is being loved and cared for, and it's a wonderful bonding experience for all.

If you're hiring a new caregiver, this person must spend plenty of time with your child before you take your vacation. Familiarize the caregiver with your home and neighborhood, including the daily goings-on and emergency procedures. Have that person accompany you to the places most often frequented, such as preschool, local market, and pediatrician's office.

Since a young child doesn't have a concept of time, tell him no more than a week before your departure about your impending vacation. If he acts upset, let him know it's OK to feel sad, and you'll telephone him while you're away.

Time-Tested Advice

❤ Make a list of important names and phone numbers, and post it by the most-used telephone in the house. Include your pediatrician, fire and police department, neighbors, relatives, preschool or day care, close friends, and parents of your child's friends. (For list of additional emergency information to keep posted by the phone, see Emergency Information List in Chapter 8, "Safety.")

❤ Show your caregiver where first-aid supplies and medicines are stored.

❤ To reinforce a sense of security, the caregiver must maintain your child's rituals and routines.

❤ For every day you're away, write out a detailed list of the child's daily schedule for the caregiver. Include routines, carpools, planned activities, and play dates.

❤ Before you go away, set up activities for your child, such as play dates. Do not expect the caregiver to make all the plans.

❤ Make sure you leave a notarized letter of consent authorizing the caregiver to make decisions regarding your child in the event of a medical emergency. Also prepare a letter of consent giving your pediatrician authority to treat your child in your absence. It will be kept permanently on file in your child's medical records.

* Stock your pantry closet and refrigerator with plenty of food for the time you'll be away. If possible, prepare meals in advance and then freeze them, labeling each package with the name of the food and date it was cooked.

* Leave a list of menu suggestions so the caretaker knows what your child likes to eat. Be specific about the kinds of foods you want your child to eat and not eat.

* Give your preschooler a calendar highlighting every day you're away. Let him mark off the calendar with a sticker each day you're gone.

* If your travels will be for an extended period of time, leave a prerecorded message on a tape for your child to hear your voice. Also, send a letter or postcard to your child before you leave so he can receive mail from you the second or third day you're away.

* To reassure your child you are fine, check in by phone. Don't call too many times in one day, as that may be a bit upsetting for the young child.

* If your child will be staying at someone else's home, be sure to pack some of his favorite toys and other transitional objects (blanket, pillow, etc.), which will give him a sense of security.

- Just before you leave, give your child a gift that you know he will like and will keep him preoccupied after you have said your good-byes. There will be less hysteria, and it will make the transition easier.

- Write a few notes that the caregiver can put daily into the preschooler's lunch box.

Index